FREEDOM CLIMBERS

FREEDOM CLIMBERS

BERNADETTE MCDONALD

VERTEBRATE PUBLISHING

Vertebrate Publishing, Sheffield
www.v-publishing.co.uk

FREEDOM CLIMBERS – BERNADETTE MCDONALD

First published in the UK and Ireland in 2012 by Vertebrate Publishing.

VERTEBRATE PUBLISHING
Crescent House, 228 Psalter Lane, Sheffield S11 8UT.
www.v-publishing.co.uk

This work was originally published in 2011 by Rocky Mountain Books of Canada,
under the title Freedom Climbers by Bernadette McDonald.
www.rmbooks.com

A CIP catalogue record for this book is available from the British Library.

ISBN: 978-1-906148-44-7 (Paperback)   ISBN: 978-1-906148-45-4 (Ebook)
10 9 8 7 6 5 4 3 2 1

Produced by Nathan Ryder, Vertebrate Graphics Ltd – www.v-graphics.co.uk
Based on an original design by Rocky Mountain Books – www.rmbooks.com

Printed and bound in Malta by Latitude Press.

CONTENTS

PROLOGUE

I have always said that Poles are gifted,
Perhaps too gifted. But gifted for what?
— GÜNTER GRASS

She was standing at the bar with a beer in her hand. What struck me immediately was her warmth. Surrounded by adoring fans, she was telling a story – about climbing, I assumed. She punctuated her tale with weather-beaten hands, but the real telling was in her face. Deep-set espresso eyes encircled by the sorts of lines that come from laughter and high-altitude winds. A broad expanse of forehead obscured by an unruly mop of wavy chestnut hair. And a smile so wide it completely melted that strong, Polish jaw.

As I approached the bar, she glanced over. "Hi. Come on. Have a beer. I'm Wanda."

Of course, I knew that. Meeting Wanda Rutkiewicz was one of the reasons I had travelled halfway around the world to this mountain film festival on the French Riviera. Antibes is a lovely spot, but not in December.

We skipped that evening's film program. Instead, we stood at the theatre lobby bar, talking, laughing, sharing stories of mutual acquaintances. She spoke of Jerzy Kukuczka, Poland's leading alpinist, who had died two years before on the South Face of Lhotse. This gentle giant of a man had been one of Wanda's dearest friends. I had met him a couple of times, once in Kathmandu on his return from the first winter ascent of Kangchenjunga, and again in northern Italy, where we had enjoyed a three-hour lunch together. There were others: Kurtyka, Diemberger, Curran. Lots of stories. Lots of laughs. Lots of beer.

As I stood next to Wanda, I was amazed at how slight she was. It was hard to imagine her shouldering a heavy pack up a mountain. She was slender, almost delicate. Except for that jaw. And of course her hands, which were muscular and rough.

I was surprised too at how she was dressed. I expected a strong style statement from this Polish star: retro, dirtbag, elegant, I wasn't sure what, but *something*. Instead, she was wearing the most ordinary mismatched array of fleece and cotton. Of course, she was just back from an expedition to Dhaulagiri and had hardly found time to catch her breath, let alone dress for a party.

As the evening unfolded I revealed my ulterior motive, which was to persuade her to give the opening lecture at the next Banff Mountain Film Festival.

7

That was part of my job as director. She enthusiastically agreed. Then we glanced over at Marion Feik, her somewhat protective manager, hovering nearby. The three of us talked and agreed that Wanda could make the trip to Canada in November 1992.

A couple of hours later, as the audience streamed out of the theatre, we were still standing at the bar. We refilled our drinks and drifted over to some tattered leather armchairs in the now empty lobby.

"So, Bernadette, I want to tell you about my plan," said Wanda. "I call it the Caravan of Dreams."

"Sounds interesting."

"I intend to become the first woman to climb all 14 of the 8000-metre peaks. You know I have done eight. I want to do the rest…"

"Well if anyone can do it, you can."

"… in 18 months."

"What? Are you serious? Really serious? I don't think it's possible."

"Yes, yes, it is possible, because that way I keep the acclimatization, don't you see? It is better to go quickly from one to another."

I put down my glass and leaned forward. "Wanda, seriously, you can't do this – it's a dangerous plan. Have you actually talked to anyone about this? Other climbers? What do they say?"

I protested as best I could. I was sure her plan was unreasonable, even though I had never climbed an 8000-metre peak. Nobody had done anything like this before. Climbers took years to collect the 8000ers, and only Reinhold Messner and Jerzy Kukuczka had summited all 14. Why was she in such a rush, I asked? What about the fatigue factor?

Marion cast me a pitying look. She had heard these objections before. Many times. I could tell from her glance that she agreed with me. But it wasn't Marion who was driving the agenda. It was Wanda's plan, and Wanda was in a hurry.

"I'm almost 50," she said, brushing her hair off her face. "I'm slowing down. I don't acclimatize as quickly as I used to. So I have to be strategic and group them together. I can do it, I know. I just need luck with the weather."

I stopped protesting. Clearly, there was no point in arguing with Wanda.

We agreed to stay in touch over the next months, between her expeditions. She would keep me updated, and I would start the publicity machine to promote her Canadian appearance.

Wanda sent me an aerogram letter from Kathmandu the following spring, 1992, just before heading off to climb Kangchenjunga. This would be her ninth 8000er. She sounded confident, determined, and eager to be done with it. I wished her luck.

Wanda never returned.

❄ ❄ ❄

Two years later I was in Katowice, the industrial heartland of Poland, where I was helping organize a film festival. It was wildly successful, with hundreds of enthusiastic people milling about, watching films and reconnecting with their friends. The atmosphere in the auditorium was electric, despite the gloomy Polish winter. The scale of the climbing community in this cold industrial wasteland astonished me; the climbers seemed hardened, rough around the edges, intense. I was intrigued.

At the end of the festival a group of climbers invited me to the local clubhouse of the Polish Alpine Association. Another dank, dingy building, windows smudged with residue from the nearby smokestacks, but inside there was warmth, light, plenty of vodka and an energy level that rivalled a rock concert.

Many of the surviving great Polish Himalayan climbers were there: Zawada, Wielicki, Hajzer, Lwow, Majer, Pawlowski and more. I knew their histories and I had the impression that these alpinists were special, even visionary. I could see it in their eyes. They were fearless about tackling new routes in the great ranges and seemed impervious to the suffering implicit in going after (and often succeeding on) unforgiving winter ascents of the highest mountains on Earth.

But there was also a palpable sadness in the room. I couldn't ignore the repeated references to those who had sacrificed their lives for the mountains they had loved. Jerzy Kukuczka was one. Wanda was another. I expressed my admiration for both of them, and my luck at having known them, albeit briefly. There were smiling nods but troubling stories, particularly about Wanda. "You were charmed by her," one of them said. "She had another side. Very hard. Calculating. She could be tough, like a bull."

I protested. Of course she needed to be tough in order to survive her lifestyle. "Yes, that's true," another climber admitted, as he pulled at his impressive mustache. "But she tried too hard. Always fighting. Difficult. Competing. We loved her, but she didn't seem to know that. She thought she was alone. She pushed us away. But we loved Wanda."

"What about Kukuczka?" I asked. "Was he a fighter too?"

"No, no, Jerzy had no time to fight. He was too busy climbing. He got distracted for awhile – the race – you know, with Reinhold Messner.

They both wanted to be the first to climb all 14 of the 8000ers. But he came back … once he was done with that. He came back to the real climbing – the big faces."

"But that's what killed him," I countered.

"Yes, that's true. But he was a real climber – Poland's best."

They talked of the changing times, of the crazy yet good old days of Communism, when the central government understood and supported the needs of climbers – at least the very best ones. They spoke with pride of the entrepreneurial skills they had honed in order to support their Himalayan habit. Climbers had risked their lives not only in the mountains but in their jobs as well, cleaning and painting industrial chimneys and scaling the slippery, unstable smokestacks that punctuated the Katowice skyline. This was dangerous work, not only because they risked falling but also because of the toxic environment. They whispered veiled hints about smuggling – how lucrative it had been. But times had changed, and now they felt cast aside from the crumbling heap of the Polish free-market economy.

It was 3 a.m. when we finally left the clubhouse. As we made our way through the damp, unlit streets, the warmth of the party stayed with me, despite the bone-chilling darkness.

Back in Canada, I often reflected upon that night in Katowice. I treasured the stories of great climbs completed, plans for the future and dear friends lost. I puzzled over the conflicting opinions about Wanda and the others. Some of these climbing heroes seemed more complicated than I had imagined them to be. Particularly with Wanda, it was hard to reconcile the warmth that I had experienced with the ambiguous portrait that had emerged. Over time, I couldn't shake the feeling that I had attended a wake – a nostalgic, bittersweet celebration of something unique: the Golden Age of Polish Himalayan climbing, an era that had passed.

I pondered the grimness of Poland's recent history. Sixty years dominated by hideous violence and oppression, massive upheaval and miraculous rebirth. The ability of this tight-knit climbing community to co-exist with such a desperate political reality, and produce the very best Himalayan alpinists in the world, was puzzling. Did the hard times forge their ambitions, or only toughen them, train them in stoicism?

And now, life in Poland was once again undergoing massive change, seemingly in a positive direction. I wondered how Polish climbers would respond. Would an easier life consolidate their strength in the mountains, or simply distract them?

These questions continued to intrigue me long after that night in Katowice. Eventually I decided to dig deeper – into the history of Poland leading up to its dominance of Himalayan climbing, and into the human contradictions of the great climbers of this era. Who was the real Wanda? Could she help lead me into the hearts and minds of this incredible group of people who, although they were shaped by their country, could not be contained by it?

This is the story of their amazing journey as they climbed their way to freedom.

CHAPTER ONE

CRUTCHES TO CRAMPONS

*May your trails be crooked, winding, lonesome, dangerous, leading to the
most amazing view. May your mountains rise into and above the clouds.*
— EDWARD ABBEY, *BENEDICTO*

The trail was rough. Boulders of all sizes tottered underfoot and treacherous ice patches lurked under a thin layer of unstable sand. The ground trembled from the roar of the murky Braldu River, far below. A gaunt, hollow-cheeked woman hobbled along, pain clouding her dark eyes. She stopped and leaned against a crumbling rock wall. Reaching into her pocket, she found two painkillers and tossed them into her parched mouth.

It was 1982. Wanda Rutkiewicz was the most famous female Himalayan climber in the world. Her specialty was all-women teams. This was to be her summer: she had assembled a group of 12 women, all top climbers, many of them former climbing partners, for an ascent of K2, the second-highest mountain in the world. There was only one problem – Wanda was on crutches. She had shattered her femur in the Russian Caucasus Mountains a year earlier and there had been complications.

Most people would have abandoned the idea of hobbling in to K2 on crutches, but Wanda, like so many Polish alpinists, had been forged to an unimaginable level of toughness and determination. K2 was Wanda's dream, and she wanted to see it through, at least as far as base camp.

Grim-faced and intent, she limped along the 150-kilometre approach march, trying to keep up with the others. Her crutches teetered on the overhanging cliffsides as she balanced on the pencil-thin trail. Hour after hour. Day after day. The villagers were dumbstruck when they saw her – this exceptionally beautiful and rather small woman – forging ahead on crutches through the Braldu Valley. The local porters, who knew her from previous expeditions, were so in awe of her bravery that they began to inscribe messages on the rocks: "Long live Wanda. Viva Wanda."

After several days she reached the Baltoro Glacier, where the trail worsened. Pebbles and boulders gave way to large talus. As each pair of crutches disintegrated from the punishing route, she would haul out a fresh set. Her hands hung with shreds of blistered skin, and her armpits were rubbed raw.

Wanda was still a few hours from base camp when exhaustion overwhelmed her. Unaware of the magnificent granite walls around her, she slumped down on a rock, massaged her throbbing leg, and silently began to weep. This was how her fellow Polish climbers, Jerzy Kukuczka and Voytek Kurtyka, found her as they made their way to K2 base camp. The indestructible, bearish Kukuczka, known by all as "Jurek," couldn't help himself: he scooped her up and began to carry her. Voytek, slender and wiry, took her crutches. Alternating loads, the two carried Wanda the remaining distance.

In truth, Jurek didn't think much of women's expeditions, even though he admired Wanda. He supposed that she viewed climbing as a competitive sport, which was why she insisted on climbing with, and being compared to, other women. He just wanted to go climbing. Most of his male counterparts felt the same. Nevertheless, Wanda was well connected and had managed to get a climbing permit for K2. If he and Voytek could tag along, they weren't too proud to do it.

Since Voytek knew her better, it was he who had negotiated their places on her permit. They wouldn't get in her way, he promised, or climb on her route. He knew it was important to Wanda that her all-women's expeditions at least be *perceived* as being unsupported by men. As far as the Pakistani authorities knew, he and Jurek were along as official photographers and reporters, as well as to protect the ladies in a Muslim country. He understood Wanda's wishes, and he respected them.

This was characteristic of Voytek. Unlike some of his more plain-spoken fellow climbers, he was thoughtful and careful about what he said. His powers of observation were impressive, not just of facts, but of nuance and attitude and feeling. Known as a "thinking man's" climber, he came from an educated and cultured background and was able to demonstrate his remarkable curiosity in a number of languages.

Now in his early thirties, Voytek came from the small village of Skrzynka in western Poland, in what formerly was German territory. There, he spent his early years surrounded by nature. A move to the war-ravaged city of Wrocław at age 10 sank Voytek into a childhood depression. Studying electrical engineering in university did little to improve his spirits. Then he encountered rock climbing. His natural aptitude for climbing on rock garnered him the nickname *zwierz*, or "animal." He immediately grasped that climbing was a kind of addiction for him. Little did he understand how serious a trap that addiction could become.

A year younger than his intense friend, Jurek Kukuczka was built solid and stocky, while the slender Voytek was coiled tight like a spring. Jurek was a man of few words. If anything caught one's attention, it was his eyes. They were warm and friendly, with just a hint of a smile. Born in 1948, Jurek, like so many of Poland's leading climbers, studied electrical engineering at university. This prepared him well for work in the coal-mining industry that dominated the Katowice area of southwestern Poland. But his life was climbing. From the first time he touched rock at the age of 17, he felt a surge of power that ultimately propelled him to the world's highest summits. And in the mountains, he was unstoppable.

Jurek, Voytek and Wanda: three climbing legends, all in Pakistan with the same goal – to climb what was widely accepted as the most difficult of the 14 peaks that exceed that magic height, 8000 metres. Their fierce resolve and tireless motivation had made these three among the most highly respected climbers in the world. Yet nothing about their position in the mountaineering world was accidental. Their brilliant careers as alpinists had begun humbly; but like so many, they were shaped by the violent devastation into which they were born – a country plagued by wars, then carved up and dominated by two stern masters: Germany and Russia. And although Wanda, Jurek and Voytek were among the lucky ones to survive, the terrors of war helped shape their resilience and toughness. For all of these elite climbers, the story was the same: history had hardened both their bodies and their minds. They weren't just climbers. They were *Polish* climbers.

❄ ❄ ❄

Four years before Wanda was born, Poland's fate was sealed. In 1939, just days before the onset of World War II, the Nazis and Soviets signed a non-aggression agreement known as the Molotov/Ribbentrop Pact. The agreement stated that the two countries would not attack each other and would handle any "problems" in an amicable manner. Initiated by Germany, the agreement was meant to minimize the threat of having to fight a war on two fronts – a situation they wanted to avoid at any cost, particularly after their experiences in the previous world war.

The "non-aggression" theme is ironic because, at the same time, the two states agreed to a secret protocol that would partition Poland and the Baltic States between Germany and the Soviet Union, providing the Soviets with a buffer zone in case of an attack from the west. This secret deal precipitated years of bloodshed and horror.

Less than two weeks after the secret protocol was signed, Germany unveiled its duplicitous strategy through an ingenious plan. On August 31, 1939, German soldiers attacked a German-language radio station in Gliwice, in the Upper Silesia region of Poland. The attack was a complete sham, for at least one of the instigators was not a German soldier at all, but a convicted German criminal who had been promised reprieve for his actions. Mission accomplished, he was mowed down by *real* German SS soldiers. The SS troops removed his blood-soaked uniform, replaced it with a Polish uniform, and left the body to be discovered by the police. The next morning the world learned the shocking news: the *Poles* had apparently launched an unprovoked attack on the Third Reich.

Germany's military pummelling of Poland accelerated after that, exactly as planned: air raids, dive-bombers, street bombs and rifle fire. In less than a week, Poland was unable to defend its frontiers. By the end of the second week, Warsaw was surrounded. The Poles were completely outnumbered: 2,600 German tanks against the Poles' 150; 2,000 German warplanes against 400 Polish. But the Poles didn't panic. They knew they only had to hold the Germans off for a couple of weeks until the Western Allies, who had recently declared war on Germany, would launch a major offensive.

That never happened.

Then, on September 17, 1939, to the complete surprise of the Poles and the rest of the world, but precisely as outlined in the secret protocol, the Soviets crossed Poland's eastern frontier. The Polish government fled Warsaw, leaving the local population to defend it, which they managed to do for another 10 days. But by then it was clear what was going on: the Germans and the Soviets were in collusion, pinching off the city. There was no place to hide. The Polish armies lost more than 60,000 men, with 140,000 wounded. The Allies never appeared. It would have been unthinkable to upset the Soviet alliance for the sake of the Poles.

Germany and the Soviets then had to divide the spoils. While the Soviets carved up the northeast, the Reich picked up the western parts of the country, where they promptly declared martial law. They designated their newly occupied territories as "work areas," offering just two types of punishment for perceived offences: concentration camps or death.

Both sides appeared to hate the Poles almost as much as they hated the Jews. Nazi military commander Heinrich Himmler busied himself crisscrossing the country in his efforts to classify, segregate and subjugate the population. Village by village, he forced each citizen to register with the Nazi authorities. They doled out identity cards and work passes and finally, calorie coupons, depending on each individual's classification.

A "first-class" person born of German heritage received 4,000 calories per day. A Polish worker got 900. A Jew, usually nothing at all.

The troops expelled Polish citizens from their homes in order to make room for German officials. Wanda's father, Zbigniew Błaszkiewicz, was living in Radom in southeastern Poland at the time. He was working as an engineer at a weapons factory when he was forced to flee rather than risk imprisonment. The soldiers gave him just a few hours to gather his meagre belongings and leave. Eager to get as far away as possible, he moved to Płungiany in northeastern Poland (later Lithuania). There, he met and married a well-educated local girl, Maria Pietkun, whose passion was translating hieroglyphics.

Almost from the start there was tension between them. Zbigniew, who was obsessed with frugality and worries about the future, confided in his diaries that he didn't completely respect his free-spirited wife. Wanda, their second of four children, was born on February 4, 1943, into a divided household and a divided country.

❊ ❊ ❊

It wasn't just the Germans who were terrorizing Poland. In the northeast, where Wanda's family lived, the Soviets were deporting Poles to concentration camps where they were used as slave labour. Throughout 1940 and 1941, scores of freight trains headed east, full of falsely convicted Polish "criminals." They were packed standing up in sealed, windowless cattle cars and transported thousands of kilometres at a time. They starved. They went mad. They froze. They even resorted to cannibalism. Those who died en route were thrown from openings in the car roofs. In all, 1.5 million Poles were deported, and nearly half never made it back. The brutality was another sad reminder of Poland's melancholy history of partition.

Between the Nazis and the Soviets, Poland was being systematically reduced to a slave nation. Completely isolated from outside help, it had no means of defending itself. Then the war changed direction when Germany attacked Russia on June 22, 1941. Incomprehensibly, the Soviets turned to the Poles for assistance. As outrageous as the idea was, answering the Soviets' call saved Poland from total annihilation – but just barely, for it was on Poland's soil that some of the principal battles were fought.

German rulers had a plan for Poland and its people, despite their preoccupation with Russia. They estimated that about 20 million of the "least suitable" Poles should be resettled in Western Siberia; about four million were suitable for "re-Germanization" because of their Germanic roots;

and the rest should simply be eliminated. The German troops confiscated private land, factories and homes – without compensation. Poland provided Germany with the ideal location for a wide array of camps: camps for "criminals," camps for deportees, camps for political and racial enemies, camps for slave labour and, finally, camps for systematic genocide. Lublin, Chełmno, Treblinka, Sobibór, Bełżec and Auschwitz: names that became forever associated with inhumanity. But this program of death was not limited to the camps. From 1940 to 1943, the Warsaw Ghetto and most of its Jewish occupants were carefully and methodically eliminated.

During the six years of war, from 1939 to 1945, more than six million Poles lost their lives – over 15 per cent of the population. Only 10 per cent of the dead were a result of direct war actions. The rest were Polish civilians, killed in executions and perished from disease and starvation in the streets and the camps. The numbers defy understanding, as do the conditions in which people struggled to survive during those years.

Those who did survive continued fighting for their country's independence, still with no help from abroad. The Warsaw Uprising, which Polish citizens launched in 1944 in order to gain back their capital, was doomed from the start. It took only 63 days for the Reich to demolish the city's historical treasures, its hospitals, homes and bridges. Mass shootings were commonplace. More than 150,000 Warsaw residents were killed, and the remaining half million were transported to labour camps. After the city emptied out, troops of German engineers came in and burned and destroyed everything that was left, with particular attention paid to historical monuments, churches and archives. The German army had taken Hitler's orders to heart when he said that Warsaw should be "razed without trace."

When the Russians pulled in a few months later, in early 1945, they didn't take long to push the Germans back and install a new president in the city – a Communist. By the time "peace" was declared on May 9, 1945, all of Poland was under Soviet rule. Liberation from the Germans was complete – but it was liberation in name only, and even then it hardly lived up to the name.

The new Soviet bosses made high-level deals and shuffled borders at will. Płungiany, where Wanda was born, was now in Lithuania and rechristened Plungė. The Polish citizens who survived were numbed by the six years of terror and slaughter. They no longer remembered what it felt like to walk in the streets without fear of being shot. Their social structure was completely altered; there was no more intelligentsia, and there were certainly no more Jews. For the survivors, each day that passed by blurred the memory of the Poland they had once known.

❋ ❋ ❋

Near the end of the war, Wanda's family home fell into the hands of the conquering Russians. By 1946 most of their personal property had been confiscated and it was clear they would have to flee. But to where? Eventually they joined Zbigniew's parents in Łańcut, in the south, not far from the Ukraine border. Once again, Zbigniew packed up his family's few pieces of furniture and clothing and set out. They weren't alone. The pockmarked roads were crammed with tanks, motorcycles, trucks laden with gas cans, and human convoys – everyone leaving some anguish behind, looking for fresh hope, a new life.

But in Łańcut, Zbigniew struggled to find meaningful work and, after the birth of two more children, the family of six outgrew the ancestral home and began to search for a place of their own. They found it in Wrocław, hundreds of kilometres to the west, where the ravages of war were still very evident. Street corners were piled with debris, and the walls of many buildings were scarred from shellfire. Dislodged roof tiles clattered down in the wind, and shards of glass in the gaping windows were bandaged over with cardboard. Some houses were completely destroyed, with just a few half-walls standing. The worst appeared as hideous, blackened, burnt-out shapes, etched against the sky. Everywhere was rubble.

The Błaszkiewiczes moved into a partially destroyed, three-level house. The water pipes had burst; the windows were broken; the walls were damp with cold; the roof leaked. But according to the authorities, it was too large for just a family of six, so they threatened to move even more people in. The highly intelligent yet eccentric Zbigniew wanted none of that. He not only refused to repair the damage but inflicted even more on the old house in order to discourage any takers.

The chaos of Wanda's home was mirrored in the continuous power struggle within the household. Zbigniew was an impatient man, uninterested in practical things, preferring instead to invent new tools, experiment with unusual varieties of vegetables in his backyard garden or tend to the goats that occupied the first level of the house. He was stingy with what little money he had, and he doled it out in dribs and drabs to Maria. When he lost all confidence in Maria's ability to budget, he delegated responsibility for the household expenses to Wanda. This, at the age of four.

It was difficult to find enough food in the shops, and the queues were endless. Luxuries like chocolate or coffee arrived only at Easter and Christmas, sent by sympathetic relatives living abroad. The stress grew too much for

Maria, who couldn't cope. Instead, she relied heavily on Wanda, the eldest daughter, who spent much of her time sweeping floors, peeling vegetables, standing in food lines and caring for her siblings. Clever Wanda soon learned that the best way to finish her chores was to delegate them to her younger brother and sister, a practice she would use frequently on her climbs later in life. "She was a very good boss," said her brother, Michael Błaszkiewicz, of their youth. "She was a *hard* boss," sister Nina Fies corrected him.

Even at this early age there was little time for Wanda to be a girl. One day, in a ruined section of the house, Wanda discovered a rag doll almost as big as her. The only thing missing was a head. She was overcome with childish joy when her parents managed to find a plastic head for the doll. It was much too tiny for such a big doll and looked ridiculous, even macabre. But Wanda the girl still had a doll, *with* a head, and for a time she was happy.

Wanda didn't mind looking after her much younger brother Michael, but her sister was a different matter. Nina was just close enough in age that she often wanted to be with her older sister, something that Wanda abhorred. "For me, it meant that my freedom was curbed," she said. Years later, she struggled to find pleasant memories of that time. "I don't remember the moments when love and tolerance were between us ... Only the regrets stay in my mind."[1] But not so for Nina, who smiled sadly as she recalled her impressive older sister.

Across the street from their home was a large wooded area, a favourite place for children to play and one of the few parts of the city that had not been assaulted. But even more fun was roaming throughout the nearby bombed-out houses, crunching broken glass underfoot and building play-houses with bricks and stones. Hide-and-seek was popular, and so was finding unexploded grenades buried in the rubble.

One afternoon in the spring of 1948, Wanda, together with a few friends and her older brother, came upon one of these grenades. They decided to put it in a firepit and light it. Since Wanda was the only girl in the group, the boys chose to exclude her from this thrilling and forbidden game and sent her home, angry and crying. She wailed her story to her mother, who raced back through the streets to stop the others. She was too late. Mercifully, the killing scene was obscured by a thick, dusty haze. Only a few hours later, there was nothing left to indicate the hideous tragedy that had occurred: all of them killed, including Wanda's brother. The emotional scars, and the capricious nature of death, never left Wanda, however. "I wouldn't be here if seven-year-old boys could bear to play with five-year-old girls."[2]

✳ ✳ ✳

Wanda's childhood was not unusual; life in Poland at this time was anything but comfortable. The first postwar government administration was called the Polish Committee of National Liberation (PKWN), and, although the personnel were Polish, they were appointed by and worked for Stalin. The Soviets first set up a sinister surveillance system to deal with spies and saboteurs. Next, they "liberated" vast numbers of landowners from their property by breaking up all private holdings larger than 50 hectares into 15- to 20-hectare plots, which they then redistributed to peasants. But not even the peasants were safe. They were subsequently ordered to share their food with worker squads, all in the name of "agrarian reform."

In the three years that followed the war, there were massive resettlement programs. Millions of people took to the roads. Some were survivors of the work camps. Others were Polish refugees who had fled the country. Still others were residents ordered to relocate and populate the recovered territories in the north and west.

A particularly tough year was 1947. The harvest failed, triggering a series of new laws and protocols created to manage the resulting panic. Centralized control grew even tighter. Economic statistics were considered state secrets, and free debate ceased. By 1948 the Soviets had successfully moulded the government into a clone of the Soviet system, not only in Poland but in all of the Soviet-controlled Eastern European countries. They closed the frontiers, tightened security to wartime levels and reintroduced conscription. They spent all the public coffers on military priorities and even set up a Soviet-style secret police to deal with any perceived transgressions.

Wanda tried to ignore the madness that surrounded her and concentrated on her studies. She sped through the grades and chose mathematics as a field for further study, a subject that seemed both interesting and practical. By the age of 16 she was enrolled at Wrocław University. When she wasn't in class, she was racing around the countryside on her motorcycle, her dark hair flying. She continued living at home with her family and earned a little on the side by tutoring students in math and physics. Eager young men frequented the family home, but Wanda seemed more interested in her professors than her classroom peers. Then, when she was just 18, she discovered a fresh new world, untouched by war.

It was a bright Saturday morning when a school friend, Bogdan Jankowski, introduced her to the sport of rock climbing at a crag in southwestern

Poland. "Wait there," Bogdan told her, instructing her to sit on a tree stump at the base of one of the routes in order to watch some of the others climb. Her turn would come soon. But when he was halfway up his route he heard a monstrous panting coming from the chimney feature next to him. He looked down and there was Wanda, climbing without a rope, already near the top of the chimney, quite frightened and struggling to complete the route. He reached the top of the cliff, tied a knot at the end of the rope and tossed it down to her. "Wanda, catch!" he yelled. Wanda caught the knotted rope with her extended hand, threw it away in disgust, and scrambled to the top on her own.

Her body seemed custom-designed for climbing: she was light and strong and she instinctively knew how to stay in balance on the rock. A photograph of Wanda striding across the meadow in front of the crag, still in her climbing harness, reveals a confident young woman, eyes flashing, arms flexed in a mock display of muscle strength, with a confident grin on her face. She gushed in her journal that she "adored the physical movement, the fresh air, the camaraderie and the excitement."

The next weekend she was back, throwing herself at increasingly difficult climbing routes during the day and sleeping in caves at night, warmed by a roaring campfire and like-minded friends. Wanda was possessed by climbing from the first moment. "I knew it would somehow mark the rest of my life," she said.[3] For many first-timers, climbing feels like a discovery of freedom. But in Wanda's world of limited self-expression, that feeling must have been much more intense. She had found an environment in which her strength and ambition could flourish, and, in the middle of a country devastated by war, she had discovered a landscape that humans hadn't yet blighted.

The Polish landscape was especially devastated in and around the city of Katowice in the southwestern part of the country. This was the area where Jurek Kukuczka had grown up, a region that changed dramatically after the war ended, because of the Six Year Economic Plan, which was announced in 1950. The undisputed darling of the plan was heavy industry – unlimited iron and steel. The centre for much of its production was Katowice. The Soviets even constructed a railway line linking Katowice directly to the Soviet frontier in order to move products from the massive Katowice Steelworks. It was here that a large community of hard-core climbers emerged, their jobs provided by the steelworks.

Despite the economic initiatives, Polish citizens were overwhelmingly disgruntled. Their wages were fixed, regardless of how much – or how little – work they did. Although they were powerless to fight the system, they practised a kind of passive resistance that ground their country almost to a halt. There was low-level cheating and slacking off, which resulted in poor productivity, shoddy standards and terrible inefficiencies. People saved their energy for moonlighting jobs or for standing in the endless breadlines. Their resentment was further fuelled by what they had endured: war with Germany, war with Russia, providing the battlefield for the war between Germany and Russia, Soviet rule, partition. They had little respect for the unearned authority that ruled them. Instead, they concentrated on their own survival.

Yet within this stifling atmosphere, Wanda saw a new world opening up for her – a world of nature and rock and friendship, and a sense of freedom, far from the grey, grimy streets. Her climbing jaunts soon extended beyond the nearby crags as she sampled the limestone of the Jura Mountains northwest of Krakow, the sandstone cliffs near the frontier with East Germany and, finally, the High Tatras, bordering what was then Czechoslovakia. The mountains became her oases of peace. Just like her attitude in school, Wanda's approach to climbing was systematic and persistent. Her sister later said, "Climbing worked like a drug on her. She never even gave it any consideration. It automatically entered her blood and was totally absorbed by it." As her confidence grew, so did her beauty. Her predominantly male climbing partners were dazzled by her radiant smile.

※ ※ ※

Wanda's first trip to the Alps coincided with her graduation from university in 1964 at the age of 21. Because of a severely infected cyst on her arm, she did very little climbing. But she found a sympathetic Innsbruck physician, Dr. Helmut Scharfetter, who not only treated her infection but assuaged her disappointment by arranging a mountain rescue course for her. He then went on to climb with her in the Zillertal Alps. His first impressions were of an intelligent young woman, incredibly attractive despite her tattered clothes. The good doctor would eventually play an important role in her life.

Shortly after she returned to Wrocław, the phone rang. It was a man from the militia, inviting her for coffee in Wrocław's best café. Wanda agreed and appeared at the appointed time. Two men in uniform greeted her, introduced themselves rather formally, showed her their identification papers and asked her to sit down. They ordered thick, strong coffee and generous portions of apple cake.

The taller of the two offered a thin smile as he complimented Wanda: "You are a climber – a very famous climber in Poland."

"Yes, I climb a lot. Maybe a little well known, but not so famous," she replied, a little wary.

The short, pale one chimed in between enormous bites of cake. "Climbing is difficult and dangerous," he gulped. "You must be very strong. And you travel a lot."

"Yes, I travel to climb. I must, if I am to be a serious climber."

They leaned a little closer, peering at Wanda with increased concentration. "You were in Austria recently. How was it? Did you meet some interesting people?"

She sat back in her chair, gaining a little distance. "Yes, of course, I always meet interesting people. Climbers, of course."

"You are a very privileged woman; you travel outside of Poland and you meet foreigners. Is this an activity you would like to continue?"

Wanda finally grasped the gist of their queries: they wanted her to work with the secret service! While they continued with their propositions, she began to seethe. Finally she could no longer contain her anger. She pounded her fist on the table and yelled, "What are you asking me to do, spy for Poland? That is completely immoral and contemptible. How could you even ask me to do this?"

Very easily, as it turned out. The Soviet surveillance machine relied upon "volunteers" like Wanda and her climbing contemporaries – Polish citizens who regularly travelled outside Poland's borders.

The neighbouring table craned their necks to see Wanda, whose eyes darkened with anger as she continued to shout and gesticulate. The men cast furtive glances at the nearby customers. They tried to calm her by assuring her that it was all just talk, nothing serious. The tall one snapped his fingers to signal the waiter, then he paid the bill, and the two men escorted Wanda outside the café, where their attitude changed. They warned her that if she ever mentioned this conversation to anyone, she could forget about further trips to the Alps – or anywhere outside Poland.

She was never approached again, but many others were. Numerous climbers revealed that not only were they expected to report in to the authorities immediately after each trip abroad, but "collaboration" was often the key to retrieving their passports for their next international expedition.

The secret service was interested in them for a number of reasons. Climbers who travelled and lived abroad for extended periods of time were prime candidates for the "Western idealistic rot," it claimed. Even worse, they could bring it back to Poland. They needed to be watched – carefully. But they could also be useful observers of the West, bringing back valuable information about politics, economies and lifestyles. Most important, climbers were easy to bargain with because they had much to gain – freedom to travel – and even more to lose – confinement to Poland. Climbers were easy targets. Most club presidents spoke regularly with the secret service, and it was common knowledge that there were informants within the clubs. Some climbers talked about the situation openly, and others did not. Some climbers were allowed to leave the country after meetings with the secret service, and others, mysteriously, were not. It is highly unlikely that any high-profile or well-travelled Polish climber managed to escape their grasp.

❅ ❅ ❅

It was on Wanda's fourth trip to the Alps, in 1967, that she first managed some serious climbing. Her partner was Halina Krüger-Syrokomska, a tiny fireball of a woman who liked rough jokes, climbed well and smoked a pipe. The Mountain Club had selected and sponsored them; it was a rare opportunity for Polish female climbers. A year later they travelled to Norway to make the first women's ascent of the steep east buttress of Trollryggen – over 3000 metres high and one of the longest rock routes in Europe. They formed a strong team: Halina had the brains, Wanda the brawn.

As two female climbers who had achieved success abroad, they returned home from Norway as minor celebrities, more so than their male counterparts who were also chalking up impressive climbs in the Alps. Although their story was a pleasant diversion to the spartan lives of normal Polish citizens, their temporary fame did little to improve their own quality of life.

From 1961 to 1968, the standard of living for most was scarcely better than during the war. In contrast, high-level party bosses and senior industrialists basked in ostentatious luxury. Their fast cars, private villas and foreign travel infuriated the people who struggled to survive on paltry earnings. The average monthly wage was 3,500 zł. per month (about USD35). Even if they had been able to travel abroad, their currency was completely useless outside the country, making them virtual slaves of the state.

Over three million housing units were constructed after the war, primarily in the urban areas. These shoddy apartment blocks were built of cement and plaster in the Soviet style seen throughout the Eastern Bloc. The workmanship was substandard and few had the luxury of indoor toilets or central heating. These structures certainly bore no resemblance to the opulent homes of the party elite.

Then, in December of 1970, the government miscalculated the reach of its power and influence when it increased food prices by 20 per cent. Just in time for Christmas. When the populace demonstrated with widespread strikes, the army retaliated. A truce was signed, but it was an uneasy one. By now, ordinary citizens were not just angry about the rise in prices. They were sick to death of the whole regime, including the mind-numbing level of censorship. The government not only controlled information, it manufactured it. The colossal party rallies, attended by thousands of cheering "supporters," fooled no one. The ridiculous posturing was an insult to people's intelligence. Particularly for educated Poles, the preaching of party lines was offensive.

The long queues, the polluted air, chronic food shortages, crumbling homes, bullying officials, the substandard living conditions: it all wore the people down. Many turned to alcohol. Depression was rampant. The streets became full of the walking dead.

❊ ❊ ❊

Wanda's family struggled. They were perpetually short of money, despite her father's futile efforts to patent his inventions. As the disappointments accumulated, Zbigniew's mistrust of people grew. He anticipated foul play at every turn. He withdrew into an imaginary world of lost opportunity and began studying Spanish in the hope of escaping Poland's austerity for sunny South America. Deeply unhappy, he eventually moved out. Wanda's sister Nina recalled that sad time: "He was so different from our mother. Mother could not recover from the problems of losing everything during the war … Suddenly she was left by her husband in a poor home without anything. Wanda accepted the role of husband, father, friend, guardian's daughter. She was the strongest person in our family."

The split was acrimonious and Wanda's parents fought over the family home. Wanda stepped in and, in her new role as unofficial head of the family, bought it with borrowed money so that the remaining family members could stay together. This created additional stress, for her priorities were now torn between her financial responsibilities and climbing.

She coped with the increasing financial pressure as well as she could, but it surely influenced her decision to marry, and marry well, in the spring of 1970. Wojtek Rutkiewicz was tall, dark and handsome, a mathematician, and the son of Poland's Deputy Minister for Health. He was also a climber, which was how they first met. They moved into the upper flat in Wanda's family home and then later relocated to Warsaw for Wojtek's work.

Three months after exchanging vows, Wanda jumped at the chance to join a Polish–Soviet expedition to the Soviet Pamirs. The nationally sanctioned trip was headed by the well-known Polish expedition leader Andrzej Zawada. Their objective was 7134-metre Pik Lenin, the highest mountain Wanda had ever attempted. It was almost like a honeymoon – except that Wojtek wasn't invited.

CHAPTER TWO

CLIMBING POLITICS

And the point is to live everything. Live the questions now.
Perhaps then, someday far into the future, you will gradually,
without even noticing it, live your way into the answer.
— RAINER MARIA RILKE, *LETTERS TO A YOUNG POET*

To be a Polish climber has never been easy, and yet the country boasts a long and colourful mountaineering heritage. As early as 1924, Polish climbers were making plans for Everest and K2. This, so soon after the country was licking its wounds from the war with Bolshevik Russia. Patriotic feelings ran high, and by the 1930s climbers had established their own Mountaineering Club. Even after World War II, the club managed to remain active, but when the Stalinist system took over in 1949 everything changed. The Soviet authorities didn't outlaw climbing completely; they just shifted it from an individual experience, which they categorized as a "relic of bourgeois alpinism," to a collective endeavour that could be manipulated by the propaganda machine. The most immediate impact was the severely restricted access to the Tatras. Climbers were forced to dodge border patrols and submit to searches and interrogations. But the strategy failed. A naturally rebellious lot, they jumped at the opportunity to climb in forbidden territory.

Under Khrushchev and Gomułka, a political thaw encouraged the Mountaineering Club to reform, but there were still plenty of rules. As soon as the Iron Curtain lifted slightly in the mid-1950s, climbers headed west – to the Alps. Desperate to catch up to their European counterparts, and dreadfully underfunded, they nevertheless stormed around the Alps and managed to put up an impressive number of difficult climbs. By the early 1960s they had discovered the Hindu Kush, the most practical combination of high mountains, easy access and cheap living. With all hope of real democratization in Poland fading, climbers gave up on realizing their potential at home. They began to look beyond its borders for ways to escape from the boredom and drabness of their everyday lives.

Ironically, the system that stifled them at home provided their ticket to freedom. The centralized government was happy to grant them permits to climb abroad, for their international successes brought glory to Poland.

The style of climbing that developed during this time was built on the classic, well-rounded model that valued not just climbing but also knowledge of mountain history, literature, art and tradition. The spiritual hub of this developing culture was not in the club office in Warsaw, but in a little mountain hut in the Morskie Oko valley in the Tatras. There, during the candlelit evenings that followed long days in the mountains, the oral tradition flourished. It was a place for storytelling, heated debates, singing and dreaming. It was a place where Polish climbers could feel free.

For those who went abroad, the exhilaration of escape was marred only by the pressure to succeed. That, combined with the climbers' solid training, dogged determination and stoicism in extreme conditions, as well as a strong streak of romantic heroism, produced outstanding results.

Climbing evolved into a pastime that people from all levels of society could enjoy. Before long, climbers were identifying themselves as a subculture within Polish society. The climbing writer J.A. Szczepański, known as the cerebral leader of Polish climbers in the first half of the 20th century, wrote, "Climbing is not a symbol or poetic metaphor of life – it is life itself."[4]

Word spread. The climbing life was a good life. Trips abroad, adventure and the underground economy that developed around climbing began to attract more and more climbers to the clubs. When the clubs merged into the Polish Alpine Association in 1974, additional red tape arose. Each climber was given an official card stating where and when he was qualified to climb. It was almost like a licence. By 1979 there were 2,400 active climbers in Poland. Clubs multiplied and soon the universities jumped on board, creating their own organizations that took advantage of centralized funding for their "sporting" activities.

One of the greatest breakthroughs was the creation of the Fund for the Social Action for Youth (FASM) in the 1970s. The fund made it possible for young people to earn extra money at a low tax rate in order to buy muchneeded things like furniture. In order to retain some level of control, the extra earnings had to be funnelled through an officially sanctioned club. The Polish Alpine Association (as the Mountaineering Club was now named) was recognized as a legitimate club, as long as it declared itself a "Socialist" organization, which it did. Climbers directed their meagre earnings through their clubs – not for furniture but for expeditions!

The clubs became micro-communities within the country. People worked *in* the clubs and *for* the clubs. They spent their free time in the company of club members who had similar interests and opinions. They kept aloof from their dysfunctional surroundings and abandoned any career aspirations. They channelled their unfulfilled hopes and suppressed energies into a passionate love of mountains and adventure. Their mountain asylums became much more than an escape from their reality; they were a way to fulfill themselves and create meaningful lives. Up in the hills, the Orwellian principles didn't apply. There, they could rely on principles that predated the totalitarian state – values that were common to all the climbers. The more successful the climbers were, the more they turned inward, developing their own ideology and forms of literary expression.

Within a very few years Poland was a Himalayan superpower and the government authorities loved it. The government's propaganda machine exploited the climbers' successes while the climbers exploited the machine. The very best were given awards and medals. Hundreds of others took advantage of the freedom to roam the world's great mountain ranges.

But the climbing community faced some disquieting moral dilemmas. Most climbers were opposed to the regime and by the early 1980s were active in the emerging Solidarity movement, which was trying to bring democracy to Poland. At the same time, they were tempted by centralized support and were forced to join clubs that openly declared themselves socialist. The authorities watched climbers closely, monitoring their movements and offering them opportunities to spy. Some accepted. Outspoken Wrocław climber Alek Lwow characterized this kind of behaviour as "obedience to the official propaganda, though rather with a view to milking the authorities, to sucking advantages out of the regime."[5] Andrzej Zawada knew this world better than most, but he defended the strategy, claiming it was certainly no worse than what Western climbers did – plaster their clothing with unsightly sponsor logos. Still, there seemed to be a collective feeling of guilt, for climbers referred to the situation as being "dipped in the manure" of the totalitarian state.

Despite the moral hand-wringing, the fact remained that the choice for Polish climbers was simple: accept government support, or don't climb at all.

They chose to climb. The more they climbed the better they became, and the mountaineering world stood in awe.

✳ ✳ ✳

When Andrzej Zawada first became interested in climbing, he joined the Warsaw Mountain Club, part of the countrywide alpine association that dated back to the 1930s, when there were no restrictions for Polish climbers. Most aspiring climbers were part of the club, which played a decisive role in developing and defining climbing in Poland – almost too great a role. The club offered advancing levels of theoretical and practical instruction. But it was also extremely regulated. A novice climber was forbidden to climb unsupervised before passing a number of tests. Progress was tracked in each climber's passbook, and at some point a qualified climber could begin going to the Tatras or the Alps to climb. But not before. Activities like soloing were strictly forbidden and a climber caught doing so could be thrown out of the club. In a bizarre display of self-censorship, the club magazine, *Taternik*, responded by not reporting solo climbs.

Not surprisingly, there were occasional transgressions despite the tight controls. Although the Wrocław club was strong and active, Voytek Kurtyka wasn't part of it, at least not immediately. Yet he climbed like a fiend, both in Poland and abroad, finagling his way across borders. The club officials were horrified when they realized that one of Poland's leading rock climbers – someone who had already made a number of notable climbs in the Alps, as well as daring first winter ascents in the Tatras – had never taken a single course of instruction. Since Voytek had occasionally travelled under the club banner and with their support, they were now liable. They hastened to install him as a fully qualified member of the Polish Alpine Association in hope no one would notice.

Andrzej Zawada, on the other hand, played by the rules and quickly became the darling of the Warsaw Mountain Club. Yet even his golden-boy status was temporarily tarnished in 1959 when he violated club rules by making a complete winter traverse of the Tatras mountain range. He had sent out a memo looking for potential partners and had been soundly reprimanded by the club, which advised him that it was too dangerous. A month later he did it anyway. They traversed about 75 kilometres, and gained and lost 22,000 metres on a route that was steep, airy and difficult. Andrzej judged it a great success and an important test of his abilities in winter conditions. The club saw it as a flagrant disregard of their rules and they refused to report it, depriving him of a significant first ascent.

Although the association allowed Andrzej a couple of climbing trips to the Alps in the years following his transgression, they withheld his passport for an expedition that he had organized to the Rakaposhi area in Pakistan's Karakoram Range. But he persisted in his efforts to win back their support, and he finally succeeded. Despite the ever-present secret service agent tagging along, Andrzej felt he had "escaped the cage that was the Polish People's Republic" when the club gave him permission to lead a trip to the Russian Pamirs in 1970. At the same time, Wanda's international reputation as a talented climber was growing, and so the club invited her along too.

Government authorities were convinced that sport could bring prestige and respect to Poland, so they supported the athletes judged most likely to succeed. This included climbers. Some funding came from the state, but institutions and businesses contributed as well. Even factories chipped in with much-needed support. The entire process was funnelled through the club's Himalayan Fund. Poland's best climbers were sent out of the country on partially or completely funded expeditions. They were chosen by an expedition leader from the club's Sporting Committee, a powerful position indeed.

But there was a fundamental difference between the state's support for athletes and its support for alpinists. Top-level football or volleyball players had all their worldly needs taken care of: a car, an apartment, a stable income. Their time was used to train. Climbers were different. Although their successes provided fuel for the propaganda machine, they nevertheless received less money. As a result, climbers had little time to train. Even though they had world-class reputations, they were treated as hobbyists or amateurs. An alpinist had to be an organizer, an outfitter, a packer, a transporter, a communicator, a diplomat, a financier, even a beggar from time to time. Alpinists did everything *except* train. And at the very end, after months of preparation, and if the weather cooperated, they climbed.

Still, financial support from the club was considered a coup for any Polish climber, so it is not surprising that Wanda's invitation to the Pamirs ruffled a few feathers amongst her extremely talented male counterparts. Jurek and many others had been climbing hard in the Polish Tatras, and Voytek was making a name for himself with first winter ascents and new routes on increasingly difficult terrain. But exotic foreign climbs impressed the association honchos the most, and it was Wanda's success abroad that attracted the attention of Andrzej Zawada.

Wanda knew none of the other climbers on the team. It was also her first introduction to Andrzej, who at the age of 42 was already well known in Poland – not only as a climber but also as a leader who could inspire, a diplomat who could smooth the way and a charming and strikingly handsome man.

With only the University of Wrocław in common, Wanda and Andrzej came from entirely different circumstances, and their leadership styles were like night and day. Andrzej hailed from a long aristocratic tradition, starting with Count A. Malczewski. A Romantic poet who is sometimes regarded as the first Polish alpinist, Malczewski did the first ascent of the lower Aiguille du Midi and the sixth ascent of Mont Blanc, both in 1818.

Although not a count, Andrzej was proud of his lineage: Philip, his law-yer father, had a doctorate in international law, and his mother was a lin-guist who translated both Russian and German. But it was his grandfather, Tomasz, who influenced Andrzej the most. Tomasz had fought in the Polish Uprising of 1918–19, and his taste for risk was equal to his grand-son's. Philip's skills were more inclined to diplomacy. When he succeeded in negotiating the terms of the amorphous German–Polish border in the 1920s, he was named the Polish consul for his efforts. The family settled into a diplomatic life in what had now become Germany. Not long after, however, he was struck down with tuberculosis and travelled to Davos, Switzerland, for treatment and the sharp, clean air. But the treatment failed; he died in 1931, when Andrzej was only three years old. His wife, Eleonora, was so terrified her children would succumb to the disease that she moved her two young boys back to Poland and as high as she could, near the Tatras. By 1939 they were living in an alpine-style chalet in which Eleonora rented out rooms to supplement her translation income.

They would occasionally visit their aunt's estate back on the German side of the border, but these trips were always fraught with angst. First, they needed visas to cross the border, and when they arrived, they were obliged to witness their helpless relatives' terror – harassment and bully-ing, incidents where the Gestapo would storm into the home, destroying furniture and ordering them about. Eventually, the family that remained was forced into work camps.

Andrzej was relatively sheltered from the horror, growing up in the pro-tective shadow of the Tatras. He wandered amongst them as often as he could, picking berries and mushrooms and breathing the alpine air. During the war, Eleonora's translating skills brought her work in the local hospital, where hundreds of soldiers whose lungs were damaged by poi-sonous gas arrived for treatment. Some nights, the brave resistance fight-ers held secret meetings in their cozy chalet. Other evenings, she hosted intimate chamber recitals with travelling musicians playing Chopin – a forbidden composer in this German-controlled area, since he was Polish.

As bad as the German occupation was, the Russian "liberation" turned out to be much worse. Russian soldiers – wounded, dirty and often drunk – would storm through the town, forcing civilians to feed them. It was then that Andrzej began colluding with some of the partisans. Still just a schoolboy, he kept a machine gun under his desk at school and grenades by his bed at night.

Andrzej, predictably, landed in prison at the age of 17. He could hear the cries in the neighbouring cells, where most of his friends were executed. Of those who survived, many were tortured. All Andrzej could do was change the dressings on their wounds. He too was interrogated by the Russian secret service, but perhaps because of his youth, they released him after a month. His mother, frantic for his safety, whisked him away to a secret location, where he finished his high-school studies. Going on to study geophysics in university at Wrocław and Warsaw, he soon joined the local mountain club, taking their courses and climbing on weekends. He went on to lead foreign geophysical scientific expeditions, for which he organized the logistics, permits and equipment, and learned about teamwork and diplomatic wrangling.

By the time he and Wanda met, he was perfectly prepared for life as an expedition leader. He had travelled widely, knew how to function within a wide range of institutional and governmental structures, and had led groups of men in situations of significant risk. In contrast, Wanda had been the CEO of her family, supervising her siblings and buying the family groceries.

But they both knew how to climb.

Andrzej was intrigued by the dark-haired young beauty as she navigated the land mines of the mostly male, multicultural Pamirs team. The men flirted with Wanda and teased her, vying for her attention. At first it was fun being the princess. But when they were reluctant to treat her as an equal member of the team, she pushed back. She tried to establish her credibility by beating them at arm wrestling and carrying heavier loads. This only alienated her more. They were used to "girl climbers": women who climbed well but who were never first on the rope, and who usually climbed with their boyfriends or husbands. But this Wanda creature – she wanted to lead and get to the summit on her own!

Disgusted at their attitude, she pronounced the entire expedition dysfunctional. Although she did get up her 7000-metre peak, she vowed to never again join an expedition of this kind. Still, it had occupied more than a month of her newly married life, so as soon as she returned home she set about getting to know her new husband and landing a job at the Institute of Mathematical Computing in Warsaw.

But by 1972 she was planning to hit the road again, this time to the Hindu Kush Mountains of Afghanistan. The team's objective was Noshaq, the second-highest peak in the range and the highest in Afghanistan, at almost 7500 metres. Situated in the Wakhan Corridor separating Russia and China from India and Pakistan, Noshaq's second ascent had been made by the Poles 12 years earlier. Thanks to the war and the Soviet grip on their country, Polish climbers were at this point lagging behind their international counterparts in the high mountains. Now they were returning for some badly needed postwar high-altitude know-how.

Wanda's experience in the Pamirs convinced her that she had to run her own show. The loss of independence implicit in accepting full financial support from the club was too much for her. So she directed some of her private earnings into the club's expedition fund and then tapped into that fund for her expedition expenses.

Another source of funding was Julian Godlewski, a wealthy Pole living in Switzerland. A great patron of Polish culture, Godlewski sponsored the Chopin competition prize as well as Olympic athletes. His other area of interest was mountaineering, a passion that funded a number of Polish expeditions to the great ranges. His endorsement was a gold stamp, for expedition leaders could then approach the official agencies. "Julian has already given us 20,000; how much will you give?"

The most difficult challenge for Polish climbers was finding foreign currency, a requirement for a portion of the expedition expenses. This was solved by inviting foreign climbers along, for they could bring hard currency to the table. In order to use Polish złotys as much as possible, the teams travelled overland to their destinations whenever they could, bringing all their own equipment and as much Polish food and gas as was practical. This strategy made Afghanistan, reachable by road, one of the most popular destinations, at least until the Soviet invasion in 1979, when the country collapsed into complete chaos.

Organizing an expedition was an overwhelmingly complex affair. It was impossible to go to a shop in Poland and buy supplies; camping equipment, tents, sleeping bags, down pants, anoraks, clothes and boots were simply not available. Everything had to be assembled from scratch. At one place climbers would buy the fabric. At another, the zippers. A mother or aunt would sew the items together. There was a shoemaker in Zakopane who handmade their boots, and the ice axes were forged in a local blacksmith shop. "We almost had to pluck the ducks and geese to get the down for the jackets," Wanda said. To add to the hassle, they needed permits for absolutely everything: a permit to buy canned food, another to buy chocolate and yet one more to take anything out of the country. Organizing *any* mountain expedition is onerous, but in Poland it took twice the effort.

After months of preparation, the team of 11 climbers was finally ready to depart for Noshaq. They travelled overland through the Soviet Union in a

Star A-29 truck barely big enough to hold them and all their equipment. Among them was an English woman, Alison Chadwick, who had married Polish climber Janusz Onyszkiewicz. Wanda was intrigued by Alison. An obviously cultured woman, she seemed measured – almost slow – in her actions, but quick in her thoughts. Wanda watched as Alison coped with the Polish team. She was from a country that respected the rights of individuals, but she now found herself in a group of people with a different culture and mentality, one that oscillated between a desire for democracy and a need for an iron fist – people who wanted individual rights but who found it hard to accept other people's ideas. "She respected our right to be different and was merely curious," Wanda remarked.[6]

As the expedition progressed, Wanda and Alison began to talk about the possibility of climbing even higher mountains. There were very few female climbers active on the Himalayan giants at this time, so they needed to gain some self-confidence. The women huddled together, drinking tea, sharing a rope and their dreams. Were they strong enough? Did they have the right skills? Perhaps the most important factor was leadership. They would need to overcome their fears and weaknesses, take advantage of their strengths and learn to make their own decisions, because indecision in the mountains could be fatal. Wanda became convinced that she and Alison could do great things together.

The Poles were not alone on Noshaq. Among the others was an American chemist, Arlene Blum, who would go on to lead the first all-female ascent on Annapurna. The Polish team succeeded on their peak, and four women – Ewa Czarniecka, Alison and Wanda, plus Margaret Young from Arlene's team – stunned the climbing community by summiting in good style. Now that they had climbed to almost 7500 metres, what would stop them from climbing an 8000-metre peak?

The remoteness, the exciting mountain, the group of friends: it all came together for Wanda on this trip. "The perils of climbing fascinated me because they released so much joy and delight in simple things, like the feel of the wind, the scent of rock warmed by the sun, the sudden relaxation of tension, or the hot tea in the cup."[7]

❄ ❄ ❄

While Wanda gained personal confidence and experience in the high mountains, Andrzej had even more ambitious plans; he wanted to carve a secure place in climbing history for all Polish climbers. The year before, in 1971, he had led a groundbreaking climb of the 7852-metre Kunyang

Chhish, in the Western Karakoram. Now, just months after his return from Afghanistan, he was leading another Polish team to Noshaq – in the dead of winter. The government of Afghanistan expressed concern about this audacious undertaking, so, before giving permission, they made an unusual demand: they wanted a letter from the Mountaineering Club stating that the club was aware of the Polish expedition plans and that it would take full responsibility for the climbers' actions. With some difficulty, Andrzej convinced the club to provide the letter.

Andrzej, more than the others, understood the significance of what he was trying. He knew the history of Polish Himalayan climbing, which had begun badly back in 1936 when the Mountaineering Club's Himalayan Committee was first created. They had initially wanted to climb K2, but when denied a permit, they shifted their focus in 1939 to Nanda Devi East, an unclimbed 7434-metre peak in India's Garhwal region. Despite dire warnings from their porters that the Goddess of Destruction would repay them if they set foot on the sacred summit, the team did just that. Within fifteen years, all of the summit climbers were dead.

After World War II broke out in 1939, climbing in the Himalaya more or less came to a halt. But the interruption lasted much longer for Poland than for other countries, thanks to the Soviet regime's stranglehold grip. Mountains were a sign of freedom – a concept the Soviets feared above all. While the Poles languished under Soviet rule, climbers from around the world summited all 14 of the 8000-metre peaks. The French started it with Annapurna in 1950, and the Chinese finished the job on Shishapangma in 1964.

The first Polish expedition to Afghanistan didn't take place until 1960. This event set off an avalanche of expeditions to the Hindu Kush, during which the future cadres of the Himalaya were trained. Andrzej felt that Poland was now ready to claim some new territory in the mountaineering world. A winter climb of Noshaq would be the beginning of that journey.

On December 29, 1972, Andrzej's team assembled at the Warsaw railway station with their three tons of equipment. Although the trip was his idea, Andrzej began the journey to Moscow with a heavy heart, worried that the objective was too ambitious. On the one hand, venturing into the high mountains in winter seemed like a logical extension of summer pursuits, just like they did in the Alps or the Tatras. But it had never been done. This was a step into the unknown.

During the train journey, Andrzej suffered with visions of heavy snowfall, lethal avalanches and frozen feet. As they chugged along through

Kazakhstan's bleak landscape, he stared out at the endless frozen fields hidden beneath a blanket of snow. The temperature dipped to −30° Celsius. The climbers had a brief reprieve when they welcomed in the New Year with Georgian champagne, somewhere near the city of Orenburg on the Ural River.

When they arrived at Noshaq, they were relieved to see very little snow. But it was cold – frighteningly cold. Temperatures hovered around −25° Celsius during the day, and 10 degrees lower at night. The hours of day-light were brutally short. As the winter storms cycled through, the climb-ers suffered in the cold; they eventually retreated to base camp to tend their cracked and frozen lips – and to pray the mountaineer's prayer.

> Bless, oh Lord, our mountain endeavours.
> In the blizzard, in the rain, in the avalanche.
> We see your power everywhere.
> Counting the sleepless hours in the bivouac,
> May we survive another night.
> The hanging shadow of the rock temples,
> Soon a ray of sunlight will shine upon us.
> May we happily make it through the day.
> From the mountaintop may we touch the stars.

Near the middle of February, Andrzej and his partner, the famously tough Tadek Piotrowski, were high enough on the mountain to consider a summit attempt. But temperatures had dropped even lower and were accompanied by a punishing wind. Then, during the night of February 12, Andrzej woke with a start. The tent had stopped flapping and was eerily quiet. He stepped outside. The mountain was windless and calm. He stood perfectly still, savouring the silence and staring in wonder at the black sky, studded with a million stars. This was their chance.

After hours of thawing out their boots and heating water for tea, they squeezed out the door of their tent at 11 a.m. They still had 800 metres to go. As the day wore on, they stopped on a snowy plateau to make some tea. Andrzej almost fainted when he glanced down and saw a dessicated black hand protruding from the snow. It was that of a Bulgarian climber, one of five who had become lost during the previous summer's Noshaq expedition. The sight of the hand rattled them, shaking their resolve. Then the sun dropped behind the ridge and the temperature plunged.

Not long after, the moon rose, bathing the mountain in a pale, ethereal glow.

They decided to continue. The summit appeared just ahead, and they radioed down to base camp that it would only be a few minutes more. When they reached the top, however, their spirits plummeted, for they saw that the main summit was still more than a kilometre away. It was now well after 9 p.m. and the wind was picking up. Just before midnight they finally arrived at the summit, faces numbed by the freezing wind. At 4:30 a.m., after 17 hours of continuous movement, they arrived back at their tent. Now it was time to survey the damage. Tadek's two big toes were frozen like cubes of ice. He rubbed them madly and stuffed them inside his sleeping bag, next to his frozen socks. Andrzej seemed to have emerged unscathed.

Despite the physical toll, they had succeeded – the first in the world to climb a mountain over 7000 metres – in winter. What would be next? Andrzej was a young and powerful climber. He was ambitious. He embraced risk and celebrated the freedom to do so. He understood the value of that freedom as one of the most important things in his life. "The wind on my cheeks, and the cold when it was winter, and the warmth in the summer, the friction of granite against my fingers…. They bring me so much joy."[8] After Noshaq his mind raced with the possibilities. Why not an 8000er now?

While Andrzej was tasting success on Noshaq and beginning the long process of rewriting Poland's place in mountaineering history, Wanda returned home to yet another family tragedy. Her father was found dead, murdered in his home, dismembered and buried in his garden. The murderers were his tenants, presumably motivated by a bit of cash. In a stupor, Maria, Wanda and Michael accompanied the police to identify his mutilated body. As she stared at the carnage, Wanda raged, kicking at the useless clumps of dirt. She swore and threatened revenge at this senseless act of cruelty, then she stormed out of the garden, slamming the squeaky gate behind her.

Faced with this brutal murder and still haunted by her older brother's violent death, Wanda became anxious and paranoid. Strangers frightened her and she began to feel that something terrible might happen to her. She knew her fears were pathological and irrational, so she tried to overcome them, placing herself in situations where she was alone, at night, in the forest, completely responsible for her own safety. Despite her efforts, she couldn't control her fears. She would stuff her head inside her sleeping bag to block out the horrifying sounds of rustling leaves, which, to her, sounded more like ominous footsteps coming closer and closer.

In addition to the deaths of her father and brother, several of Wanda's early climbing partners had already been killed in the mountains. Perhaps it was an overexposure to premature and sudden loss of life that prompted her, and other climbers, to ignore their own mortality rather than succumb to the trauma. As the deaths multiplied, those who survived began to feel immortal. But in her more realistic moments, Wanda admitted that even though she could never escape her addiction to climbing, "It may be the path to death." Wanda had begun to embrace a dangerous philosophy. She not only rejected the societal values that disgusted her but she also accepted that her commitment to climbing might come at the price of self-sacrifice. This attitude seemed to permeate the Polish climbing community as they pushed themselves harder and longer at increasingly difficult and dangerous routes. The harder they pushed, the better they became. Their success in the mountains grew. As did the casualty rate.

Fresh from her victory on Noshaq, Wanda travelled to the Alps in September of 1973. Voytek and Jurek were there that year, too, turning heads with their first ascent of the Polish route on the North Face of the Petit Dru near Chamonix, France. Wanda was in Switzerland, with her eye on the notorious North Face of the Eiger. She took two strong women climbers from Poland with her because, as her confidence grew, so did her preference for female climbing partners. She cited two reasons. One was that she had more opportunity to lead (both physically and figuratively) with women partners. "I don't feel I own a route unless I've had to conquer my fears and take my own risks," she said.[9] Wanda knew of many good female Polish climbers at the time, but most of them climbed with male partners. Her experiences with mixed-gender climbing had provided her with only a limited amount of leading and decision making, both of which she craved. With women climbers, she could be the boss.

Her second justification had more to do with competition. Wanda had grown up playing competitive sports, and she thought it was unfair to be ranked against other male climbers: she would always appear weaker. She was a competitor by nature, and she wanted an equal field. She set out to build a group of competent, self-sufficient Himalayan female climbers with whom she could climb, and against whom she would be compared.

When Wanda, together with Danuta Wach and Stefania Egierszdorff, climbed the difficult and dangerous North Pillar of the Eiger, they returned to Poland as celebrities. Journalists were drawn to Wanda's eminently quotable style: "You don't appreciate the full flavour of life until you risk losing it." News of her adventures in the free world excited other Polish climbers, giving them hope and determination to taste freedom for themselves.

Wanda was thrilled. But when the cameras stopped flashing and the reporters moved on to other stories, reality set in again. There was never enough money or time to relax or train between expeditions. For Wanda, it was straight back to work.

Then there was her marriage. It was now blindingly clear that, although climbing had initially drawn her and her husband together, it was now tearing them apart as Wanda became increasingly focused on her annual expeditions abroad. She later admitted that her decision to go on that first expedition to the Pamirs so soon after marrying Wojtek probably sealed the fate of their marriage. She and Wojtek divorced after only three years together.

Some people criticized her for her lack of commitment to married life, but her approach was hardly different than that of her male counterparts, all of whom were away from home for months at a time. She seemed to approach climbing – and life in general – "like a man." She was independent, with clear and obvious ambitions, and she counted on her spouse's support. For this, she was judged quite harshly. Perhaps because she had been forced into a patriarchal role in her family after the deaths of both her older brother and her father, an attitude of dominance and responsibility felt natural to her.

Although Wanda enjoyed what some describe as a meteoric rise in her climbing career, there were a few setbacks. At least, perceived setbacks. The importance of being included on official Polish expeditions cannot be overstated, so it's not surprising that Wanda felt insulted and ignored when Andrzej failed to invite her on his 1974 winter Lhotse expedition. Her accomplishments were the best among Polish female climbers at the time: hard routes in the Tatras, both winter and summer; the Eiger; Trollryggen; and two 7000-metre peaks. She later heard rumours that she had been excluded not because of her lack of experience but because of her excessive ambition and drive. The assumption was that she would have wanted the summit too badly, perhaps threatening the success of some male members of the team. Another woman was asked to go to Lhotse instead, although in a subordinate role.

The team did not reach the summit. Andrzej later called the failure "the biggest disappointment of my life because we got so close to the top [8250 metres]."[10] But despite his personal frustration, Andrzej understood the power of the media. He managed to spin the Lhotse story as a great success, the first time anyone had climbed above 8000 metres in winter.

In the 1970s, Poland's mountain clubs were still almost exclusively male. A rising star in that world, Leszek Cichy, explained the situation as he remembered it thirty years later. "To tell the truth ... women in the mountains was something new," he said. "The men sort of treated it as ... an attempt at taking part in things that, until now, were things only done by men, such as trips to the poles, conquering space, climbing unconquered peaks.... So maybe we were a bit ... um ... selfish?" Disliking this state of affairs, Wanda decided to take things into her own hands.

The year 1975 was declared International Women's Year, so Wanda decided to organize a women's expedition to the highest unclimbed peak in the world – Pakistan's Gasherbrum III. A number of Polish climbers were convinced that she wanted not only to climb the peak but also to prove that a woman could *lead* an expedition to one of the highest mountains in the world. With the official support and endorsement of Pakistani President Bhutto's wife, Nusrat, Wanda was under enormous pressure to succeed.

Located in the spectacular Karakoram Range, the mountain sits amidst a group of six Gasherbrums, all above 7,000 metres and two of them reaching the magical 8000-metre mark. The complex plan had Wanda leading a group of 10 elite women climbers on Gasherbrum III, while the prominent Warsaw climber Janusz Onyszkiewicz led seven men up Gasherbrum II.

The concept proved confusing right from the start. Alison, Janusz's wife, was under the impression that the men were there as "an emergency support team" to deal with any problems that might arise between the local Muslims and the women's team. Janusz later admitted that their fears about the Muslims were amusingly unfounded. "They didn't regard our ladies as women, but as white men of the female gender."

Among the women invited by Wanda, two had already established themselves as a strong climbing team within Poland: Anna Czerwińska and Krystyna Palmowska. They had met Wanda a couple of years earlier while climbing at a Warsaw training crag, and had been impressed by Wanda's conviction that the future of Polish women's alpinism demanded a broad range of experience. In order to get the full support of the alpine association, female climbers needed more than just a few important

Tatras climbs under their belts, she told them. They needed an international reputation as well.

The men and women planned to share a number of camps along the way, sharing the work as they went. It was an ingenious strategy, and it worked, although not immediately. Some on the team doubted Wanda's ability to lead such a large expedition, and Wanda was a little naïve about how a group of motivated, ambitious and strong-willed women would respond to her sometimes bullheaded approach. When she ordered them to carry double loads to save porter fees, they just ignored her.

Despite her high expectations of others, she was at least as tough on herself. Leszek, 23 at the time, recalled having breakfast with Wanda at one of the higher camps on the mountain when she suddenly felt ill, possibly due to altitude. She ran out of the tent and vomited, came back in, cleaned herself up and declared, "Okay, it's time to go up." Not a hint of self-pity was allowed, and certainly not a rest day. Wanda hadn't scrimped and saved, organized and strategized and travelled halfway across the world to go on vacation. She was completely focused on one thing – the top. It didn't matter to her how terrible the task was. You had to do it. Gasherbrum III had become her *idée fixe*.

But she wasn't always tough. After a particularly hard day of trail-breaking in the deep snow, one of the climbers saw her collapse into a puddle of tears when her camera malfunctioned. Another time she exploded in frustrated anger when her tent poles wouldn't cooperate. She was full of contradictions: strong yet weak, stoic but emotional, hot and cold.

Her success on the mountain did not come easily, particularly with human relationships. Everything started to unravel when climbers began choosing partners, not always to Wanda's liking. Another complication arose when Saeed, the expedition's liaison officer, fell in love with the soft-spoken, blond and beautiful Krystyna, and convinced her to take him with her to the top of the mountain. Alison was particularly frustrated and surprised by what she saw as Wanda's dogmatic attitude, and her husband, Janusz, had serious issues with Wanda's strategy on the mountain, which he saw as flawed. Krystyna defended her, insisting that Wanda was more pragmatic than dogmatic, adjusting her strategies as needed in order to succeed.

Their disagreements were laid bare in a documentary film about the expedition called *Boiling Point*. In a particularly tense scene, the cameras rolled as the two leaders, Janusz and Wanda, argued about the timing of their summit attempts. Janusz stated that they should have tried for the summit three weeks earlier. Wanda defended her decision, saying, "I don't see that the participants are so exhausted," adding that she felt just fine. He retorted, "I wasn't talking about you since you're indestructible. I just wanted to say that the plan of attack is damned risky." He continued his barrage of criticism: "I'm not the leader, because you are, unfortunately, and that's why there are only seven people [left to climb] after seven weeks. In order to be the leader you have to reach a certain level of intelligence and honesty and you haven't reached either."

"End of discussion," Wanda said, looking down.

Late that night she left her tent for a solitary stroll. She needed to clear her mind. The mountains were illuminated by a rising moon, and the continuous murmuring of a nearby stream calmed her jangled nerves. She gazed about for almost an hour before returning to her tent to write in her journal. "This is *my* place. More than any other. I belong in these mountains.... There are not enough words to communicate this world. Words are unimportant. Silence is best."

Wanda felt she needed to be strong, so she ignored the obvious tensions in the group. She made the conscious decision to be hard-nosed; if people didn't like her, it didn't matter. She assessed the expedition dynamics as a microcosm of Polish society: people cried for democracy, but they needed the opposite – tough, directive leadership.

By the end of the expedition, most of the climbers had turned against her. Some of that dissension came from an incident on summit day. Up until the last moment, Wanda insisted that only she and Alison would make the first summit attempt on GIII, as an independent female rope team. Halina Krüger and Anna Okopińska were to follow a day later, as the second summit team. There was never any mention of the possibility of including men on the summit team. But through the binoculars, the climbers at base camp could clearly see that four people (two of them men) were climbing to the top.

"Hello Wanda, hello Wanda, over."

"Everything is fine up here. We are making a summit attempt, over."

"Wait, just tell us, are all four of you going for the top?"

"At this moment the decision is for us to go up, the four of us."

With that announcement, base camp erupted in guffaws and looks of disgust. "So she camouflaged it to the end," Anna snorted. "If she had said openly that the four of them, including two men [Janusz Onyskiewicz and Krzysztof Zdzitowiecki], were going to the summit, nobody would have breathed a word.... We got duped."[11] It was then that, instead of following the climbers up GIII, Anna and Halina changed direction and became the first all-female rope team to climb an 8000-metre peak – GII. It all worked out in the end, but not without a bitter aftertaste.

The men had already climbed GII, provoking Alison to later comment that the much publicized Ladies' Expedition to Gasherbrum III had succeeded in putting three men on the summit of Gasherbrum II! But Wanda ignored the gender politics and was ecstatic about their collective success as well as her own personal development: "You seem to absorb a greater intensity of experience in the short space of one expedition such as this than you can in years of your ordinary life below.... The Gasherbrum expedition hardened me physically and mentally, and prepared me for my future ventures."[12]

Wanda's insensitivity and shifting priorities on the Gasherbrum III climb eventually became a trademark style that would plague almost all of her climbing expeditions. But despite the accusations that she was selfish and that she didn't take others into account, it's hard to imagine her ever having climbed in the Himalaya had she been quiet and subservient. She was certainly not yet as inspiring a leader as Andrzej, but she was a born fighter. She seemed to be stimulated by a combative atmosphere. The weak link in her leadership style was her inability to motivate people to work together. This may have been in part because, unlike Andrzej, Wanda did not lead from below. Even though he climbed well – and sometimes high – Andrzej saw his place at base camp. Not Wanda. Wanda led *and* climbed. And sometimes her personal ambitions superseded her ambitions for the team. Although she was clearly not a perfect leader, she undoubtedly instilled confidence in the women on her team. She emboldened them to feel that they had the power to create their own future. They could climb. They could lead. They could do whatever they wanted. And they could do it with – or without – men.

Wanda agreed that she considered herself not only a leader but a summit climber as well. She later admitted that if she were to manage a team again, she would curb her own ambitions in order to better lead the group. But instinctively she knew she was a visionary, not a manager.

❊ ❊ ❊

Wanda's credibility was even more severely tested when she returned from the expedition and insisted the Gasherbrum III climb had been an "all-female" ascent, without the help of porters – or men. Yet others pointed out the numerous men on the mountain, many of whom had helped equip the climb with fixed ropes and assisted with setting up the camps. There were even rumours that the two men on her GIII summit team had stopped and waited so that the "ladies" could summit first. The exaggerated all-female claim obviously meant a lot to her and was likely a reaction to the perceived snub from the 1974 Lhotse team, which had invited Anna Okopińska instead of Wanda.

The Gasherbrum expedition caused a temporary rift in Wanda's friendship with Alison and Janusz. But time healed the wounds, and when Janusz was imprisoned in 1981 for his work with the Solidarity movement in Poland, Wanda thought back to his leadership on Gasherbrum II in a positive light: "quiet, thinking, democratic ... a solution for many, not for one." Unfortunately, there was little time to mend her friendship with Alison, who was killed on Annapurna just three years later.

Wanda's return journey passed through Rawalpindi, where she met the famously authoritarian German expedition leader Dr. Karl Herrligkoffer. He was planning a German-Austrian-Polish assault on the 8126-metre Nanga Parbat in 1976. Her reputation had caught his attention, so he invited her to join.

The climb was a short-lived effort. Soon after they began ascending Nanga Parbat's mammoth Rupal Face, one of the Austrian climbers, Sebastian Arnold, fell to his death. Karl ordered the entire team to recover his body and then called the expedition off. Wanda felt it was an inappropriate response to the tragedy, that no dead colleague would want the rest of the team robbed of their chance to summit. She wasn't the only team member who felt that way, but her reaction was perceived as somewhat harsh, and her reputation as a "hard woman" grew.

CHAPTER THREE

CLIMBERS WITHOUT BORDERS

People gravitate towards environments that
reward their hereditary inclinations.
— E.O. WILSON, *CONSILIENCE*

The possibility of death is always present while climbing in the high mountains, as real for experienced climbers as it is for novices. When they first begin to climb, climbers rely on luck more than experience. Over time, the balance shifts to experience, which – in theory – should eliminate the need for as much luck. It's true that some objective hazards can be avoided by strategy, tactics and experience, but others claim lives, seemingly at random. Every alpinist knows this, and all are forced to deal with this knowledge in their own way. Jurek believed so strongly in his God that he felt sure He would protect him. Wanda's initial confidence came from her own inner strength, a source that could not, in the end, sustain her. For Voytek, it was Christ's example – not as a religious figure, but as the ultimate martyr – that instructed him in an attitude of calmness and grace when faced with his own mortality.

As a child, Voytek and his father argued about many topics, including religion, a subject that was fundamental to his father's being. Voytek refused to accept the Christian doctrine. He was so horrified with the idea of heaven and hell that he perceived it as a kind of religious terrorism. His father reproached him, insisting that, even if he refused to believe in Jesus Christ, he should at least acknowledge Christ as a great human being. Voytek's blunt reply shocked him. "How can you call a great human being someone who claims he is a God? Either you are a God, or you are a human being!"

Many years passed before Voytek experienced any inkling of compassion for the figure of Jesus Christ. It was during a musical performance of *Jesus Christ Superstar* that he began to appreciate Christ's character – a being who suffered, and who understood that his death was near. The intriguing part for Voytek was that, even though Christ didn't understand *why* he had to die, he seemed to accept its inevitability with an elegant serenity. Voytek was moved by the Christ figure. Even inspired.

One of Christ's lines from the musical, "Now I'm sad and tired," particularly resonated for him. "At some moment in everybody's climbing experience, you grow weaker," Voytek explained. "You *were* inspired, but *now* you're sad and tired. Sad and afraid. There is a point when the inspiration leaves and the tiredness and sadness arrive." Climbing a big mountain inevitably produces unpleasant sensations that have to be managed. To be a climber, one has to deal with difficult situations and feelings of despair – even abject terror. Overwhelmed by a sudden change of weather, a moment of hallucination, the onset of fatigue or the loss of a friend, an alpinist has to dig even deeper for motivation at these times of sadness. To be a climber, one has to accept that gratification is rarely immediate.

For Voytek – a man who would eventually become one of Poland's greatest alpinists, and one of the very few who would live long enough to reflect on his brilliant career – that gratification was slow in coming.

While still young, Voytek and his family moved from the countryside to the war-ravaged city of Wrocław. Like Wanda and Andrzej, he was disheartened by the drab, crowded streets. The move was initiated by his father, Tadeusz Kurtyka, a well-known author who wrote under the pseudonym Henryk Worcell. Tadeusz had achieved critical and popular success with his very first effort, a volume of stories about his days as a waiter in a well-heeled restaurant in the historical and scholarly city of Krakow. *Bewitched Circles* reflected his observations of the prominent patrons who frequented the restaurant, and its publication caused quite a stir in Poland. A somewhat withdrawn man but a keen observer, he next turned his attention to the Germans who lived in the Wrocław region, just prior to their repatriation to Germany. For Tadeusz, the city of Wrocław represented access to publishers and to a literary cultured life. To Voytek, it was hell.

Slumped up against his bedroom window, he would stare glumly at the rain-streaked streets below, yearning for the colours and smells of the forest. He slipped into a form of childhood depression and became plagued by nightmares in which he encountered a strange ghostlike being with a horrifyingly evil soul. Voytek would stand in front of it and try to make contact. Defiantly, he would take one or two steps toward the creature and then awaken – screaming. Each night he would take one more step. The closer he went, the more vivid the dream, and the greater the fear. The nightmare seemed a harbinger of his later feelings of deep primal fear: fear of falling, fear of dying. Each time he faced that fear in the mountains, the memory of his childhood dreams resurfaced.

Voytek graduated from high school and, like Wanda, enrolled at Wrocław University in the electrical engineering department. Just like Wanda and Jurek, from his very first moments at the base of a rocky crag, Voytek knew he was onto something special. "When I came to the rock, I put my hands on it and they contracted automatically. I just started moving up."

He finished university and left Wrocław in 1971. For a time he tried to work as a television repairman, but he was unable to muster any interest in the trade. It so disgusted him that, when he needed to fix his own television set only a few months later, he called a repairman rather than do it himself. He tried again to overcome his hatred for manual labour with a stint as an engineer in the Polish steelworks. That didn't work, either. Traditional jobs bored him silly. As with his approach to climbing, Voytek brought an intellectualism to all aspects of his life. He needed complexity, problem solving, route finding and other challenges to retain his interest.

It was at this time that Voytek discovered a more interesting way to make a living. Like most Polish climbers travelling to and from Asia on expeditions, he began dealing in "trade." Food, outdoor equipment and cheap goods from Poland could be sold for hard currency in Asia, and that hard currency had enormous purchasing power back in Poland, which was still under a completely artificial Soviet economic system. Voytek later broadened his business model by importing sheepskin coats and other quality products from Afghanistan. These he sold in France, in partnership with his French climbing friends.

The sheepskin coats, very much in fashion at the time, were well-made garments with elaborately embroidered details and a flattering shape. He would buy them for around $30 and sell them for a whopping $150. It was easy to live in Poland on a mere $25 a month, so the profits more than sustained his lifestyle. He thrived within the myriad systems he abhorred, scheming and strategizing about permits, money and passports, and staying ahead of the laws that prohibited black-market trade. He took considerable pride in his business, both in terms of the lifestyle it allowed him and the ease of the work. He soon abandoned any thoughts of working in the electronics field and focused his sights on the mountains.

The last half of the 1970s saw Voytek travelling the globe, his lifestyle facilitated by his unofficial import-export business. In order to access his passport for these international jaunts, he would have to prove he had enough foreign currency to live outside the country. This he did quite handily, with his hard-currency bank accounts topped up regularly by those cozy – and lucrative – sheepskin coats. In addition to climbing hard new winter routes in the Polish Tatras, Voytek blasted up difficult lines in the Alps and in Norway.

Most Polish climbers, even those who engaged in smuggling, were perennially short on cash. Particularly when abroad, they were forced to scrounge for food and accommodation. The climbing mecca of Chamonix, France, was hideously expensive for the Poles, who earned a reputation for "getting by" that superseded even that of the English, who were fighting their own battles with unemployment and poverty.

On one trip to Chamonix, a group of penniless Polish climbers found a lovely campsite that appeared strangely empty. It had just one sign overhead: *Camping Interdit.* They congratulated themselves on their good eye for campsites, set up their tents, and wandered into town. An officious gendarme, who had been keeping a close eye on them, came over to make their acquaintance.

"*Bonjour, mes amis.* Where are you camping? You are not in the campground."

"Oh yes, we are in the campground," they answered.

"Which one?"

"Why, it's just over there. It's the one called *Camping Interdit.*"

Although economic and political upheaval created barrier after barrier for the young climbers, it seemed to whet their appetite for even more adventure. Shoplifting in Chamonix wasn't unheard of, but, although most itinerant climbers visiting the French climbing town participated in this unofficial sport, it was a serious offence for the Poles; they were official representatives of the Polish Alpine Association. Still, compared with the monotony of life in Poland, starving in the Alps felt like a higher form of existence.

Even the Tatras presented bureaucratic hurdles. The mountain range straddles the border between Poland and what was then Czechoslovakia; only 30 per cent lies within Poland. Crossing that mountain frontier was illegal, but there were so many tempting new routes to be climbed on the other side that Polish climbers found it hard to resist. Besides, there was a distinct pleasure in ignoring the so-called "Friendship Border," and most active climbers boasted at least half a dozen illegal climbs on the forbidden side each season.

It was a blazing hot summer morning when young Katowice climber Grzegorz Chwoła slipped across the frontier to try one such route. He normally wore a construction helmet when he climbed, but his brother had recently sent him a proper climbing helmet from Italy. It was bright orange.

On this occasion, Grzegorz offered it to his girlfriend, who was accompanying him on the climb. She carefully packed it at the top of her rucksack. Into his pack he stuffed his old, scuffed and sun-bleached, black, construction helmet.

They rose early, drove to the trailhead on the Polish side and hiked up and across the undefended border without incident. They dropped down to the base of the 150-metre cliff. She opened her pack to take out the precious helmet. It was a hot day and her hands were slippery with sweat. She fumbled. The helmet fell out and tumbled two hundred metres to the valley below – into Czechoslovakia! Grzegorz swore. They was no other option but to pack up and hike down – four hours of scrambling over detestable talus slopes and through scratchy scrub brush in hot, humid summer temperatures. Finally the ground levelled off and there it was, teetering between two boulders. Undamaged, and still very orange. Next to the helmet was a cool mountain stream. Dripping with sweat, they stripped off and dove in.

Two minutes later, a border patrolman arrived. It was the notorious Captain Bagniak, famous for his strict adherence to the rules.

"Good morning. Your passports, please." The captain stood close to the two, respectfully averting his gaze.

"Ah, good morning, Captain Bagniak," said Grzegorz. (This was not his first border incident.) "It's good to see you again."

"Please, I would like to see your passports."

They had passports but from the wrong country, and they were sadly lacking visas. Of course, there was also the problem of their clothes, which were scattered over the nearby bushes. They begged to be let off, spinning a tale about an orange helmet falling out of the pack on Polish soil and escaping into Czech territory.

The captain wasn't buying it; he was overheated from the summer sun, just as they had been before their refreshing dip, and was in no mood for discussion. He ordered them to dress and then hauled them off to a series of police stations where they were interrogated, thoroughly chastised, and finally dumped at the Polish border. They returned as minor heroes – *with* the orange helmet – but *without* their new route.

❋ ❋ ❋

Despite all the obstacles, Polish climbers persevered, even thrived, both in Poland and abroad. Voytek had emerged as a particularly talented climber and, back in 1972, had made his first trip to Afghanistan, Poland's favourite high-altitude training ground. The objectives of the Krakow Club trip led by Ryszard Kozioł were two giant peaks over 7000 metres: Acher Chioch and Koh-e-Tez. Despite his impressive climbing skills, Voytek knew very little about climbing at this altitude; his experience was in the much lower Tatras and Alps. He had read a few accounts of high-altitude climbing and had a vague recollection about Camp I, Camp II and moving up a mountain in stages. But there he was, a young man in his twenties in the Hindu Kush, a couple of 7000-metre peaks nearby. With naïve enthusiasm, he approached them just as he climbed back home in Poland. Alpine style: no pre-stocked camps, no bottled oxygen, no fixed lines.

Still, the climbers knew enough to first acclimatize their bodies to the rarefied air. That accomplished, they climbed Acher Chioch by a new route on its Northwest Face, followed by a three-day ascent of the North Face. The Acher Chioch climb was one of the very first technical alpine style ascents in the high mountains – a relatively unheralded climb compared to Tyrolean climber Reinhold Messner and Austrian Peter Habeler's history-making alpine style ascent of Gasherbrum I, also known as Hidden Peak, three years later in 1975. Although the Hidden Peak route was not as technically difficult as the one on Acher Chioch, it topped out at just over the magical 8000-metre mark, capturing the imagination of the entire mountaineering community.

The Polish appetite for the Hindu Kush reached epic levels in the next few years. In 1976 there were 13 Polish expeditions and 151 climbers. In 1977 the numbers rose to 22 expeditions and 193 climbers. They climbed 102 summits that season and made 29 first ascents. The Hindu Kush was now firmly established as the Polish school of high-altitude climbing.

Voytek was also part of Andrzej's 1974 winter attempt of Lhotse, but the big national expedition scene didn't suit him. His aversion was verified the following year when he was included in a K2 East Ridge expedition led by another prominent expedition leader, Janusz Kurczab. The team came within 200 metres of climbing a new and difficult route along the airy crest, but Kurczab's leadership style was "excessively democratic" in Voytek's opinion, with endless discussions and secret ballots about who would go where, when and with whom. Even though Andrzej was more spontaneous in his approach, Voytek felt stifled by the unwieldy and hierarchical expedition-style atmosphere, and he instinctively knew that he needed to discover a new way for himself.

❅ ❅ ❅

Voytek continued to climb abroad, and in 1977 he returned to Afghanistan, this time with a young British climber, Alex MacIntyre. A product of the flower generation, Alex was a wild-looking creature with an unruly head of curly black hair, sparkling blue eyes and an appetite for hashish. Together with Anglo-American climber John Porter, they were part of a climbing exchange that Andrzej had arranged between the Polish Alpine Association and the British Mountaineering Council. Since climbers from both countries increasingly rejected the ideological barriers between them, the next logical step was to go climbing together. Besides, high unemployment in Britain and low salaries in Poland gave none of them much incentive to stay home.

The climbers met in Warsaw and headed off by train to Moscow. For five days they rolled along the endless plains, across the Volga to Orsk, then slipping down between the Aral and Caspian seas to the ancient city of Termez on the Amudarya River, which formed the border with Afghanistan. Their expedition budget was minimal since prices in Afghanistan were as low as they were in Poland. But still, some foreign money was required. The Poles provided the train tickets, equipment, food and organizational experience. The British brought hard currency. The system worked for everyone.

As the train rolled along, they exchanged climbing terminology and off-colour jokes, all the while enjoying an impressive array of Polish delicacies. There was one small problem: the foreigners lacked permission to travel to Termez, where the Russian invasion of Afghanistan would be staged in just 18 months. In order to get past the frequent checkpoints, Porter – now called Porterwich – and MacIntyre – known by all as MacIntyreski – were ordered to keep their mouths shut and to simply nod their heads in response to any questions.

The subterfuge worked well until they reached the Afghan frontier, where the border guard demanded their passports. Neither John's nor Alex's contained the required stamps. The guard exploded in a froth of spittle and demanded that the two "British spies" be incarcerated. The discussion continued for several days, and it looked like the international climbing exchange was over. The Brits would need to go back to Moscow in order to clear this thing up, and the Polish Alpine Association would need to do some serious fence-mending when they all returned to Warsaw.

Exasperated by the delay, Voytek motioned the guard aside. "Look, let's consider some possibilities here," he began. "If you report this indiscretion, you will have days and days of paperwork and you will probably be severely reprimanded by your superior." The guard nodded his head. That would certainly be the case. "Why not just forget the whole thing," Voytek appealed. "All you have to do is approve their passage and we will go on our way and you can have a nice day here, with no problems." Weary from arguing, the guard weighed the two options for only a few moments before concluding that Voytek's solution was best. With a scowl on his face, he provided the necessary travel documents and waved them onto the ferry, with a stern reminder to keep their heads down and their cameras safely stowed, as well as to avoid looking at absolutely anything.

They piled into the trucks waiting on the other side, giddy with relief at their victory over officialdom. With renewed energy and optimism, they began hatching a plan for a fierce objective – the Northeast Face of 6868-metre Koh-e-Bandaka in the central Hindu Kush. The face, which John described as "massive – ugly, yet compelling," had already repelled a Polish team the year before.

But first they had to convince Andrzej, because Bandaka was not on the agenda. As leader, Andrzej was responsible for the entire team, and he would face a mountaineering tribunal if anyone were injured or killed. He had already endured this interminable ordeal after two previous climbing fatalities, so he knew it was serious, particularly when foreign climbers were involved. Bandaka wasn't even in the same valley as Andrzej's objectives on Koh-e-Mandaras. But Voytek and the others argued their case, and Andrzej finally caved in; he could see the excited gleam in their eyes and he understood. When the trucks reached Zebak, the team split: Andrzej and his partners continued on to the Mandaras Valley, while Voytek, Jan Wolf, John and Alex piled off to begin their four-day march to Koh-e-Bandaka base camp.

As the climbers watched the forbidding wall – 2200 metres of unstable rock and toppling ice séracs – their enthusiasm cooled, only to be replaced by fear. The horrifying rumble of rockfall was so continuous that the normally laid-back Alex was driven to a near-panic state. It was the arbitrary nature of the rockfall that unsettled him the most: one millimetre to the left and it was just a whining sound near your left ear; one millimetre to the right and your head exploded.

After a five-day acclimatization climb, Jan developed bronchitis. The remaining three team members paced back and forth at the foot of the wall. It bore down on them, dauntingly. "An affair with a big wall is never a wham-bam," Polish writer Tomasz Hreczuch wrote, describing the process, "but always a banter, taking a vast amount of patience."[13] His patience waning, Voytek began to consider retreat.

One evening at base camp, he left the tent to walk – and think. His solitary ramble turned into a rare experience that profoundly influenced his relationship with nature. As he wandered about, stopping to gaze at the immensity of the wall, he had the powerful sensation that the mountain landscape surrounding him was a kind of living creature. Yet, at the same time, he had the desperate feeling that there was no way to approach it. "I was so close, but it wasn't responding to me," he said. It was as if this special place were trying to speak to him, or maybe it already had, and he had missed it. He wasn't sure which was true, but the phenomenon, frustrating though it was, transformed his Bandaka climb into one of great spiritual intensity.

The three climbers studied the patterns of rockfall and icefall activity on the wall. They debated their strategy and finally, after a frank and difficult discussion between Voytek and John about the risks involved and their chances of survival, decided to head up. They spent six days on the wall, which steepened up the constantly changing rock – from rotten sandstone to a metamorphic rock cathedral – then continued on the upper half of the face with its massive slabs and arêtes, and finally the 700-metre summit icefield. They were forced to be creative in their approach. Each day, as the sun warmed the Northeast Face, the ice that glued the notoriously loose rock into place would melt, sending down a torrent of stones. So they waited until mid-afternoon, when things had settled down, to start climbing. Despite the unusually late starts, the talented trio still averaged 12 pitches of climbing per day.

Three days up the wall, they gathered at a belay to discuss their options. They counted up their few remaining pitons, which they were using to pound into the rock fissures for protection. They had enough to go up but not enough for a retreat down the face. They could pinpoint the very moment when their options narrowed, and, at that juncture, all their tension drifted away. They were infused with an inner calm of complete commitment. The last 700 metres of ice was topped by a complex maze of leering, teetering séracs, through which Alex found a way.

Their success on the difficult and dangerous 60-pitch climb stood out as one of the most impressive routes done in the Himalaya up to that time. They had pooled their individual expertise to find the key that unlocked the face, and, more important, they had conquered their fears. The trio was spurred on to another challenge the following year – this time, in India.

❅ ❅ ❅

Changabang is a 6864-metre peak in India's Garhwal Himalaya region. The geometric precision of the triangular peak offers no easy route as it is guarded on all sides by immense walls of granite and ice. Located on the rim of the Nanda Devi Sanctuary, the mountain almost eluded them because of complications with their permit. For days, the group clawed their way up the chain of command, trying to navigate the complicated web of the British-style bureaucracy so enthusiastically embraced by Indian authorities. Finally, they reached someone for whom this waste of time was just too tiresome. He gave them their permit.

The west side of the mountain had been climbed two years before, but Voytek, Alex, John and another Polish climber, Krzysztof Żurek, wanted a new route on the South Face. Taking just 35 pitons, three ice screws and a small selection of equipment for protection, as well as food for eight days, they climbed the imposing 1700-metre wall in one continuous push, sleeping at night in hammocks dangling in the thin air, or on narrow ledges hacked out of the icy slopes. It was exciting, airy stuff, with a number of heart-stopping 25-metre falls. After eight days of climbing, Voytek knew he had discovered his own way: there would be no more big expeditions for him. He loved the flexibility, the commitment, the creativity and the independence of a small team. Most important, he knew now what really inspired him: elegantly arching, technical lines on steep, massive geometric blocks of rock and ice. And with his financial independence, he knew he had the freedom to follow the path that made him feel alive.

CHAPTER FOUR

THE KNUCKLE

*Love unto exhaustion, work unto exhaustion, and walk unto
exhaustion…. The only mortal danger for the spirit is to
remain too long without it. The world is made of fire.*
——MARK HELPRIN, *A SOLDIER OF THE GREAT WAR*

Celina Ogrodzińska, a dark-haired young woman, was just looking for a
cup of coffee when he caught her attention. It was a damp, chilly day when
she and her girlfriend wandered into a café in Katowice, only to find every
table occupied. As they turned to leave, three young men rose and offered
their seats. One of them was Jurek Kukuczka. The girls accepted and sat
down. The men took another look and thought better about leaving.
Would it be okay to join them? Yes, of course.

As they warmed their hands on the hot mugs of coffee and chatted
with the boys, the rather shy Celina remained quiet. She preferred to
watch and listen. One of the three guys seemed intriguing: quiet, warm,
a bit mysterious, with kind, inviting eyes. An hour later, they rose to leave.
Two of the young men offered Celina a ride home. She went with Jurek.
And so it began.

On their first date to the Katowice Mountain Club, she met his "tribe."
It was immediately clear to her that this was his second home and that his
heart was in the mountains. The next weekend they climbed at a nearby
crag, an activity she would never repeat because of her fear of heights. But
the camping, the stories, the bonfires and the relaxed camaraderie were
seductive. Celina understood the draw of climbing and felt welcome.

Like Wrocław, the Katowice club was another Polish stronghold of
climbing. During the week Jurek would attend lectures to learn the
theoretical aspects of the sport, and every Sunday he would learn the practical art of climbing. At the end of a few months he earned his rock-climb-
ing certificate. Then it was off to the Tatras for a strenuous two-week
course, which he also passed. Now he was ready to lead-climb. At this
point in his career, Jurek was just a novice, but a promising one. A confirmed athlete, the former boxer had a body that responded easily to the
requirements of climbing.

He stayed on for weeks in the Tatras, climbing increasingly difficult routes. A year later his carefree existence was interrupted when he was conscripted into the army, an event that he described as a "major disaster in my life." The army stole two years of his life, but as soon as he could, he scurried back to the Tatras.

Almost immediately, Jurek encountered death in the mountains. He was climbing in the Tatras in winter with a friend, Piotr Skorupa. Halfway up what was considered to be the hardest unsolved climb in the range, Piotr fell to his death. Just three weeks later, Jurek was back, making several first winter ascents.

Jurek didn't go often to the Alps due to his tenuous financial situation, but he managed a couple of trips with Voytek, whom he had encountered, climbing in the Tatras. Then in 1974, a regional Silesian team invited him along on an expedition to Alaska's Mt. McKinley, where he suffered from altitude sickness at just 4500 metres. Still far from his goal, he crept into his tent and howled in agony, shocked that his strong young body could be so struck down by lethargy and pain. He eventually reached the summit, although only through sheer willpower and an amazing capacity to suffer.

Again, in the Hindu Kush in 1976, Jurek became ill at altitude. And again, thanks to utter single-mindedness, he reached the summit of the 7000-metre Koh-e-Tez, alone.

Throughout this time, he and Celina dated. "I liked his attributes," Celina recalled. "He was very quiet and balanced, not too high-strung or nervous." She watched Jurek's increasing obsession with climbing and was aware of the hazards of loving an alpinist. "I was thinking all the time about him being in the mountains, because I knew it was possible to die there. I tried to stop thinking about that, but it was in the back of my mind that this sport could be dangerous."

For his part, Jurek saw a woman with whom he wanted to make a life – an attractive woman but also traditional and deeply religious. They would have children, raise a family and grow a garden. They would thank God for their many blessings. With Celina, he could do this – and climb. Or could he? Managing both was a difficult manoeuvre, one that eluded many of his Polish climbing friends, and climbers everywhere. Wanda had already lost her first partner, as had Andrzej. The companionship of the larger climbing family was warm and inclusive, but the intimacy and pressures of a real family were different. Celina and Jurek both understood the risks. And instinctively, Celina knew that the success of a marriage with Jurek would depend on her. She would be the one left at home. She would raise their children. She knew that Jurek was a good man, but she would only have a part of him; the rest belonged to the mountains. Yet they loved each other, and after three years of dating they married on June 22, 1975.

❉ ❉ ❉

There had already been a few Polish expeditions to the great ranges: Wanda's expedition to the Gasherbrums in 1975, the 1974 winter Lhotse attempt, Kurczab's expedition to K2 in 1976, and a tragic expedition to Broad Peak in 1975 in which three of five climbers died while descending from the Central Summit. Now Jurek joined the 1977 Katowice Mountain Club expedition to the East Pillar of Nanga Parbat. After one look at the route, they changed their plans to the Rakhiot Face, where they were turned back by the rock band just above 8000 metres. Jurek left the mountain a sad, defeated man.

Then the Polish Alpine Association applied for a permit for Lhotse for 1979. In case that didn't come through, they also asked for Kangchenjunga Central and South summits. Amazingly, they got all three. Now they had a problem. What to do with all these permits? Adam Bilczewski was leader of the Lhotse trip and asked Jurek to join them, despite his painful experience in Alaska and his failure on Nanga Parbat.

Like every other Polish climber, Jurek now had to figure out how to pay for his climbing trips; his was a "made in Katowice" solution. Growing up in the industrial heartland of Poland, he was surrounded by the towering smokestacks of the steelworks. These smokestacks had to be periodically cleaned and painted, and it was here that Jurek, and an entire generation of his contemporaries, found their entrepreneurial niche.

Jurek was good at – and proud of – his negotiating skills. He even wrote about the time he and another climbing friend first entered the director's office at a steelworks plant in Katowice. They were there to make some serious cash, for they were slated for Lhotse. The office wall featured the national emblem, and the bookshelves heaved with works of Lenin. Through the streaked window they could see a tall smokestack, the reason for their meeting.

Jurek wasted no time in offering his services to paint the thing. The director jabbered on about a big company in Katowice that could do the job. At the same time, the director knew that the company in question would charge a small fortune for the work. And it would be slow. So he tossed out the all-important question: "How long do you think it would take you to paint it?"

Jurek gazed out the window at the towering corroded chimney. He had known, even before setting foot in the director's office, exactly what the answer would be, but he furrowed his brow and considered the situation. "About two weeks? We might be able to manage it in one."

The director chuckled at Jurek's naïveté. "It would take more than a week just to put up the scaffolding," he threw out.

"We don't use scaffolding," retorted Jurek.

"How do you do it?"

"With ropes."

This was now a really interesting situation. And it demanded a decision. The director knew the chimney needed painting – and soon. Regulations demanded it. He also knew how long it would take the official painting contractor to do it: at least four times as long. He didn't know these two young guys in his office, but they might just be able to solve his problem quickly and cheaply. It was a risk, though. He needed time to think. In the meantime, he couldn't let them get away; he needed to stall.

The director offered coffee.

They accepted.

Jurek sensed that the coffee routine was just a way of gaining time. He had seen this tactic before. It was obvious they had been sent down from heaven for this "very important person" and his rusted, leaning chimney. They had him! Jurek also knew the amount of money he would be asking for the job: 1 million złotys. This was the equivalent of 200 average monthly wages – a huge amount. But it was exactly what they needed to get to Lhotse.

"You must realize that we are a state organization ... impossible for us to contract such a job to ... private individuals," the director said.

This, too, they had prepared for. The payment would be to the "Youth Social Action Fund," and they had the regulation book with them, ready for his inspection, should he require it.

"Okay, fine, fine. I will still have to consult the legal department. In which case, when could you start on this chimney?"

It was, as they say, a win–win situation.

❊ ❊ ❊

Jurek's first exposure to India was a shock. Their two-dollar-a-night budget placed them in rock-bottom Bombay hotel rooms: dirty cubicles with a bed of boards and rats scurrying in the corridors. Initially Jurek shied away from local food and refused to drink the water. Yet Coca-Cola was too expensive. As time went on, he relaxed a bit and began to enjoy the local cuisine and people, shedding his European mistrust and fear of Asia.

At Lhotse base camp he once again had to face the crippling effect of altitude sickness. Situated at 5400 metres, it was just high enough to make his head pound and his stomach heave. But within a few days, he discovered that by continuing to move and work and exert, the pain eased. The continuous activity forced him to breathe deeply, circulating oxygen and blood into his sturdy, untiring legs. For Jurek, hard work seemed to be the answer.

As they made their way up Lhotse, Jurek couldn't ignore the fact that their route was the same as one would take to Everest, at least as far as 7300 metres. At that point, the two routes split: turn left for Everest, right for Lhotse. He began to fantasize about switching mountains. After all, Everest was higher. But their permit was for Lhotse, and that's what he had been invited to climb. Besides, his head still throbbed.

When he realized that Everest wasn't his to dream about, he looked back at Lhotse and let his imagination run wild. What about climbing it without oxygen? At that time, most people thought climbing a Himalayan giant without oxygen would result in permanent brain damage. "You'll see, you'll lose half your grey cells and become a moron," his teammates warned him at base camp. This was a sobering thought. But Jurek wanted more than the summit of Lhotse. There was a part of his character that rejected the idea of playing for low stakes. "For me it is the high bid or nothing," he said. "That's what fires me."[14]

Two of the four summit climbers opted for bottled oxygen. Andrzej Czok wanted to climb it oxygen-free. Jurek did, too, but in order to hedge his bets, he decided to carry up two bottles of O_2 and a breathing apparatus, just in case. Ten extra kilos on his back.

All four started up: two using supplemental oxygen, and two not. After the first hour there was little distance between them. Jurek decided to dump his load. He moved more easily without the extra weight, but after three hours the gap widened between those with oxygen and those without. Above 8000 metres now, the distance grew even more. Jurek concentrated on his breathing and his rhythm. Ten steps. Rest. Lean on the ice axe. Breathe deeply. Don't sit down. Ten steps. Rest. Lean on the ice axe. Breathe deeply. Don't sit down.

On the summit, he gasped convulsively, then fumbled in his pack for a pennant from his first Scout Mountaineering Club and another with the Katowice emblem. He felt no summit euphoria, just the knowledge that he needed to take a few photos and turn around and get down.

When he reached Camp III and had a chance to drink some tea and soup, he paused to reflect. He listened to the complex machine of his body, which had so nearly ground to a halt. Now it slowly calmed down. When the others started down the next day, Jurek declined the offer, preferring to stay on the mountain. He was acclimatized now, and the carbonated fog had left his brain. It felt wonderful being high on the mountain, so why rush down? For the first time he felt healthy and strong on a high mountain – a taste of the life that lay ahead of him – a life at altitude.

As the climbers walked back down through the Khumbu Valley, proud of their success, they stopped to camp at the village of Namche. While they were unpacking their packs, two Sherpas came running up the trail. "Mr. Messner is coming! Mr. Messner is coming!" they yelled. Jurek watched in amazement as the Sherpas pitched Reinhold Messner's tent, laid his dry clothes out, hung a lamp and prepared his bedding. Soon the great man appeared. Jurek was surprised and relieved to realize that the climbing superstar behaved like a normal human being.

After some pleasantries about where the Poles had been and where Reinhold was going (Ama Dablam), their talk turned to Nanga Parbat. Jurek told him about their expedition two years before, when he had reached a col at around 8000 metres on the mountain and there had found a torch (flashlight).

"A torch?" Reinhold asked.

"Yes, an ordinary torch. I could not understand how it had got there, as this was a new route," Jurek answered.

Reinhold was visibly shaken. He told Jurek how he and his brother Günther had climbed the South Face in 1970 and had then become separated. He was sure that this col was where Günther had changed the batteries. This was a welcome bit of information, because Reinhold was facing severe criticism and speculation that he had "left his brother" on the other side during their descent. This torch might prove his claim that Günther had died on his way down the Rupal Face. He asked Jurek for the torch, as well as a few words about how and where he had found it. For a book that he was writing, he added.

By December 4, 1979, Jurek was home. He called Andrzej Zawada the next day to give him the good news. He had proven himself at altitude on Lhotse and he wanted more. Andrzej was just the man to make that happen. He congratulated him and then made his offer: Everest in winter. Everest! Jurek had stared at it, even lusted after it, and now he was being offered it – in winter. But there was a catch. He would need to leave in two weeks. As appealing as the offer was, and it was almost irresistible, Jurek had to decline. Celina was pregnant and the baby was expected in January.

She had already miscarried a baby girl, so Jurek needed to be there for her.

But Andrzej had a consolation prize: he had another Everest permit for the following spring, so Jurek could join that expedition if he was interested. They would try a new route, and that excited Jurek.

Maciek Kukuczka was born on New Year's Eve, 1979, and Jurek was there for his first son's birth.

CHAPTER FIVE

HAT TRICK ON EVEREST

What is a mountain? An obstacle; a transcendence; above all, an effect.
— SALMAN RUSHDIE, *THE SATANIC VERSES*

All mountain landscapes hold stories: the ones we read,
the ones we dream, and the ones we create.
— MICHAEL KENNEDY, *ALPINIST*

By the late 1970s, Everest had already seen a number of important ascents. New Zealander Edmund Hillary and Sherpa Tenzing Norgay first climbed it by the South Col route in 1953. It would be nearly a quarter century later, in 1975, that the first woman, Junko Tabei, would make a successful ascent, the same year the expedition led by British climber Chris Bonington astonished the climbing world by cracking the secret of the massive Southwest Face. Three years later Reinhold Messner and Austrian Peter Habeler shattered the perception of what was possible when they climbed the tallest mountain on Earth without bottled oxygen.

The British, Austrians, Japanese, New Zealanders, Nepalese and many more – all had made their mark on Everest. But no Pole had yet stood on its summit. They were hungry for Everest, not just as individuals but also as a nation.

Politics, once again, had played a role in this disappointing history. There had been no opportunity to leave the country for the major ranges in the 1950s and 1960s immediately following World War II. The Socialist system hadn't allowed it, eliminating any chance of making the first ascent. And while the other major Everest firsts were toppling, Poland's climbers were just beginning to hit their stride. Somehow, they would need to accelerate their learning curve if they were to catch up with the rest of the world's climbers on Everest – and surpass them. The Polish Alpine Association understood this as well as the climbers did, and it was prepared to support their efforts.

At the same time, Wanda's reputation was growing. She was back in Pakistan in 1977 to attempt the 8126-metre Nanga Parbat, and then she returned to the Alps the following year to climb the North Face of the

Matterhorn – in winter. This all-women's ascent was regarded as quite a notable achievement in the Alps at that time. She was now widely respected as one of the world's leading female alpinists. Invitations came often, particularly from Europe, where she had established a good network of climbing friends. Her life had become completely focused on expedition climbing: preparing, training, raising money, travelling, climbing and recovering. She confessed in her journal that the only time she could completely relax and be herself was when she was on a mountain. It was there, in camp, in the clean mountain air, surrounded by like-minded people and away from the problems of Poland that she felt most at home.

In 1978 Wanda hit the jackpot. Her Everest opportunity came, not from the Polish Alpine Association but from Germany, when she was invited by Dr. Karl Herrligkoffer to join him on top of the world. He had assembled a large international team to tackle Everest's South Col route, and he wanted Wanda as his assistant deputy leader. His choice rankled some team members who felt she wasn't up to the job, an assumption she attributed to a good old-fashioned case of male chauvinism. Wanda was much too strong to crumple in the face of this kind of condescension. This was her chance to climb the highest mountain on Earth; a few unsupportive men wouldn't stop her. Still, she couldn't help feeling that they were against her from the beginning.

Karl was well aware of the strife amongst his team members, "the like of which I had never experienced on any of my many expeditions," he reported in his account of the climb. The root of the trouble was the perceived discrepancy between Wanda's emancipated and self-confident attitude and her inability to share tasks and burdens equally with her male colleagues. "The discussion deteriorated into the most naked display of unfeeling masculine selfishness that I have ever witnessed," he concluded.

The difficulty began when Wanda was assigned to the second summit team. One of her responsibilities was to keep an eye on a female German climber in the group. When it became clear that the woman could climb no higher, Karl asked Wanda to take her down to base camp. Wanda refused. She wasn't here to guide; she had come to climb. Exasperated, Karl threw up his hands and said, "Do what you want, then." She continued up.

The conflict continued up the mountain all the way to the South Col at around 7900 metres, when deputy leader Sigi Hupfauer ordered Wanda to carry an extra oxygen bottle to the top. She protested that she was already loaded down with the extra weight of her film equipment. He exploded with some sharp words and, together with the other climbers, walked away. She was alone, abandoned by her fellow climbers, so near the top yet utterly terrified. But Sherpa Mingma was standing nearby and offered to carry the oxygen bottle for her, a gesture others on the expedition later interpreted as proof that women were too weak for Everest.

Wanda did complete the climb, however, joining her not-so-friendly teammates on the top of the world about 15 minutes after their arrival. There must have been some kind of hypoxic forgiveness, because summit photos show Wanda being embraced by Willi Klimek. Yet the show of solidarity dissipated into thin air on the way down. When she arrived at Camp IV at the South Col, she was unable to find her sleeping bag. As she wandered around in a near state of collapse, nobody offered to help. Finally, Austrian climbing legend Kurt Diemberger offered her his sleeping bag, reasoning that his portly frame could better withstand the cold night they were sure to endure. Wanda fled the expedition as soon as she reached base camp, happy to have made the summit but desperate to leave.

She had climbed to the top; nothing else mattered.

There was nothing particularly unusual about this expedition, despite Wanda's disgust. Karl had chosen his climbers for their experience, not their compatibility. As was the case with many of his previous expeditions, the climbers never coalesced as a team. Each one was as motivated and ambitious as the other, and Everest was Everest. Although their behaviour toward Wanda certainly displayed some chauvinistic tendencies, it was at least as much about sheer competition. There were only so many who would make it to the top, and this driven, self-confident woman, catapulted into a leadership position, displayed all the makings of a prima donna to these men.

But from Wanda's perspective, their actions – and her isolation – made her more determined than ever to mount her own women-only expeditions in the future. After Everest, she was convinced that a woman could never assume an equal role in a mixed-gender expedition, and she was tired of fighting for what she felt were her rights on the mountain.

Her style, when faced with a problem or disagreement, was confrontational. Particularly on a mountain, she refused to back down or consider a compromise. For Wanda, compromise signalled weakness. But the constant fighting and holding her ground was tiring; even someone as resolute as Wanda grew weary of it after a time.

Consistency wasn't Wanda's strong suit, either. While she was often hard-nosed, she was also perfectly capable of using her feminine charms to her advantage. Legions of stories exist of her enticing male climbers to assist her with particularly difficult or onerous tasks. On one K2 expedition, a British team's doctor was completely captured by her charismatic beauty and responded to her screams for help when she discovered a tick in her thick hair. After she burst yelping out of her tent, he and his teammates rushed over, carefully combed through her tangled mane and finally snagged the offending creature. Another time, while Mexican alpinist Carlos Carsolio waited 17 days for his Pakistani climbing permit, Wanda sashayed up to the authorities in Islamabad, clad in her best summer dress, makeup and heels, and triumphantly returned with her permit in a matter of hours. She knew how to work the system if she wanted to. But it obviously hadn't worked on Everest.

Her erratic behaviour, veering from ardent feminism to wily sensualism, fuelled great stories but frustrated those close to her. They never knew what to expect. Teammates and colleagues didn't know if they would be faced with the toughness of an equal-opportunist or the softness of a romantic. Wanda was nothing if not unpredictable.

Despite the bitter aftertaste, her Everest victory was significant and she knew it. On October 16, 1978, she had become the third woman to climb the mountain, the first European woman, and the first Polish climber. Throughout the climb, regular press reports had arrived at the Polish Alpine Association. "Wanda's on the South Peak … Wanda's at the Pass … Wanda's on the South Col … Wanda's going up … Wanda's on the top!" And while these breathless reports continued to arrive from the mountain, Poles were also awaiting news of a different nature. The world's eyes were focused on Rome as the Vatican's cardinals elected a new pope; a Pole was on the short list.

Wanda returned home from Everest nervous about Polish climbers' reactions to her success. She even queried the alpine association secretary, Hanna Wiktorowska: "What do the guys say? Are they angry?" There was certainly a bit of teeth-gnashing that it was a Polish woman – not a man – who had climbed Everest first, but most were silent on the matter. Some Polish climbers who had harboured Everest aspirations lost interest in the peak now that a Pole had climbed it. Some even came up with a little ditty: "First Wanda climbs the peak – then the rest of the clique."

At about this time, Alek Lwow summed up Wanda's celebrity status by categorizing Polish alpinism into three levels: 1. men's alpinism, 2. women's alpinism, 3. Wanda Rutkiewicz. "She has her own category," he laughed. Still, it irritated many that Wanda was getting all the attention while their ascents of the Central and South summits of Kangchenjunga that same year – two unclimbed 8000ers in one expedition – went relatively unheralded.

On one hand, their frustrations were warranted; from a mountaineering perspective, their ascents on Kangchenjunga were more difficult and more important than her Everest ascent – they were true "firsts." At the same time, they insisted on a more purist approach to alpinism: climbing for themselves, not for fame. At least that's what they said. Wanda was clearly a self-promoter as well as a climber. She knew Poland's place in mountaineering history just as well as the next person; Everest had been there for the taking. She had taken it. First.

Hanna Wiktorowska had little sympathy for the complainers. "I always said that she had enough strength and determination for not five, not 10 but 25 women," she said. "She just knocked everybody out."

Even more auspiciously, Wanda's summit day coincided with that of Poland's Karol Cardinal Wojtyla's election as Pope John Paul II. This fact alone elicited the kind of publicity that a professional climber could only dream of, like Edmund Hillary's Everest gift to the young Queen Elizabeth II, whose coronation coincided with the announcement of his reaching the summit.

❀ ❀ ❀

Pope John Paul II visited Poland in June of 1979. Nobody could have predicted the response: the nation's sense of pride was boundless. This, after decades of humiliation. Millions of Poles poured onto the streets in a countrywide release of emotion. Finally, they were in the presence of a real leader. The Pope was not a puppet of a foreign power but a man whose authority was based on his own values. He didn't criticize or reproach but spoke of love, forgiveness and faith.

Suddenly, this country, tragic in so many ways and invisible to most of the world, was on the international stage. Their economy was a mess; their politics, a sham; but where it really counted – their deep religious faith – they were leading the world. The surge in Polish self-confidence was enormous.

Because their big days coincided, it was arranged that Wanda and the Pope would meet during his visit. When she presented him with a small rock from the summit of Everest, he responded, "It must have been God's will that we should both be set so high on one and the same day."[15] The two joyful and uplifting events marked a turning point in Poland, as people rediscovered hope and strength.

Outside Poland, too, confidence grew. Based on its shiny new profile, thanks to Pope John Paul II's election, the vast community of Poles living abroad was now more aware of Poland and its problems, and this expatriate community was throwing its support behind the people, not the ruling party. Poland was suddenly visible. The new-found support prepared the country for the next decade – the 1980s – and the most overwhelming changes they could imagine.

Wanda had climbed Everest, becoming the first Pole and the first European woman to do so. But Andrzej was more ambitious than that. He wanted to stretch the boundaries of what was considered possible: he dreamed of climbing the mountain in winter.

Polish climbers have always found good training ground on the multi-pitch cliffs of the Tatras, where winter climbing is almost as popular as rock climbing. "Who did the first winter ascent?" is a question as common as "Who did the first ascent?" Routes in the Tatras are primarily mixed climbs, requiring a constantly changing palette of rock and ice techniques combined with devilishly canny route-finding skills. The climbs are difficult, both technically and psychologically, because there are few opportunities for climbers to build safe belays, the method used to secure a climbing partner to the wall.

With heavily mittened hands, a winter climber in the Tatras first clears off the light, feathery snow to reveal whatever weakness might exist on the rock beneath – perhaps a small ledge that might hold a cramponed boot. Then he reaches up and swings one of his ice axes – *thunk* – and it finds its mark, a narrow fissure between the rock and frozen earth. Another swing, but this one bounces off a rib of stone hidden by a small drift of snow. He struggles to maintain his balance and then reaches up, swings again, until he finds a reliable purchase. Now he needs to move up and away from his last secure crampon placement, carefully stepping onto the cleared-off stance. He redistributes his weight between his arms and legs, never losing his balance. Straightening his legs to gain maximum height, he repeats these moves over and over, inching his way up the snow-covered terrain.

This is winter climbing in the Tatras – priceless experience for winter ascents in the world's highest mountains.

An equally valuable sub-skill that Polish climbers acquire in the Tatras in winter is how to survive a bivouac (an unplanned night out on the mountain, often without shelter). Bivouacking became so commonplace (and popular) in the 1970s that top climbers began to compete with each other to see who could do it most often. Specific rules developed: bivouacs inside tents didn't count; using a bivouac sack subtracted one point; sticking one's legs in a backpack scored the highest points. The eventual leader of the "bivy competition" was Andrzej Heinrich, a notoriously tough Himalayan climber who boasted hundreds of bivouacs.

With all of their winter training in the Tatras, plus their climbs in the Hindu Kush, Poles seemed ready for more. And although a lot of interesting things had already been done in the Himalaya, not one 8000-metre peak had been climbed in winter. Andrzej knew from his winter success on Noshaq and the near miss on Lhotse in the winter of 1974, where they had reached 8250 metres before being turned back by a ferocious storm, that 8000 metres in winter was possible. He craved a new accomplishment on a world-class scale, and he knew that Polish climbers could pull it off.

But the Nepalese authorities were not so convinced. They forced Andrzej to wait two years, until 1979, for his winter Everest approval. The permit finally arrived in Poland on November 22: they were scheduled to begin climbing on December 1! They would have to leave almost immediately. The next weeks were pure madness as Andrzej scrambled to get enough funding from the Polish Alpine Association to fly all the climbers to Kathmandu; there was no time to travel overland by truck. The pressure was fierce to get to the base of the mountain.

Andrzej believed that good equipment was the basis of any successful expedition. But at that time in Poland he couldn't just pop down to an outdoor-equipment shop with a credit card. Neither of those things existed. With considerable effort and some influential contacts, he was able find down clothing, fixed lines and mediocre tents in Poland. But the gas stoves, ice axes, lightweight carabiners, oxygen cylinders and climbing ropes had to be imported, and quickly. He had designed a high-altitude climbing boot in anticipation of this climb and now commissioned a bootmaker to manufacture several pairs as fast as possible.

If anyone could pull it all together, Andrzej could. Magnetic and charismatic, he was already a well-known lecturer capable of stunning his audiences with fantastical stories that sent a clear message to aspiring climbers: the world is waiting for you. He galvanized people and boosted their self-confidence as well as their belief in his ideas. He even succeeded in attracting the interest and generous support of wealthy Polish philanthropist Julian Godlewski.

There were many climbers who, after an encounter with Andrzej, were convinced that they too could do something really impressive in the Himalaya. He would have no problem getting climbers for his team, but he knew he would need to choose carefully. He drew up a list of Poland's 40 top climbers and sent them each a questionnaire, querying them on their level of interest in either the winter expedition or the one planned for the following spring, for which he had a second Everest permit. From that list, he chose both teams. Krzysztof Wielicki, an ambitious and daring climber from Wrocław, was among those slated for the spring attempt. Then three of the winter team members had to beg off for personal reasons and Krzysztof got his chance to go in winter.

❄ ❄ ❄

Born in 1950, Krzysztof grew up in the small village of Szklarka Przygodzicka, which is near the sea and surrounded by forest. It was an environment in which he flourished. He loved the outdoors and joined the Boy Scouts. ("A beautiful little uniform," he recalled.) Scouting became his most important influence, and for two intensive months each summer he led the scouting life. He learned about nature, orienteering, how to make a fire, camping and fishing.

In addition to the practical skills, he learned how to function in a group, how to prepare and share food, and how to respect personal boundaries within the confined spaces of camp. He also learned about leadership. Even the older scouts respected him; he seemed a natural leader. Scouting provided him with the best possible educational base for his future life in the mountains.

Though his upbringing was in sharp contrast to Wanda's, their lives converged at the university in Wrocław, where they both studied electrical engineering. They were members of the Wrocław Mountain Club, and Wanda, who was a bit older, taught him some of the basics on their climbing excursions to the crags.

Krzysztof was a bit of a daredevil, and in his very first climbing season he fell and broke three lumbar vertebrae. The doctors stuffed him into a plaster corset all the way up to his neck. Now he faced a family crisis: his brother was about to be married and his mother didn't know that Krzysztof had taken up climbing. In order to attend the wedding, he asked his friends to bring his street clothes to the hospital. He escaped over the hospital balcony, sliced off the top part of his cast with a knife in order to hide it and then changed his clothes, arriving at the ceremony just in time.

His unfortunate luck continued when, three years later, he was hit by falling rock in the Italian Dolomites. The impact destroyed his helmet and he lost consciousness for a few moments. But instead of retreating, he continued up and slept out just below the summit, dripping with sweat and blood. The next day a local doctor stitched up his head and warned him not to climb – good advice that Krzysztof promptly ignored.

Instead, he went to the Afghan Hindu Kush in 1977 and joined Alek Lwow and Jurek Pietkiewicz to climb a new route, alpine-style, on the 7084-metre Koh-e-Shkhawr. He now felt ready for a bigger challenge. He had proven climbing skills and obvious nerves of steel, and he clearly knew how to suffer. As well, he understood how to function well within a group. Andrzej Zawada was confident he would make an excellent addition to the 79/80 Everest winter team.

One of Krzysztof's teammates was Leszek Cichy, a tall, fair-haired climber from Warsaw. Leszek was a university lecturer, but his modest $20-per-month salary did little to hold him back in Poland: he jumped at the chance to escape to the Himalaya, even if it was in December. Leszek was young and fit, but he wasn't a likely candidate for the summit team. That didn't bother him. Like Krzysztof, he was just happy to be included on the expedition and to support the efforts of the more experienced climbers.

By January 5, the Polish team had set up base camp on the south side of the mountain. Within 10 days, the first three camps were ready and the team began to wonder why no one had tried this before. At this point the extremely cold temperatures and screaming winds of an Everest winter set in. They retreated to base camp and waited for the worst of it to pass.

Andrzej had earned valuable experience from his previous punishing winter climbs, and he knew how important it was for cold, tired climbers to slip into a hot bath once in a while. So for Everest in winter he had come prepared, with a plastic bathtub from Warsaw. Because of the temperatures, the plastic soon cracked, but Andrzej replaced the tub with an enormous aluminum basin bought in Kathmandu. There was no problem keeping it full of hot water, since a fire burned constantly in the kitchen, melting blocks of ice for tea and for cooking. Climbers returning from high on the mountain wallowed in the warmth as they thawed their frozen bodies.

Dominating the camp were two 20-metre radio aerials, each made of aluminum. Climber and technical whiz (and Wanda's first climbing instructor) Bogdan Jankowski was on hand to ensure that the aerials worked. Bogdan was also responsible for three long-distance transmitters, eight radio telephones and tape recorders used to record communication between camps, a gas-driven high-voltage generator, dynamos and batteries. Somehow, Bogdan kept it all working.

He also sent daily bulletins to the outside world so that Polish citizens could follow the team's struggle on Everest. But the messages flew both ways. At the Polish Alpine Association, Hanna was inundated with important family messages that she was asked to forward to the climbers: "Zosia has got one tooth up, one tooth down … what's new on the mountain? Are you remembering to wear warm socks?" Bogdan's communications centre was so effective that months later, during the spring climbing season, a parade of foreign climbers could be seen lining up to use it.

But all the technology in the world was no match for an Everest winter. For weeks the shrieking wind battered the climbers, eroding their strength and their will. Finally, there were only four climbers who remained strong enough to function in the otherworldly conditions, including the two youngest on the team: Krzysztof and Leszek. Andrzej moved them about like chess pieces, looking for the magical combination. He was convinced it was a psychological barrier rather than a physical one that was preventing them from climbing the mountain.

By February 11, Krzysztof, Walenty Fiut and Leszek had reached the South Col. Leszek dropped down to Camp III shortly after. The remaining two had a sturdy American tent, but its complicated pole assembly was impossible to erect in the wind. So they made do with a simple one-pole affair that they set up amidst the debris-strewn and wind-stripped col. The tent was so inadequate that they were forced to hold it up all through that terrifying night. Base camp talked to them until dawn, encouraging and comforting them, willing them to survive. The next morning, Leszek suggested that Walenty and Krzysztof should continue climbing up since they were so near the top. His comment was greeted with howls of protest from the rest of the team. From their all-night radio transmissions, they knew that the two had reached their limit; going up would be suicidal.

Andrzej sensed that this was a critical moment: there was an imperceptible shift in mood.

Krzysztof had frostbite in his feet, so he dropped down to Camp II to recover. Walenty continued all the way down to base camp. Andrzej realized that the situation had spiralled out of control. "How powerless is any leader at moments like these?" he asked. "If I wanted to save the expedition, there was only one thing to do, and that was to attempt the climb myself." Andrzej had not yet been as high as Camp III, and now he was proposing to climb the mountain. It seemed a preposterous idea, but within two days he and another teammate were on the South Col.

Andrzej was not likely to get up the mountain, but he had to make the gesture in order to salvage team morale. After all, it had been his idea to climb this giant in winter in the first place. Increasingly, it appeared that his dream had been unreasonable, but like a good military general, he needed to lead by example if he wanted his troops to do the impossible.

The chess game continued: up and down, sideways and diagonal. But the climbers were worn down and time had run out; their permit expired on February 15. The orders from Kathmandu were clear: no more moving up the mountain after the 15th. From that time on, their job would be to clear their camps off the mountain and descend. Andrzej knew they couldn't climb it by the 15th, so he sent a porter off to relay a message to the Ministry of Tourism, asking for an extension. What he didn't know was that the porter was fed up with the whole expedition: the cold, the wind and the endless effort. Unbeknownst to Andrzej, the porter's request to the authorities was for just two more days. Two more days and the suffering would finally be over.

Two days is all they got. Andrzej and the others were back in base camp, so the youngsters, Krzysztof and Leszek, were the only ones left high on the mountain. "I was never supposed to be the person to go to the summit," Krzysztof said. "I just happened to be in the right place at the right time." When the news came that they only had two days, they knew there was no choice: Poland was Poland, and Everest was Everest. They had to climb it.

Krzysztof and Leszek reached the South Col for the second time on February 16. That night, the temperature reached −42° Celsius. The sky was cloudy and the wind continued to roar. On the morning of the 17th, the last day on their permit, they started up, lightening their loads as much as possible by taking just one oxygen bottle each. Step by step, they inched up the slopes. Krzysztof could no longer feel his feet, but he kept plodding on, drawing on his reserves. The two hardly spoke. They didn't need to. They knew what was expected.

The rest of the team waited – and watched. From that moment on, it was impossible to sit still at base camp. "The tension was unbearable," Andrzej said. "Hope and despair followed one another at each passing moment. As the hours passed and there was still no word over the radio telephone, our anxiety was overwhelming." At 2:10 p.m. they radioed up. "Hello. Hello, Leszek. Krzysztof." No answer. They began making bets: would they make it or not? They jokingly considered cutting off their digits. Maybe their sacrifice would bring good luck. Should they cut off one finger or two?

At 2:25 p.m. Leszek's voice boomed in over the radio: "Do you copy? Do you copy? Over."

"Negative, say again. Say again."

"Guess where we are!"

"Where are you? Over."

"At the summit. At the summit."

"Hooray, hooray, at the summit. Kisses, hugs. A world record. Over."

The base camp climbers screamed and shouted, but Andrzej raised his hands to silence the commotion. He needed to be certain that they were at the true summit. His voice crackled over the radio: "Hey you, can you see the triangle?" The two summit climbers assured him that they were standing next to the triangle, and they promised to leave a maximum-minimum thermometer on the summit to prove they had been there.

Andrzej fired a message back to Hanna at the Polish Alpine Association. She had been waiting for hours, anxious and worried. "Today on the 17th of February at 2:30 p.m. the Polish flag appeared on the highest point in the world. Thereby the Polish team set a record in winter climbing. Best regards from all the participants. Zawada. Over."

Both Leszek and Krzysztof admitted that if the goal hadn't been Everest in winter, they would have given up weeks earlier. But the objective – and Andrzej's leadership – had inspired them to the highest level of performance. Their effort had been tremendous. Yet the top of Everest wasn't the end of their winter journey: they still had to get down.

By the time they reached the South Summit, their supplemental oxygen was depleted. They could feel their frostbite deepening in intensity, and the blowing snow stung their faces and obscured the visibility. Their welding goggles proved useless in this environment. Then their headlamp batteries malfunctioned, so they were now forced to continue the epic descent in complete darkness. Krzysztof lagged behind Leszek, losing his way as he struggled to continue moving on his frostbitten feet. He tried every possible way to walk: backwards, sideways. Finally he crawled.

After finding the tent, Krzysztof's first priority was his feet. He spent the night warming them over the flames of his stove. Over the next days the two managed to crawl and climb down the rest of the mountain to base camp, where they were received as heroes. For Krzysztof, the moment when he and Leszek arrived in Everest base camp would mark the most marvellous experience in his mountaineering career. Around him, his friends were weeping tears of joy. Although they had not stood on the summit of Mt. Everest, they felt that his success was their own.

No subsequent trip to the Himalaya could match this one for good atmosphere, strong leadership and team effort. It was quite a start to Krzysztof's Himalayan climbing career.

Back in Poland, people had been monitoring the climb on their nightly evening news for weeks. Krzysztof and Leszek were instant national heroes. But there were tinges of jealousy in certain sectors of the international climbing community. The bad feelings can be partially attributed to some confusion with the initial radio transmission, which mistakenly reported that they had made the ascent without a permit. For the next two years, Reinhold Messner insisted they hadn't climbed it in winter. This was because in Nepal at that time, the winter season officially ended on February 15, two days before their summit day. But Himalayan historian Elizabeth Hawley supported the team's claim, saying, "I am not amongst these quibblers." When Hawley and climbers from other countries endorsed the climb, Messner accepted the fact that they had climbed it, but *illegally*. Then the Nepal Ministry of Tourism produced a certificate stating that they had climbed it within the "official" winter window. Finally, Messner said, "Okay, I give up. They *did* climb it in winter."

Even the Pope weighed in, with a letter dated February 17, 1980:

> I express my happiness and congratulate my compatriots on their success in achieving the first winter ascent of the Earth's highest summit in the history of winter Himalaya climbing.
>
> I wish Mr. Andrzej Zawada and all the participants of the expedition further successes in this excellent sport which so brilliantly demonstrates the "royal" nature of the human being, its cognitive skill and will to rule God's creation.
>
> Let this sport, which demands such a great strength of the spirit, become a great lesson of life, developing in all of you all the human virtues and opening new horizons of human vocation.
>
> For all the climbs, including the daily ones, I bless you all.

> Vatican, 17th February 1980
> Pope John Paul II[16]

PHOTO: JERZY PORĘBSKI

Cieszę się i gratuluję sukcesu moim
Rodakom, pierwszym zdobywcom najwyższego
szczytu świata w historii zimowego himalaiz-
mu.

Życzę Panu Andrzejowi Zawadzie i wszyst-
kim Uczestnikom wyprawy dalszych sukcesów
w tym wspaniałym sporcie, który tak bardzo
ujawnia "królewskość" człowieka, jego zdol-
ność poznawczą i wolę panowania nad światem
stworzonym.

Niech ten sport, wymagający tak wiel-
kiej siły ducha, stanie się wspaniałą szkołą
życia, rozwijającą w Was wszystkie wartości
ludzkie i otwierającą pełne horyzonty powo-
łania człowieka.

Na każdą wspinaczkę, także tę codzienną
z serca Wam błogosławię.

Watykan, dnia 17 lutego 1980 r.

Jan Paweł pp. II

W.Panowie
Andrzej ZAWADA
i Uczestnicy Himalajskiej Wyprawy

The Pope's letter congratulating the Everest in Winter team on their success.

Poland was not yet finished with Everest. Andrzej had a second permit for the mountain and he intended to use it. But what could they possibly do that would match Wanda's accomplishment, or the more recent first winter ascent? There was only one solution: a new route. And for this effort Andrzej needed Jurek on his team.

Jurek had missed out on the winter climb because of the birth of his son, but he was ready to go in the spring of 1980 and travelled to Kathmandu with his teammates, impatient to begin. There were problems, however: they had no money, their leader was still in Poland and their permit was mysteriously missing. They weren't sure how long it would take to sort out the confusion over the permit, so rather than wait around for Andrzej to arrive, the team headed off for Everest base camp, calling themselves a "trekking" group.

Over the years, Andrzej had earned a reputation for being a bit untidy – even disorganized – at times, at least when it came to paperwork. In the middle of his impressive mountain library sat a huge desk, covered in paper. Stacks of it, piles of it, file folders full of it. He would eventually find the documents he needed, but it didn't surprise Jurek that there might be a delay with the permit. It was probably on Andrzej's desk, back in Warsaw.

Once at Everest, the team began climbing, still without a permit. By the time Andrzej arrived in mid-April, *with* a permit and a liaison officer, they were already at Camp III. Now they were legitimate. They were attempting a new line on the South Face between the South Pillar and the Southeast Ridge. At Camp IV, at around 8000 metres, they faced a vertical rock barrier. This would be the crux. Jurek estimated it to be Grade V in difficulty – extremely technical and steep. "To climb this at that altitude took so much out of me that at one stage the effort made me simply wet my pants," he said later. "At times my vision blurred."[17]

He and Rysiek Gajewski pushed through the difficulties and fixed ropes so that the next pair of climbers could establish the last camp at 8300 metres. Since the team was fixing ropes the entire way up the mountain, their progress was painfully slow. It eventually became clear that they didn't have enough time to fix ropes all the way to 8600 metres, which is where they would reach the relative safety of the ridge. Jurek suggested going for the summit from Camp V, without any fixed ropes. Andrzej Czok added one more element – they should do it without oxygen. This would be risky.

Next came a long discussion about who would be the first to try for the summit. There were nine Polish climbing stars on the team, all of whom were capable – and motivated. But this was a large expedition organized in the traditional style; it was up to the leader to decide. Andrzej had an innate ability to sense the mood in a camp, and to alter the mood if necessary – to lead without appearing to lead. He could convince climbers that his plan was their idea, even if it wasn't. Climbers who didn't agree with him initially would often see the wisdom of his decisions later. They respected his judgement. Those who climbed most frequently with Andrzej were affectionately called "The Zawada Boys," a nickname they didn't mind.

After suggestions were presented from each climber about who should go up first, there was a long, pregnant silence. Finally, Andrzej spoke. It would be Jurek and Andrzej Czok who would go first because they were in the best physical shape.

Excited, the two headed back to their tents to prepare for their summit attempt. The next morning Jurek felt strong as he powered up the fixed lines all the way to Camp V. There, they had to decide what to do about oxygen: should they use it or not? While they made tea and rested, base camp radioed them frequently, urging them to use bottled oxygen to make the climb safer and increase their chances of success. Reluctantly, the two turned on their oxygen and slept.

They left the last camp at 5 a.m. Jurek set his oxygen flow at one to two litres per minute. They moved slowly because of the deep snow and steep rock steps and reached the South Summit at 2 p.m. Jurek's lungs began to tighten and he struggled to breathe. When he tried to turn up the oxygen flow he realized that the cylinder was empty. So was Andrzej's. They looked at each other. Up or down? They indicated up, even without oxygen. They radioed base camp to inform them of their decision, no longer interested in advice from below. "They were *our* lungs, *our* patches of blackness whirling in front of the eyes, *ours* to be or not to be," Jurek reasoned.[18]

They reached the summit at 4 p.m. They had hoped to find the maximum-minimum thermometer and papal rosary left by Leszek and Krzysztof on their winter ascent just a few months before, but a Basque team had taken them. Jurek and Andrzej planted a Polish flag and started down an hour later with only the Basque flag as their souvenir. In his oxygen-depleted state, Jurek moved as if in a mist, as if he were beside his own body. It was 9 p.m. – 16 hours after starting out – when they collapsed into their tent.

When they stumbled into base camp the following day, they were inundated with congratulations and good wishes. But there was an underlying tension that permeated the camp. Despite Andrzej's strong leadership, there had been some bad behaviour. It turned out that two of the climbers,

Genek Chrobak and Wojciech Wróż, had tried to make a rogue ascent of the peak without informing the others what they were up to. The era of Himalayan climbing in which everyone on the team automatically felt like a winner, regardless of who got to the top, had come to a resounding end. Now the individual's accomplishments mattered more than the team's. It was the leader's job to hold the team together and manage everyone's expectations, by whichever method worked. Sometimes the leader succeeded, but not this time.

When Andrzej discovered what had happened, he called everyone but the summit climbers off the mountain. The expedition was over. Seven Polish climbing stars had just been denied their chance at the summit of Everest by a new route. The mood at base camp was a far cry from the jubilation earlier that winter. The climbers were stoic, but their disappointment was bitter and Jurek could feel it deep inside, like a splinter.

Their return to Poland was victorious. There were reporters at the airport and gold medals for outstanding achievement in sport. Even though this ascent didn't receive as much public support as the winter climb or Wanda's ascent, their new route garnered great respect within the climbing community. Jurek arrived back at his factory to be welcomed with a placard greeting the "conqueror of Everest."

Poland had redeemed itself on Everest. Wanda had established a record as the first European woman on the summit. The Poles had climbed it first in winter. And now they had established a new route. The Polish Alpine Association was satisfied.

But not everyone was pleased. Some highly placed government officials were tiring of Everest victories, and the propaganda specialists began watching the climbing community closely. They were suspicious. Even though Poland was basking in the reflected glory of the Pope, and of Wanda and the other Everest climbers, the fact remained that these were *individuals*. And individuals receiving this much attention was surely a dangerous trend. The authorities were in a testy mood – for good reason, as it turned out.

CHAPTER SIX

SOLIDARITY TO MARTIAL LAW

The price of anything is the amount of life you exchange for it.
— HENRY DAVID THOREAU, *WALDEN*

Poland teetered on the brink of chaos in the summer of 1980. When the party imposed an increase in food prices, a rash of strikes broke out in factories across the country. Of course, strikes were illegal and the party tried to subdue them with the usual combination of bribes and threats, a strategy that had worked in the past. Not this time. Nobody had counted on one particularly persistent individual, Lech Wałęsa.

Born the same year as Wanda, the electrician from the Gdańsk shipyards had already been jailed dozens of times for his underground activities. When the latest strike began at the Lenin Shipyard, Wałęsa jumped over the back wall and assumed leadership of the strike committee. Twenty thousand workers were barricaded inside the walls, and thousands more were outside the gates, cheering them on. Not just Poland's but the entire world's eyes turned to the Lenin Shipyard.

Over the next few days Wałęsa's team negotiated an agreement that applied to strikes occurring across the country. Nothing on this scale had ever been attempted before, and from it came the Solidarity name and the slogan that electrified the country: "Workers of all enterprises – Unite." The birth of the free trade union was Poland's first big step in the long road to democracy.

Despite all the excitement, daily life continued its austere rhythm. Women stood in line for hours to buy their frustratingly small rations. Men faced similar queues at the gas stations. The only positive thing about all this standing around was the time it provided ordinary citizens to talk. And talk they did: about the war, their families, the ruling party, Solidarity and, of course, their hopes and dreams. As their emotional bonds to one another strengthened, so did their determination to create change. Over time, the Communist-style Socialist regime began to fathom just how difficult it was to destroy the traditions and dreams of the tenacious Polish people.

Meanwhile, Polish optimism soared when another of their countrymen, writer Czesław Miłosz, received the Nobel Prize for literature in 1980. Once again the world's eyes turned to Poland. First the Pope, now the Prize.

❄ ❄ ❄

While the country enjoyed a renewed feeling of confidence, the recent Everest heroes basked in the glory of their success. But amidst the euphoria and Wanda's shiny new, post-Everest profile, her personal life was a shambles. Fame is not an attribute that grows from within; it comes from outside, from a particular public perspective. As Wanda's fame burgeoned, she became increasingly isolated from other Polish climbers. Wanda attributed the cold reception to jealousy. Others blamed it on her strident feminist stance.

At the same time, some of the women climbers she had nurtured and encouraged were becoming well known and more accepted by the climbing community. Anna Czerwińska and Krystyna Palmowska had developed into a powerful climbing partnership, with a number of Himalayan giants on their horizon. It seemed that Wanda's vision of a strong Polish women's Himalayan climbing team was coming to fruition, but not with her.

Although she was now famous, Wanda's personal finances were a mess and she moved frequently from one bland apartment to another. Living alone, she seemed unable to maintain any kind of serious emotional commitment, despite her many casual friends. Like a nomad, she dragged her clothing, her important photographs and her climbing equipment around, everything in a perpetual state of disarray. She lost her ability to think clearly in this chaotic atmosphere, and gradually she drifted into a panic-stricken state. At night she slept fitfully, consumed with worry and doubt. Her days were unproductive as she strained to remember what promises she had made, and to whom. She was a tired, worn-out, thin and unhappy young woman. But still, journalists wanted to speak with her. What was it like on the top of Everest? What were her plans? What was next for the famous Wanda? "The more I had to tell the same stories again and again, the more alien they sounded," she said, "as though they had nothing to do with me at all."[19]

Because of her fame, a publisher approached her later in 1978, suggesting she write her autobiography. She agreed, not realizing what was involved. Deadlines came and went. To the publisher it appeared that she didn't care, but the simple explanation was that Wanda wasn't a writer. She had no idea what hard work it would be and how much time it would take to write her story. Finally, in frustration, the publisher enlisted an established journalist, Ewa Matuszewska, to help her. Ewa was fascinated with the world of climbing and was flattered to work with such a famous woman. "She was a flash lady," she recalled. "She enjoyed luxury, like perfume and nice clothes."

They began to meet daily: lunch, tea, long walks, interviews and recordings. They became friends in the process, but the work progressed so slowly that the publisher lost patience and threatened to cancel the deal. Ewa suggested a two-week intensive period of work in an isolated location, far from any distractions. Wanda agreed, so she used her high-level connections to gain access to a government military resort on the Baltic Sea. Arrangements still had to be "fixed," despite the progress of the Solidarity movement, and coupons were required for everything: gas, hotels, food. The resort was perched on the edge of the moody, slate-coloured Baltic, and the two women spent their days striding along the stark and deserted beaches. They talked about the mountains, climbing, writing, relationships. Ewa recorded every phrase.

While the two of them struggled to save the book deal, Wanda realized that her love affair with climbing had faded. She concluded that the only solution for her was to stop climbing completely. Everest seemed a logical conclusion to her career, short as it had been. But she had no road map for a new life; climbing had defined her up to this point. Not only had it defined her, it had filled her life. Now there was a void. Wanda was used to excitement and danger. She relied on regular surges of adrenaline to keep herself motivated. She decided that she needed to find a replacement for climbing.

Like many other climbers, she joined the Solidarity movement. She rekindled her interest in listening to the hard, clean sounds of contemporary music. These were interesting activities, but not exciting. A keen and aggressive driver, the next year she took up car racing with some money she had earned from a film. There were only three sports that American writer Ernest Hemingway judged worthy: car racing, mountain climbing and bullfighting. Now, all Wanda lacked was bullfighting.

One afternoon, while visiting some friends, she remembered she needed a set of special tires for her car, an almost impossible acquisition at that time. But Wanda was accustomed to getting what she wanted, so she asked for a phone book and dialled up Poland's leading tire manufacturer. It took just the mention of her name to get through to the director, who was thrilled to not only talk with Wanda but also send her a full set of new tires. She knew how to use her name when she needed to, and he had a cocktail party story for weeks to come. Her friends laughed in amazement at the influence she still wielded.

Before long, car racing had lost its shine and – predictably – Wanda began climbing again. This passion that had consumed her since her teenage years was far too difficult to remove from her life. Her first forays were just to the Tatras. Then, in 1981, she began organizing an extremely ambitious women's expedition to Pakistan's highest peak and the second-highest mountain in the world, K2. For this project, she received some intriguing and mysterious support.

On February 4, 1981, a few friends gathered at Wanda's apartment to celebrate her birthday. After a couple of hours of eating and drinking, they heard the doorbell ring. A young man, a stranger to all, stood there politely, asking for Wanda. When she appeared at the door he handed her a sealed envelope. She cautiously took it and slipped her thumb along the seal. In it was a large sum of money – from an anonymous donor! Wanda and her friends spent the rest of the evening trying to figure out who the donor might be, finally settling on a certain wealthy Zakopane woman who had shown great interest in Wanda's climbing career. This envelope of cash provided the seed money for her first K2 expedition.

That spring she joined a group of international climbers for a training climb of Mt. Elbrus in the Caucasus. Organized by the Soviet Alpine Federation, the group consisted of alpinists from all the social democracies of the Soviet bloc: Czechoslovakia, Bulgaria, East Germany, Russia and Poland. Absurd regulations and a distinct Soviet style permeated the camp, which resembled a military installation more than a climber's campground. Each morning the climbers would receive their "climbing orders" for the day. Each evening they would carefully report their progress in the training logbook.

Since the Solidarity movement had exploded in Poland, it had become fashionable to wear a small Solidarity pin in one's lapel. All the Polish climbers sported one. The Russians adored wearing little emblems and suggested a pin trade. The Poles were somewhat amused by the request and asked if the Russians knew what the Solidarity pins represented. Yes, they whispered, they knew.

After the official welcome reception, at which some very fine Hungarian cognac was consumed, the Poles came up with a naughty plan: the Russians could have the pins but only after climbing on top of a Hungarian equipment barrel and loudly announcing three times: "Brezhnev be gone!" Most of the Russians – especially the Georgians – were happy to oblige. After each performance, Wanda, the most famous climber of the bunch, would pin the Solidarity pin on their lapel.

But one climber refused to cooperate. It turned out he was a director of the sports commission – an official representative of the government. But the poor fellow secretly coveted one of the troublesome pins. What should he do? He and Wanda huddled for a few minutes and appeared to come up with a solution. Wanda escorted him to another room. Everyone waited in silence. When they reappeared, Wanda pronounced that everything had been done according to protocol, and she had awarded him the pin. Nobody knew for sure what had happened in there, but the Russian was smiling and there was a Solidarity pin in his lapel.

A few days later the laughter and games came to an abrupt end. As they were climbing, a team member fell and hit Wanda from above, catapulting her down the slope an astonishing 200 metres. She knew immediately that it was serious; her femur was shattered.

A rescue team lowered her off the mountain, placed her into an ambulance and raced off to a nearby hospital. Doctors opened up her leg, inserted a metal clamp, and set the fractured bone. As soon as she emerged from the anaesthetic, Wanda sensed a problem with the manner in which the bone had been set. She begged the doctors to take another look, possibly even reset it. They disagreed with her assessment and refused. But Wanda was correct, and it wasn't long before she learned that she would need to have it rebroken and then set properly. Desperate to leave the hospital, she finally achieved her goal by going on a hunger strike.

When her brother Michael first saw her after the accident, he was shocked by a tired, grey-faced woman clad in a bloodied track suit and obviously frightened, convinced she would never return to the mountains. Worse, she could end up crippled by her injuries. Michael, and all who knew Wanda, understood that this would surely destroy her.

❄ ❄ ❄

In sharp contrast to Wanda's devastating situation, Voytek was half a world away, in Nepal at the base of Makalu's West Face. Solidarity hadn't disrupted his import–export business, and he was carrying on as usual with his life as an international climber. But at the moment, he needed a partner. He had long ago abandoned the large-scale expedition model, preferring small, lightweight teams. This made things very flexible: he could try Makalu, or he could go somewhere else. It really didn't matter. The important thing was to climb.

Jurek was poking around in the garden at his country home, admiring the spring growth, when a letter arrived from Nepal. "Jurek! Come over.

I've been below the West Face of Makalu with Alex MacIntyre and some others. It did not work out; we only got to 6700 metres. But I'm certain that it can be done. Or maybe the South Face of Lhotse? … I'm counting on you! —Voytek."

Jurek grinned. He was so easy to convince. He borrowed some money from the Katowice club and lined up for the coupons he would need to buy supplies, which were well beyond the normal monthly quota of two kilograms of meat and one kilogram of sugar. Next he went shopping, but the shops were empty. He next tried the warehouses, which were crammed full. He asked in amazement what all the stuff was for. "These are *government* reserves," the warehouse manager explained. What he really meant was that they were reserved for important government officials. But with his magic coupons, Jurek was in business, too.

As he left the Supersam warehouse, his trolley laden with canned meats, an aggressive passerby accosted him. "You selling that? Where did you get it? Give it to me, I'll pay you well." Jurek finally managed to muscle through the crowd and transfer his treasures into the back of his car. But then he had to repeat the process back at his flat, carting box after box of scarce delicacies from his car into his cellar as unobtrusively as possible. Rumours floated around about "that Kukuczka on the ninth floor" who was some sort of black marketeer. The rumour was not without merit since climbers were known to sell some of their meat provisions, even before heading off to their climbs. That was one of the perks, as was eating all that good food while climbing. It was a well-known fact that climbers ate much better while on expedition than at home.

Jurek hunkered down in his cellar, packing the cans of mouth-watering sausages and sweet, fatty ham into dozens of barrels, each meticulously labelled so that he wouldn't lose track of the ones containing his favourite delicacy: pig's knuckles. The precious barrels made their way to Makalu base camp, where Jurek and Alex MacIntyre – and even vegetarian Voytek – devoured them with relish. Teased by his teammates, Voytek clarified that he was a vegetarian the way most Poles are Catholic – when it's convenient. It was on this trip that Jurek earned a new nickname, "The Knuckle," due to his voracious appetite for pig's feet.

They decided to stay on Makalu rather than move to another mountain, so they went to work. They fought their way up the technically demanding face until around 7800 metres, at which point they came to a particularly difficult 500-metre rock barrier, some of it overhanging. It was a critical moment. "There comes a specific moment on a climb when no one talks to anybody else, but we all observe one another, watching the will to win gradually die," Jurek recalled. "The pace drops; everything goes slower, with greater resistance."[20] Voytek broke the tension, admitting, "I see no chance. We won't do this." Jurek urged them to continue, perhaps on a slightly different route. But Voytek had had enough, and, as he was the most experienced member of the team, his opinion prevailed.

They went down. At base camp Jurek persisted. He agreed with Voytek that the wall was beyond them, but felt that the mountain wasn't. There was still a chance for the summit. The mood had changed, however; neither Alex nor Voytek was interested in anything other than their original objective, a new route on the West Face. Jurek was particularly disappointed with his old partner, Voytek. He seemed increasingly inflexible, and now that the original goal had disappeared, he had lost all his drive. But surely this mountain was worth climbing, regardless of the route. Jurek pushed again. Voytek pushed back. Finally, Jurek said, "In which case, I shall try on my own." Voytek was taken aback, but he knew his friend's mind was made up. He said nothing.

The audacity of Jurek's statement was extreme. His altitude performance had been indifferent, in both Alaska and the Hindu Kush; he had not summited on the Nanga Parbat expedition; he had suffered on Lhotse and had used supplemental oxygen on Everest. Now he was proposing to climb an 8000-metre peak alone, without oxygen, on a route he knew nothing about.

He started up around noon with the intention of getting to the base of the face. There, he would take a look at what lay ahead, bivouac for the night and then decide what to do. He arrived at the foot of the wall at 3 p.m. There seemed to be no particular reason to stop, so he started up the wall with his little bivouac tent. Conditions were excellent and, as the evening turned to night, a full moon lit his way. At 11 p.m. he found a partially buried, abandoned tent from a previous expedition. Delighted with the find, he dug it out of the drifted snow and crawled in.

He slept until 11 the next morning, a prudent time to go back down, he reasoned. He made some tea at a leisurely pace and then packed up to descend. Yet when he crawled out of the tent he was amazed to discover that, although the wind still howled, he was face to face with a blazingly clear, cobalt-blue sky. He put on his crampons, lifted the pack onto his back and paced. Back and forth. Up or down?

Jurek headed up. He climbed toward the Makalu La at 7410 metres, where he found the tent he had stashed on their previous climb. After a good night's sleep and in lessening wind, he left the next morning and started up the unclimbed Northwest Ridge. Jurek had no idea what he would find on the ridge, or if it was even passable. At 8000 metres he dug a platform in the snow and pitched his tent. He crawled in and had just begun brewing tea when he had the strange sensation that he was not on his own, that he was cooking for two people. He even felt compelled to talk to his strange, ethereal visitor. The altitude and effort had begun to take their toll.

The next morning, his phantom companion gone, he continued up the ridge with only his camera, 10 metres of rope, three pitons, two ice screws and his protective clothing. He fully understood the level of commitment he was making. There could be absolutely no mistakes. There would be no second chances. He was completely on his own.

When he reached a technically difficult section, he resorted to rope-soloing. He would pound a piton into the rock, attach the rope to it, then climb the 10-metre length of rope, pound in a second piton, attach the top end of the rope to that piton, then climb down to the first piton and re-climb the section, now secured to that upper piton. It meant he could never fall more than 20 metres at a time, assuming the piton would hold. But the process was time-consuming and strenuous; he was well above 8000 metres now, and the lack of oxygen was debilitating.

At 4:30 p.m. he was on the summit. He left a plastic ladybird toy belonging to his son, snapped a couple of pictures and knew he had to get down – fast. Night was moving in, and the moon wouldn't be up for a few more hours. Although the sky was awash with twinkling stars, they didn't shed much light. He made it to his tent late that night and to base camp the following afternoon. As he walked in, tired, grey and hollow-cheeked, Voytek walked up to him and asked, "So, how was it?"

"I got to the summit," Jurek replied. Enough said.

While he rested and drank and stuffed himself with pork knuckles over the next few days, a thought occurred to him: this was his third 8000er, and he was the only Pole to make that claim. He couldn't help but daydream about the possibility of more 8000ers.

The Makalu climb gave Jurek and Voytek an inkling that, despite their apparent synchronicity on the highest mountains on Earth, their values and their approach to those mountains were not perfectly matched. Jurek appeared to have a greater capacity for risk than Voytek, who seemed more focused on a specific objective rather than on reaching a summit by any route and at any cost. Their actions and decisions on Makalu had demonstrated some fundamental differences. And these differences created potential for conflict.

✻ ✻ ✻

Success in the mountains and the resulting optimism amongst Polish climbers reflected the growing popularity and influence of the Solidarity movement. Nothing seemed impossible as individual citizens rediscovered their potential; Polish climbers were ample proof of that. But this fundamental shift in mood alarmed the authorities, who had grown weary of trying to contain Solidarity activities. They finally decided on a military solution to take back control of Poland. The troops moved in on the night of December 12, 1981, and by the early morning of the 13th, Polish citizens awoke to streets filled with tanks.

Their spirits collapsed. No one knew what would happen next. All the shops and offices closed. Nothing worked: phones and buses were a thing of the past. It appeared that they would have to start all over again, just like after the war. Jurek recalled the mood. "We felt trapped … I felt as if I was in a cage."

Tens of thousands were arrested on trumped-up charges and thrown in jail. Krzysztof, an active Solidarity supporter, spent that first night of the backlash driving around the city, checking on the safety of fellow Solidarity members. He then raced back to his apartment, destroying and hiding documents until the morning dawned. Many of his friends were arrested. Internment camps were the order of the day, with frequent beatings and deaths. With martial law in effect, freedom of movement and speech became a dim and distant memory. The army had effectively declared war on Polish society. Like so many of his countrymen, Jurek lost heart.

✻ ✻ ✻

Martial law drove the country's standard of living even lower. Poland's GNP suffered a 15-per-cent drop. The national debt reached USD 30 billion and the gap between what people earned and what they could buy widened. Not that it mattered much, for there was very little to buy. Despite the fact that Poland was full of natural resources, the country plunged into a period of unproductive chaos and serious food shortages. The USA then introduced economic sanctions against Poland and the USSR, demanding that the situation be addressed.

✻ ✻ ✻

Wanda was on a lecture tour in East Germany when the military took over the country. She had been scheduled for another operation on her leg upon her return to Poland, but, due to the unrest, the surgery was cancelled. At a loss, she called up Dr. Scharfetter in Innsbruck, hoping that since he had helped her in the past he would agree to do so now.

The doctor had divorced his wife a few years before and was living with his two sons in the mountains of Tyrol. A large, gentle and now lonely man, he was charmed by Wanda's visit and encouraged her to stay in the West. His sons devoured her wild, adventurous stories, and she badly wanted to leave Poland. Why not? she thought. Better this marvellous man than the tanks on the streets at home. Within a few months they married. She was now an Austrian citizen and could travel freely on her brand new Austrian passport. Dr. Scharfetter arranged for her surgery and nurtured her throughout her long convalescence. Impatient to get back to the mountains, she used her time to plan a K2 expedition for the summer of 1982.

With martial law paralyzing Poland and the disappearance of the usual expedition funding sources, Wanda instead tried her hand at soliciting sponsors. She soon found a powerful advocate for her idea in Reinhold Messner. She accompanied him on his lecture tours, reaping the benefit of his strong endorsement as he introduced her to his sponsors. Even with crutches, her charming enthusiasm was infectious and corporations responded with generous cheques. The sponsorship support, together with her anonymous donor's contribution, left her as well funded and well supplied as she had ever been.

Wanda was not the only one bent on climbing K2. Despite martial law in Poland, the climbing community was determined to show the government that they weren't intimidated. They knew that climbing had kept them going throughout all those difficult postwar years. Now they were resolved to continue climbing regardless of the costs. Yielding to the authorities would have killed their spirits. By challenging martial law, the climbers undermined confidence in the authorities and, more important, protected their own values. They were Polish climbers: if they wanted to go abroad to climb, they would do whatever was required to make that happen.

Wanda and her team of women climbers had come to K2 for the Abruzzi Ridge. Because Wanda's leg had been slow to heal, it was clear she would not be climbing – a difficult reality for someone so motivated. But she was also a leader. If she could get a women's team to the top, that would have to do for now. Although Voytek and Jurek were listed on Wanda's permit, they had agreed to climb independently and were hoping for a new route on either the East or South Face. Janusz Kurczab had also assembled a sizable team of some of Poland's strongest to tackle a new route on the Northwest Ridge. Amongst them were Krzysztof Wielicki and Leszek Cichy.

Voytek had already attempted the difficult Northeast Ridge in 1976, but it was the first time for Wanda and Jurek to view the magnificent peak. The effect on them was electrifying and overwhelming. For Jurek, the sight of this geological wonder – this near-perfect pyramid of rock and ice – produced a degree of anxiety that he had never before experienced. He knew the mountain's propensity for killing without discrimination. Even martial law seemed mundane compared to the terror of this giant.

Wanda's team began working its way up the Abruzzi Ridge. Jurek and Voytek needed to acclimatize before attempting their route and had promised to stay out of Wanda's way, so they headed over to nearby Broad Peak. They had no intention of climbing to the summit, but, privately, they weren't excluding the possibility. Their official reason for being on the mountain was to "take photos" for the women's team.

With little fuss they made their way up the mountain – all the way to the top. Of course, this was illegal, since they had no permit for Broad Peak. The "stolen climb" brought Jurek a particularly sweet satisfaction; it felt like his own personal mountain, made more precious because he and Voytek couldn't tell anyone about their illegal ascent.

But they did, if reluctantly, the very next day. Reinhold Messner was on his way up, and although he didn't recognize Jurek from their previous meeting, he knew Voytek well enough to strike up a conversation. He asked where they had been. Voytek was careful in choosing his words in response, mentioning something about "acclimatization" and an area "near the summit." Messner pressed harder. He wanted to know if they had climbed the peak. Voytek persisted with his vagueness about being "quite high." Messner understood the subtext of the answer and nodded with a grin as he agreed offhandedly to Voytek's request to keep the information to himself.

Back at K2, the pair made little progress on their East Face. They switched to the South Face. No luck there, either. Wanda's team was struggling, too, perhaps because she was leading from below, her crutches never far away.

Krystyna Palmowska, a member of Wanda's team, was irritated with her for pushing them too hard. Wanda's leadership style, developed on Gasherbrum III, was landing her in trouble once again. She had set the bar unnaturally high by walking into base camp on crutches, and now her expectations of her teammates were enormous. She seemed to have the ability to distance herself from her body, regarding it as a tool with which to accomplish a task. She transferred this same philosophy to the people she managed, and her attitude incited defiance. "Nobody likes to be treated like an object that is there only to serve a purpose," Krystyna complained.

Then tragedy struck when Halina Krüger died suddenly of heart failure at Camp II. After 69 days on the mountain the women finally gave up. Despite the tragedy, Wanda was almost defiant as they retreated. The world's most beautiful mountain had mocked their dreams and ambitions. She would have to come back and settle the account.

Meanwhile, the larger and very experienced male Polish team, led by Janusz Kurczab, climbed their route until they reached its final step, which they tried to bypass on its northern side. This is where the trouble began. They collided with a Japanese team climbing on the North Buttress and were forced to negotiate a high-level agreement on how to divide the terrain. The Japanese traversed to the right and tagged the summit just before the weather broke. The Poles almost made it, but had to give up at 8200 metres.

All three defeated Polish teams headed back to Islamabad, only to discover that news of the Broad Peak climb had leaked. Disgruntled authorities grilled Wanda about the unauthorized ascent, but she stuck to her story: Voytek and Jurek were merely two photographers getting pictures of K2 from the lower flanks of Broad Peak. Her story seemed to satisfy the officials.

Before returning to Poland, they travelled from Islamabad to Delhi, where they unloaded some of the smuggled Polish goods and picked up clothing and coffee to bring back to Poland. It was in Delhi's Polish Embassy that a young Polish climber, Artur Hajzer, met the K2 teams on the final leg of their homeward journey. Artur was impressed and even a little intimidated by the array of Polish stars before him: Kurczab, Wróż, Cichy, Wielicki and Kurtyka. He was particularly struck by Voytek's lean face and dark sunglasses and recalled that the elusive and already famous climber would spend entire days in silence, stuck to his beach chair, listening to jazz on his Walkman and sunbathing his obviously beautiful body.

When the sun went down and the climbers gathered around the dinner table, the famous climbers spoke. The rookies, Artur included, listened. It took little prodding, according to the young climber. "You didn't have to convince Wielicki to talk about his expedition," Artur said. "He felt the need to talk a lot about it." Artur was curious about why the expedition had failed. They hadn't lacked food or equipment. Their official reason for backing off K2 was bad weather, but Artur knew that the Japanese team, which was there at the same time in the same weather, had made it to the summit.

Krzysztof talked about being at a high camp with three other climbers, two teams of two. At this moment one of the climbers developed obvious signs of altitude sickness. He couldn't build a coherent sentence and had a particular problem with verbs. "Shovel," "Platform," was the best that he could muster. By the next morning he was worse. They tried testing his cognitive ability with multiplication tables, but by now his head was pounding. He clearly needed to go down, yet nobody wanted to descend with him. They were poised for a summit attempt; leaving high camp would be the end of that. Krzysztof explained that, after some difficult and tense discussions, he finally offered to accompany the sick climber, even though he wasn't his partner.

Krzysztof stopped talking and the room went quiet. The young climbers were puzzled by this selfless decision. Krzysztof's story didn't resonate with them. Surely he wouldn't have given up the summit so easily.

After refilling his teacup, Krzysztof clarified that his offer to descend was perhaps not as generous as it seemed. He knew that this summit attempt had very little chance of success. The peak was too far away. Why waste his energy? He could go down now and save himself for another attempt, all the while appearing like a generous teammate ready to sacrifice himself for the cause. Krzysztof's assessment of their chance at the top had been correct: while he was accompanying the sick climber down the mountain, the summit attempt failed. He had been right, but had he been honest?

Krzysztof continued his K2 stories, but Artur stopped listening, struggling with what he had just heard. He was confused and disappointed to learn that in the mountains it was possible for respected climbers to be dishonest. For years he had been taught quite the opposite, a loftier set of values about clean choices and behaviours while climbing. He already had a few years of climbing experience, and he thought he understood the ethics of climbing and the sense of brotherhood on the mountain. "Would it turn out that, on the *highest* mountains, everything changed," Artur wondered? "Could theory and practice be so different?"[21]

CHAPTER SEVEN

TOGETHER OR ALONE

Mountains inspire our highest selves. When we encounter mountains in wild places we experience the peak of our own humility. Whether we are standing at the summit or paying respects from below, we are flushed with awe. Perhaps this is the beginning of religion.
— TERRY TEMPEST WILLIAMS, *EXTREME LANDSCAPE*

I have never found a companion that was so companionable as solitude.
— HENRY DAVID THOREAU, *WALDEN*

Voytek thought he had found the perfect climbing partner in Alex MacIntyre. Alex, with his wild mane of curly black hair and his round-faced charm, contrasted sharply with Voytek, who was lean like a knife. Their characters differed, too, for Alex, with the exception of his terror of rockfall, seemed more or less unflappable. Voytek was twitchy, nervous and full of angst.

He marvelled at Alex's imagination in the mountains, as well as at his pre-climb strategy, which was to drink heavily the night before. Alex seemed to approach the great things in his life with a hangover. He reasoned that the mass destruction of brain cells *prior* to climbing at altitude actually left fewer of them to be destroyed by the absence of oxygen *during* the climb – an amusing theory that held just an ounce of logic.

Alex's acclimatization strategy, described in an article for *Mountain* magazine, was even more preposterous. His first suggestion was to eat large amounts of garlic. Other possibilities included "making love for hours on end in a series of two-knuckle push-ups and hopping up big hills on one toe, to the strains of Wagner from your free, portable, lead-weighted Japanese microcassette."[22] Voytek and Alex stormed through the Himalaya with a landmark alpine-style ascent of Dhaulagiri's East Face and two alpine-style attempts on the unclimbed West Face of the 8485-metre Makalu, the second attempt with Jurek in 1981.

Voytek had a new idea that he wanted to share with both of them – a traverse of Gasherbrum I and II in the Karakoram. It was a bold plan with a lot of unknowns, but these three were certainly the ones to pull it off.

They agreed to give it a try. A week before they were to meet, Voytek was at the Polish Embassy in Delhi. A group of climbers just back from K2 arrived.

"Voytek, did you hear about Alex?" one of them asked.

"No. What about Alex?" Voytek answered. Dead silence.

"What about Alex?" he repeated.

"Alex is dead, on Annapurna."

Voytek had last seen Alex at the end of their Makalu trip, when they had agreed to launch their next adventure as soon as possible. He had written about Alex's special qualities in *Mountain* magazine: "Will I ever see you again? Oh yes, in a week I'll see Alex with all his dominating tranquility and confidence, which, when I look back through my mountains and even more through my anxious returns to the plains, I was always so lacking and longing for. I'll see him again and he'll make me believe for a while that I can seize this tranquility again."[23]

Except that now he was dead.

Stunned, Voytek turned to Jurek as his partner for the Gasherbrums. Despite the loss of Alex, and their differences on Makalu, Jurek and Voytek formed an almost unstoppable duo. They had both moved steadily upward through the impossibly strong Polish climbing fraternity and had emerged on top. They were the best of the best, a microcosmic dream team, so in tune with each other that they hardly needed to talk. With completely different personalities, they managed to co-exist for weeks, almost like an old, comfortable couple. Other climbers watched them cohabiting small tents, cooking and eating together, managing the stress of altitude and danger, and somehow negotiating their way through difficult, emotionally charged route-finding decisions. All of this, despite their contrasting styles. Voytek was the "idea guy" and Jurek brought confidence and drive. Recognizing their individual strengths was the key to their success as a team.

Voytek laughed at their differences. "When I was in pain all over, I would notice Jurek showing some *small* signs of suffering. When I was already *deeply* afraid, Jurek still did not feel any fear for a long time. When I experienced *dreadful* fear, Jurek was only slightly worried." Voytek's meticulous planning and preparation balanced Jurek's more intuitive and aggressive approach. Voytek's slender frame and his greater technical climbing skills complemented Jurek's incredible strength and power. "Jurek was the greatest psychological rhinoceros I've ever met among alpinists," Voytek said, "unequalled in his ability to suffer and his lack of responsiveness to danger. At the same time, he possessed that quality most characteristic to anyone born under Aries – a blind inner compulsion to press ahead. Characters like that, when they meet an obstacle, strike against it until they either crush it or break their own necks."[24]

For three years they dominated Himalayan climbing. They were as happy as they could possibly be, for they were living their dream. Krzysztof Wielicki described their partnership as "magical."

❉ ❉ ❉

To help finance the magic, Voytek and Jurek perfected the art of "international trade," scraping together just enough money to pay for their adventures. Like many Polish climbers, they bought cheap goods in Poland and Russia – athletic shoes, titanium ice screws, down sleeping bags and Bohemian crystal – and took them to Asia along with their climbing equipment, selling the goods for hard currency. Upon their return to Poland, they brought back hard-to-find products to sell to their Polish customers, as well as pockets full of foreign cash. American climber Greg Child recalled being accosted by Polish climbers trying to relieve him of his high-tech American tent and equipment at absurdly low prices. Greg felt they were sometimes overly insistent – even rude – about the prices, trying to impose feelings of guilt: foreign climbers should feel obliged to cooperate since Westerners were rich and the Poles were poor.

Some Western climbers urged the Poles to defect. Why not? What did they have to lose? A lot more than was first apparent. The Poles had worked out an economic system within their dysfunctional country, and, although it seemed bizarre to foreigners, it worked for them. More important, they were Polish; Poland was their home. They joked about defecting, but very few did.

The large army-style truck convoys of climbers that headed to Asia were crammed with "equipment" ostensibly to be used on their climbs. But even the border agents knew what was going on, and the frontier shenanigans sometimes approached the absurd.

Wrocław climber Alek Lwow explained his preferred method of dealing with border guards: "We drank with them." After a certain amount of imbibing, the customs agents would eventually hand over the all-important stamp to the soberest member of the group and tell him to certify the paperwork. Many climbers returned to Poland richer than when they left. Climbing wasn't just a hobby. It wasn't just a lifestyle: it was a *living*. They could buy food, clothing, cars, even houses with their illicit profits.

A well-known story has it that one alpine smuggler allegedly left Poland with a pack of chewing gum, sold it in India and continued buying and selling goods back and forth across various Asian borders until he finally returned with enough money for a Mercedes Benz!

Smuggling had become a big and lucrative business for Polish climbers. But from time to time there were problems.

※ ※ ※

Jurek and Voytek arrived at the India–Pakistan border near Amritsar in the summer of 1983, their truck fully loaded with climbing equipment and food for their Gasherbrum expedition. But their barrels held more than equipment: a few had whisky. The normal routine was to arrive at the border, pass through Indian customs, drive through a 200-metre no-man's-land, unload the trucks, reload the barrels into Pakistani trucks and, finally, pass through Pakistani customs.

This time was different. The Indian customs agents were suspicious and uncooperative. They ordered the pair to unload their trucks at Indian customs and then insisted on opening and inspecting every single barrel. Voytek protested. "Come on. We are *leaving* your country, not entering it." The officer mumbled that he was just following orders. After a somewhat cursory glance into each barrel, he trundled off to his commanding officer and reported that all seemed okay. The officer snapped at him, accused him of shoddy work, and insisted on doing it all over again, this time together.

Barrel by barrel, they rooted through the contents, all the way to the bottom. Voytek and Jurek felt queasy. Whisky was not considered "necessary food provisions," and it certainly didn't qualify as climbing equipment. They had a lot of it. Jurek walked around the corner, sat down on the ground and lit a cigarette, resigned to the looming catastrophe.

He heard shouting. It was Voytek. "What are you looking for?" he screamed. Jurek could hear the anger and fear in Voytek's voice. "You want to see everything? Fine. Be my guest!"

There were three barrels left. Each held several bottles of whisky, carefully and tightly swaddled in sleeping bags. Voytek had insisted on personally packing these barrels and had been irritatingly fussy about how they had been wrapped. He grabbed one of the guilty barrels and began tearing out its contents, including a sleeping-bag-clad bottle of whisky. Miraculously, the bundle remained intact and the bluff succeeded. The customs agents had stopped to watch the tantrum and concluded that they were wasting their time. Surely this half-crazed climber had nothing to hide since he was ripping the barrels apart himself. They abandoned their search and let the two go.

Voytek and Jurek extricated themselves from the Indians and approached Pakistani customs.

"Do you have any alcohol?"

"No, sir, we do not."

The wily pair retrieved their stamped documents and sped off, visions of Asian prisons fading away, glistening mountains slipping in to take their place.

But their problems were not yet over. When they arrived in Islamabad they had two important tasks. The first was to sell the whisky for enough cash to finance the trek to base camp. The second was to obtain and pay for the Gasherbrum permits.

Selling the whisky was easy. Voytek knew the where and how of that. It was even fun in a stealthy kind of way: the darkness of the early-morning hours brightened by the little lamps; a shot or two of vodka as they rummaged through the barrels; choosing the items to take to market that day. They toasted each other and laughed. They felt like pirates on the high seas.

Next, it was over to the Ministry of Tourism for their permits. Strangely, there was little talk of the Gasherbrums but rather an inordinate amount of interest in Broad Peak. Perhaps it was the Ramadan-enforced fast that made the official so grumpy, or maybe it was just the stifling heat.

"How was it, gentlemen, last year on Broad Peak? Did you get to the summit or not?"

Of course they *had* climbed Broad Peak in 1982, but without a permit – and without reporting it.

"What summit?" Voytek responded. Wanda had reported in after the expedition and had allegedly smoothed things over. Apparently not completely. Maybe it was Messner's book about his Broad Peak climb that had leaked the story. The official insisted that the paperwork on Broad Peak was not complete and that he would appreciate it if Voytek and Jurek could do that – now.

Jurek watched Voytek wriggle like an eel, talk and explain and, finally, scribble a barely legible, extremely vague, written report. After a few hours of careful posturing, they walked out in triumph; they now had a permit for *one* of the Gasherbrums.

As soon as they reached base camp, they initiated the second half of their plan: a letter asking for a permit to climb the *second* Gasherbrum. This had been their strategy all along, but they were playing a game of absent-mindedness in order to avoid paying for both permits up front; they first had to unload their remaining articles for sale. They were banking on their application letter reaching the tourism office at just about the time they actually climbed their second peak. And they were also assuming they would receive a "yes" from the officials. Theirs was a complex juggling act: whisky, customs officials, black market, tourism officials, forgetfulness. It was all about cash flow.

After all the deal-making and near misses with authorities in various countries, the climbing was a welcome relief. They did a couple of acclimatization ascents to stretch their legs and expand their lungs. Then they made a complete traverse of Gasherbrum II, the peak for which they actually had a permit. Now they felt ready for the Southwest Face of Gasherbrum I.

A Swiss team leaving the area gave them their extra food: all 300 kilograms' worth. Jurek was in heaven. He loved to cook and he loved to eat. As it snowed day after day, he experimented with the new provisions. Sardines with cheese sauce, chocolate fondue, bacon with potatoes. They plowed their way through the mountains of treats, and the increasingly complex and bizarre menus became the focal point of each day.

When they weren't eating they talked: about future expeditions together, family, politics and, of course, food. Jurek could talk about food endlessly: his favourite kind of herring, the savoury *golonka* – a special kind of Polish ham – and best of all, pig's knuckles. As each day passed, their appetite for conversation receded, until it was only food that interested them. After two weeks of bad weather, with only the ravens to entertain them, they retreated into their respective tents, trying to avoid irritating each other. Voytek read. Jurek mostly slept.

It was obvious to both Jurek and Voytek that the accumulation of new snow on the face of Gasherbrum I had laid a deadly trap for them. Jurek woke up in a cold sweat each night, plagued by recurring nightmares about crossing the huge, snow-laden bowl on the face. His thoughts turned to home. After three weeks of this torture he began to lose interest in this place, and this face.

Then the weather cleared. Not just a temporary clearing, but a strong high-pressure system that promised several days of reprieve from the storms. They crawled out of their tents and stood staring at the face, at just one spot – an immense, concave, sinister-looking bowl, dangerously loaded with snow. To cross it would be suicidal. As they stared, they noticed a flicker of movement at the topmost point of the bowl. White moved against white. It billowed. It grew. A muffled roar reached them as they watched in amazement at the massive avalanche ripping down the mountain. Although the bowl wasn't completely clear of snow, at least there was a lot less of it. They looked at each other and agreed without a word. Tomorrow they would go up.

But their time was running out, and the porters were scheduled to arrive the very next day. What to do? They were perfectly acclimatized and the weather looked good. So did the mountain. Voytek concocted an ingenious plan to hide their passports and money and draw a map of the mountain with an arrow to indicate their whereabouts. This, they hoped, would be found by the porters, along with some food left out for their use. Hopefully it would be enough to keep the porters in base camp for the few days required to attempt the unclimbed face.

At 3 a.m. on July 20 they started off. Almost immediately they had to cross the frightening basin of snow. Voytek described the experience: "We switched off our brains and moved steadily into danger. Ten minutes later we emerged."[25]

They climbed for two more days and were poised for the summit when a final complex headwall forced them to rappel back down for one last bivouac. Then the unthinkable happened. One of Voytek's crampons fell out of sight down the slope. This was a serious situation. They minced their way down to the bivouac to consider their options. The next morning, despite the setback, they decided to continue up rather than retreat. Shortly after starting out, Voytek heard Jurek's jubilant curse. He had found the crampon! It had fallen just a short distance and was caught on a clump of snow.

When they reached the South Ridge they faced more difficult climbing. Above 8000 metres now and severely stressed, Voytek began hallucinating. An unknown man appeared, heavily burdened with a pack and heading the wrong way. Voytek attempted a conversation with the stranger, but he was non-responsive.

He eventually faded away and Voytek and Jurek pushed on, reaching the summit at 7:30 p.m. Voytek looked out at the vast undulating sea of Karakoram peaks and sensed a vague, yet intensely familiar, affinity to a great and enormously calm universe. He was completely at peace with himself.

Jurek reminded him that their day was not yet over; they had a date with their porters. They raced down the mountain to the waiting men who, with great restraint, had avoided using any of the precious food supply. But, mysteriously, the money that had been carefully stashed was missing. No worries. They were down, they were safe, and they had porters.

Back in Islamabad, they had to report their climbs to the Ministry of Tourism. They hadn't heard a word about their second permit but assumed that all would be resolved when they offered to pay the fee. They assumed wrongly. The officials were incensed that they had gone ahead and climbed two peaks when they had permission for only one. Jurek and Voytek explained their forgetfulness and begged for forgiveness. After 10 days of haggling, they finally obtained the required documents and the officials let them leave the country.

Upon their return to Poland, the pair expected, and received, recognition and praise for their remarkable achievement: two new routes on two 8000ers, climbed by a two-man team in alpine style. Of course there was one small outstanding issue – payment for that second permit. Jurek and Voytek presented an invoice to the Polish Alpine Association and hoped for the best.

Most, but not all, of the committee agreed that the permit fee was a small price to pay for such a great Polish mountaineering achievement. There was one dissenter within the alpine association who wouldn't let the Gasherbrum issue die, and Jurek and Voytek feared they might be grounded within Poland.

Andrzej Zawada had also run into occasional problems regarding his previous expedition finances. The officials seemed particularly antsy about equipment, since much of it belonged to the alpine association. If 10 tents left the country, 10 were expected to return. Andrzej and others would explain that this one had fallen into a crevasse or that one had been blown apart by the wind. But those excuses seldom satisfied the bureaucracy. Perhaps they had heard about the smuggling. Perhaps they thought that the tents were less likely to be in a crevasse and more likely to be in a Kathmandu shop, commanding an outrageous price!

Eventually the alpine association paid the permit fee and left Jurek and Voytek alone, albeit with a strong reprimand.

❊ ❊ ❊

The dream team returned to Pakistan in 1984 for Broad Peak, this time *with* a permit. Or so they thought. The original plan was to link up with a Swiss team on their way to the mountain, but when they reached Islamabad a problem arose. The officials, perhaps remembering their transgressions of previous years, refused to allow them on the Swiss permit. Scrambling for an alternative, they ran into Janusz Majer. Nicknamed the "elephant," this tough, young, black-haired and heavily bearded climber from Katowice was leading a Polish team to Broad Peak, so they transferred to his team. They had already climbed the mountain, but this time they wanted to try a traverse of all three of its peaks before heading over to take a look at Gasherbrum IV.

Janusz's Broad Peak team included Krzysztof Wielicki, famous for his winter Everest ascent. In fact, there was no shortage of stars at base camp. The highest film team in the world was there: Austrian alpinist Kurt Diemberger and British climber Julie Tullis. Climbing legend Reinhold Messner was there, too. And three of Poland's brightest stars: Jurek, Voytek and Krzysztof.

Jurek and Voytek's original plan was to ascend Broad Peak's unclimbed South Ridge followed by a complete traverse of the entire peak. Their first reconnaissance of the South Ridge route revealed its impracticality and difficulty, so they retreated and spent several days debating the alternatives. Although Jurek wasn't pleased with the decision, they finally settled on Voytek's choice, which was to head up the North Face to the North Peak, then continue along the ridge to the Central Peak, on to the Main Peak and finally down the West Face route.

But they had a problem: his name was Krzysztof Wielicki. Krzysztof had proven to be a bit of a climbing prodigy. He was talented, fast, ambitious and smart, a combination that contributed to his justifiably high opinion of himself. He would almost certainly not be satisfied with an ascent of the normal route of Broad Peak, which was the Polish team's objective. Voytek was convinced that Krzysztof wanted to join them on their ambitious traverse. Voytek wanted a twosome for that committing climb, not a three-some. It was a tricky situation.

The three climbers eyed each other. Krzysztof with his sad, heavily lidded eyes, his deceptively soft voice, his keen sense of ironic humour, his world-weary face partially hidden by an unruly mustache, agitated, always busy, too much energy, flitting from one tent to another. Even Krzysztof recognized his nervous mood: "I was restless at Base Camp and could not find anywhere to put myself." Voytek, in contrast, focused on his plan, and, when he wasn't attending to chores that contributed directly to its execution, quietly retired to the privacy of his tent, reading, listening to music and writing. Jurek cooked.

They strutted around base camp for some time, talking about this and that, without actually confronting the issue: would it be a twosome or a threesome on the traverse? Finally, Voytek asked Krzysztof, "What are your plans?"

"Oh, I have a plan, don't worry."

But what was it? Voytek's discomfort increased. The tension grew. At this point Voytek had a moment of brilliance and approached Krzysztof with an idea. "Why don't you go up the mountain very quickly," he suggested. "I'm sorry not to invite you with us; we are a team of two, but you can do something equally daring. You can fix the camps in advance and then go up in just one day to the top."

At first, Krzysztof rejected the plan as impossible. But he didn't dismiss it completely. Privately, he thought he could probably do it, but one thing worried him: fainting. What if he ascended too quickly? Even though he was built like a bird – 80 per cent muscle, bone and sinew – he worried that the huge physical output, combined with extremely thin air, might cause him to pass out.

Two weeks passed. Voytek approached him again. "I have my own plan," Krzysztof insisted. The next day he went over to Voytek's tent and announced that he was going to climb the peak in a day. It appeared that Krzysztof had come up with the idea himself. Voytek swallowed his first response and mumbled, "Okay, that's a very good idea."

Voytek and Jurek headed off on their grand traverse and forgot all about the gamesmanship at base camp. Their hands were full. They had launched a real adventure and had placed themselves in an unknown position with an uncertain outcome. The level of commitment was colossal. Once they were past the difficult climbing up to the North Peak and had dropped into the saddle before the Central Peak, retreat would no longer be an option. If a storm moved in, they would be trapped.

There, high on the ridge between the two summits, Voytek had one of the most ethereal experiences in his entire mountain career. They were bivouacked at around 7600 metres, and it was still early in the day, about 3 p.m. Jurek had wanted to go a few hundred metres lower, but Voytek felt sure they would have problems putting up the tent, so he insisted on the early stop. "The view was so amazing, so fantastic, you could see absolutely all over the world," he said. "I remember it just like a delirium – walking and walking around – I was simply unable to go into the tent. It was a fantastic experience with a rare quality. It was deeply spiritual. Of course mountains are always beautiful, but this was different."

Although he was with Jurek, the luminosity of this experience was not shared. They were so accustomed to each other that they felt no need to talk. So the more practical Jurek remained in the tent, preparing water and food, while Voytek wandered around in an aesthetic euphoria. With each shift in light, the mountain features became almost prismatic, revealing deeper, more hidden shades of beauty. Voytek struggled to explain the intensity: "Beauty is some kind of laser connection to higher worlds. That is what I learned, just in the middle of our traverse, between the lower and middle summits."

The next day the wind grew stronger as they climbed the interminable, undulating ridge to the Central Peak. As they clung to its summit, they now faced the problem of descending safely to the col on the other side. By now, the wind velocity had increased to a horrifying scream, and as they descended on five, long, shaky rappels, it felt as if they were rappelling into a cold, cruel hell.

They trudged up to the Main Summit the following day, and then, while descending via the normal route after days at extreme elevations and constant exposure to danger, Voytek momentary lost his focus. Traversing above Janusz's Camp II at 6400 metres, he came across an old fixed line, which he grasped just for a moment for balance. It broke. He began skidding down the icy slope faster and faster. His crampons and ice axe barely scratched the marble-like surface; it took a terrific effort to gain a purchase and slow down before he was catapulted off a cliff. Strangely, the significance of his recovery brought no particular sense of relief. It just *was*.

Despite the exposure, the weather and the near miss, both Voytek and Jurek attained a level of calmness on that high, airy traverse that made them willing to accept whatever the elements and the mountain required of them, including the ultimate sacrifice. They understood and treasured the precious quality of those five and a half days of climbing the 10-kilometre ridge. They knew that their greatest motivation came from routes just like this: routes that demanded the ultimate commitment.

When they returned to base camp, everyone congratulated them and expected them to collapse into their tents to rest. But Jurek was hungry. He marched over to the cook tent and whipped up a massive pot of spaghetti, enough for the entire camp. Later that night, instead of retreating to the comfort of his tent, Jurek joined a post-dinner card game that went on into the early hours of the morning. Krzysztof shook his head in admiration: "Physically he was unbreakable."

❅ ❅ ❅

While they had been on the traverse, Krzysztof had climbed Broad Peak in 22 hours and 10 minutes, the fastest climb in the history of 8000-metre peaks and the first one-day ascent. Nobody had even attempted anything like that on a Himalayan giant. Over 3000 metres up and over 3000 metres down, in one day.

He started just after midnight on July 14, 1984. Into his small pack he placed some extra woollen clothing and a windproof suit, a plastic sheet, two pitons, one ice piton, three tapes, a camera and film, one headlamp, a spare battery, a bit of food and two litres of orange juice. He stepped out of his tent, adjusted his headlamp and knelt down on one knee, attaching his razor-sharp crampon firmly to his boot. Then the other. He pulled the outer mitts over his liner gloves, grabbed his two axes and started off. He was transformed into a climbing machine, a finely tuned instrument intent on delivery.

The full moon illuminated the ghostly white slopes. The air was bitingly cold. Despite a brisk pace, Krzysztof couldn't stay warm. He began to lose feeling in his feet, so he stopped at Janusz's team's Camp II to drink some juice and wait for the sun.

Frustrated and impatient at the loss of two hours, he burst off at sunrise, racing up the slopes. He was guided by the tracks of his teammates, who were farther up the mountain. At 4 p.m. he reached the top, where, alone, he took some time to assess what he had done. "When you are alone in the solitude your thoughts are different," he said. "More than at any other time in my life I start to miss the companionship of another human being.... One has to learn how to cope with loneliness." This was not an aesthetic, cerebral experience but a sprint – a sporting effort. His only option was solitude, for nobody could keep up with him. He took some pictures, collected some stones and started down, passing his friends as he raced down the mountain. He reached base camp at 10:30 p.m.

Inside his tent he finally stopped moving. His entire body vibrated. His eyes darted about, looking for – what? Everything was precisely as it had been when he left it in the morning, 22 hours and 10 minutes earlier. Strangely so. Nothing had changed except that a new record had been set. Krzysztof had proven to himself that he could cheat his body for a while, ascending so quickly that it didn't have time to "catch on" and react to the lack of oxygen. But he hadn't done it blindly. He knew that if there had been any interruption or delay during his sprint – some small injury or problem with altitude – the effect on his body could have killed him. He knew his body well, however, and he had listened to it carefully.

For the next two years, Voytek and Krzysztof never discussed their experiences on Broad Peak. Voytek felt uncomfortable about Krzysztof's decision to climb the mountain in a day, so he didn't bring it up. But he wished there could have been some personal connection between what he felt had been *his* idea to solve the obvious problem at base camp and Krzysztof's subsequent success. At the simplest level, Voytek wanted some appreciation for the idea. A few years later he was astonished to overhear an interview with Krzysztof. "I must say, Voytek had the idea of my going up Broad Peak in one day," Krzysztof stated on national radio.

Voytek was delighted. He grabbed the telephone and called him to thank him for acknowledging the idea and for mending a potential tear in their relationship. He was painfully aware that one of the biggest challenges on climbing expeditions was the management of egos and ambitions. "We were all stars at Broad Peak: Jurek, Krzysztof and me," he said. "In this case I was really proud. We came out of this trip without losing our friendship. We managed our egos. We each managed to do something interesting."

Although Krzysztof was criticized by some for his mountain racing style, his defence was simple: he wanted to climb the mountain in an original way, so that is exactly what he did.

❄ ❄ ❄

Jurek and Voytek's Broad Peak traverse was their last great climb together. Immediately following the climb, the tension between them began to build until it finally exploded. They had been eyeing the West Face of Gasherbrum IV for a couple of years. Most people believed that the massive, steep and technical face was impossible for a two-man team, but Voytek had convinced Jurek that there was a plausible route. Once Jurek was convinced, he wouldn't let it go.

There are multiple – and conflicting – versions of the blow-up between the two. Some climbers in the area reported that the weather was deteriorating; others said it was perfect. Some thought Voytek seemed overly anxious about the face, while others felt Jurek had lost interest because Gasherbrum IV was shy of the 8000-metre mark. Amidst the confusion and strong words, it's certain that Jurek told Voytek about his emerging plan to climb all the 8000-metre peaks, a goal he and Reinhold Messner held in common, and it's equally certain that Voytek lost respect for Jurek's aspirations at that point.

Voytek expressed his disdain for 8000-metre-peak collecting in *Mountain* magazine, where he wrote that peak-baggers were "pathological victims of emotional consumption." He was disappointed that Jurek would fall for such a trap. His irritation approached the absurd when he taunted, "I am sure one day some crazy guy will do all of them in one year. All you need is one helicopter and good luck with the weather. Look, idiots, it's easy." He proved the possibility with Swiss climbers Erhard Loretan and Jean Troillet in 1990 by racing up new routes on Cho Oyu and on Shishapangma's Central Summit in just six days. In theory, that would leave 359 days for the remaining 12 summits. He admitted he was just poking fun with his comments, but he insisted it was theoretically possible.

On a more serious note, Voytek tried to give some perspective to the painful split with Jurek: "By 1984, Jurek and I were a bit tired with each other. We still had good relations, but the main problem was very simple. He was in competition with Messner with the race for all 14 of the 8000-metre peaks."

But it wasn't just the 8000-metre plan that bothered Voytek; it went much deeper than that. Jurek had often said that climbing was a kind of sport, and that in sport you have to prove you are the best. This should not have been surprising, since Jurek had been a competitive boxer in his youth. But competition was totally alien and distasteful to Voytek, at least in the mountaineering context. For him, if you had to prove you were the best, you were already lost as a human being. The competitive aspect inherent in a "sporting" approach worried him because it seemed the inevitable precursor to suffering. Not physical suffering – he was no stranger to that. He was referring to emotional and intellectual suffering. For Voytek, ambition and ego always led to suffering. Climbing helped free him from his admittedly strong ego.

Voytek was motivated by what he called the "classical opposition of the urge for self-preservation and the need to test mortality." For him, climbing was a complex and unique way of living the interwoven elements of sport, art and mysticism. Success or failure depended less on brute force than on inspiration. Harnessing that inspiration was the challenge. "It arises and vanishes like the urge to dance and remains as mysterious as the phenomenon of life itself," he said. He likened the collecting of summits to a kind of profane materialism, where the climber needs to possess the mountains rather than accept – and be accepted by – their mysteries.

The two climbers finally agreed to disagree. Jurek would climb 8000-metre peaks and Voytek would search for interesting lines. Voytek admitted that at least Jurek was completely honest about his ambitions. He even wondered if this could mean that Jurek's intentions were purer than his,

for he himself constantly struggled to understand and articulate his motivations. It was an interesting consideration. But the battle between the
two stars was fierce and, sadly, final. They never climbed as a two-man
team again. Although they remained friends, Voytek summed it up with,
"Our climbing partnership was like a broken marriage; we no longer found
each other attractive."

❄ ❄ ❄

After Jurek and Voytek fought about Gasherbrum IV in 1984, they left the
area via different routes. In a burst of frustrated energy, Jurek ascended the
unclimbed 6700-metre Biarchedi on his way out. Then he headed for the
Masherbrum La, a seldom-crossed col. He had been assured that it was
passable but that he might want to bring a 10-metre length of rope just in
case. After navigating the maze of crevasses at the top of the glaciated pass,
a dangerous manoeuvre for one person, Jurek could see a tantalizing
meadow at the base of the glacier. But between him and that soft, appealing carpet of green was a tumbling icefall: hundreds of house-sized blocks
of ice leaning against each other in a haphazard and precarious mess. He
tiptoed his way through the chaos and finally reached the last block. He
threaded an ice screw, attached his rope and tossed the end down. It was
five metres short of the glacier ice below.

He took off his pack and threw it down to the glacier. He snapped his
rappelling device into place, inserted the rope, and slowly started lowering
himself down the full length of the single strand of rope. Maybe it would
stretch. With his ice axe in one hand, he inched down, glancing over his
shoulder, straining to see if the rope was anywhere near the ice. It wasn't.
Suddenly he was at the end. He slipped off in a fraction of a second, flying
through space. He landed with a thud, threw his ice axe into the slope and
stopped. He had been lucky; he had landed on solid ice rather than a shaky
snow bridge. He shook himself off, grabbed his pack and raced down to
the meadow, where he flopped down on the grass, happy to be alive.

In fact, Jurek was as happy as he'd ever been. The Masherbrum La adventure had given him almost as much satisfaction as the Broad Peak
traverse had. No arguing, though, and no negotiating. Every decision had
been his to make. He sighed, breathed deeply of the thick, oxygen-rich air,
and drifted off into a contented sleep.

❄ ❄ ❄

While Jurek savoured his Masherbrum La experience, Voytek returned directly to Poland, where he remained a peculiar figure in Polish mountaineering. Although his name was still not widely recognized by non-climbing Polish citizens, the rest of the world considered him to be the top Polish alpinist, possibly the best in the world. He had changed the nature of Himalayan climbing by proving that it was possible to climb difficult routes on big mountains in small teams: his record would ultimately include 13 great faces in the Himalaya, six of which were 8000ers.

Even though he was unrecognized by the general public, almost every Polish alpinist had an opinion of Voytek. Leszek Cichy, Krzysztof's Everest partner, described him as the greatest personality in Polish rock climbing, in addition to his Himalayan achievements – a man who created a certain aura of mysticism around the mountains. The ever-practical Krzysztof described him as "less of a gung-ho type, like myself." Another climber thought Voytek was "a bit more intelligent" than most climbers. Many referred to him as an enigma, one who avoided risk while climbing the most difficult Himalayan faces. Messner referred to him as "intelligent, sensible and human." All of these statements were true, making Voytek one of a kind: a man so complex that, even while resting, he was processing an enormous volume of information and ideas – intellectually, emotionally and physically.

After each great climbing adventure, Voytek's perspective on everyday life was totally changed. The mountains worked like a giant broom that swept away all the junk, all the trivialities, all the burdens of his daily life. Voytek came back from the mountains an immaculate and transformed person. His experience mirrored that of Norwegian explorer Børge Ousland, who explained his passion for extreme solo expeditions to the polar regions: "Because they strip me away ... I become like an animal. I find out who I really am." In such a manner, Voytek seemed more receptive to the beauty of life and the surrounding world after an expedition. He became more accepting of life's negative aspects: getting weaker, getting older, getting sick.

But the feeling never lasted, and eventually he would need another adventure to cleanse himself and to repair his spiritual delamination. He struggled to find catharsis in other activities, such as gardening, family life or nature. But ultimately it was climbing, and the force and power he sensed in the big mountains, that allowed him the mystical experience he had come to crave. He hesitated to call that force a *God*, because he was not a religious man; he likened it more to an animistic response.

Through climbing he discovered the most elementary and basic truths about himself: who he was, what he was, where he was going. This understanding changed his vision of life so fundamentally that he articulated it in a paper he presented at the Katowice Mountain Film Festival in 1988, and subsequently wrote about in several journals. He called it the "Path of the Mountain."

The idea for the path came from the philosophical and religious traditions of the East: the Buddhist Middle Path and the Samurai Path of the Sword. He drew heavily on the Samurai path, noting the many features it had in common with climbing: "Confrontation with death, the requirement of courage, striving for psycho-physical perfection or the notion of style and sense of honour."[26] It represented a way of living that was defined by a code of ethics and a system of practical considerations, such as diet, meditation and breathing. By observing these guidelines, the mountain path could help lead one to a higher level of enlightenment, even perfection. For Voytek it was mountaineering that opened the door to this kind of self-actualization, which was a combination of physical and spiritual growth.

He treasured the intensity of what most would consider negative experiences – fear and anxiety, exhaustion, despair, hunger and thirst – for after each extended period of adversity came a sense of calmness and confidence. A kind of peace.

The mountain landscape was an important factor in the path because it was in this context that Voytek felt such a concentration of the *truth* of nature that he felt he could even sense the *essence* of nature. By "essence" he meant the physical diversity found in the mountains: the rocks, scree, water, ice and all their variations. In the three-dimensionality of the mountain landscape he could fully appreciate the subtlety of nature. The view from the plains, in contrast, was only two-dimensional for him. But returning from those extreme elevations highlighted another miracle of nature: the colour green. Voytek, like so many mountaineers, marvelled at the reappearance of life after coming down from the biological void of the world's highest places.

It was the emotional connection he felt with the dramatic mountain landscape that articulated his philosophy of the mountain path the most. For Voytek there was power in that landscape that suggested the existence of a soul. "This impressive power invokes a desire to be a part of that soul," he wrote. "Experiencing the mountain landscape touches our deepest selves."[27]

❄ ❄ ❄

While Voytek and Jurek struggled with their diverging styles, Wanda was having troubles of her own. By 1985 it was clear that her heart was in the Himalaya, not back in Austria with her husband, Helmut. His idiosyncrasies had begun to irritate her. A confirmed naturalist, he eschewed many acceptable comforts (such as soap) and allowed his menagerie of pets to have the run of his house. He criticized Wanda for being corrupted by sponsorship and nagged her to be an amateur climber rather than a professional, an idea she abhorred.

Austria had been convenient during her numerous leg operations and rehabilitation, but it felt confining now that she was healthy and strong. She had toyed with the idea of children and family life but had often confided in her sister Nina that, although she wanted kids, it would have to be after the *next* expedition, not now. She sometimes mused about what her life would have been if the mountains hadn't captured her. Would it have been easier, more "normal"? Her friend Ewa found the image of Wanda with babies preposterous: "Everything was about the mountains … if she had had a normal life … she definitely would have gone crazy." Nina felt otherwise and was sure that Wanda wanted the same things that many women wanted: a house, a husband and kids. But she understood Wanda's dilemma. Wanda couldn't afford to have a family. The price would have been too high for her.

Helmut admitted they had both been pressured by Poland's political situation into a too-hasty union. But after three lonely years of marriage to Wanda, his assessment of her was bitter: "No amount of tolerance could make life possible with someone like Wanda. She was an egotist, totally inconsiderate of others, and wanted only admirers around her who would unreservedly support her and work themselves to death in her causes."[28] He regretted her lack of emotional depth and, over time, concluded that she was incapable of strong emotional ties. Although Wanda initiated the divorce, he agreed immediately.

Once again Wanda was alone. She moved back to Warsaw and earned her keep by lecturing and writing about her climbing. She was now, without question, a professional alpinist.

She was back in Pakistan in 1985, this time for another giant, Nanga Parbat, the ninth-highest mountain in the world and the one with the cheapest permit. She was climbing with her three K2 partners: Anna Czerwińska, Krystyna Palmowska and Dobrosława Miodowicz-Wolf, known by all as Mrówka. All but Mrówka summited.

To casual observers, the team's ascent of Nanga Parbat was a landmark achievement for female alpinism. But the inside story was somewhat different. By this time there were clear signs of rivalry amongst the best Polish women climbers. They were strong, ambitious and strategic in their objectives; there were still so many "firsts" to be won. Wanda felt exploited by her partners on Nanga Parbat, complaining that she had been forced to shoulder too much organizational responsibility, leaving her little energy to climb. Her partners disagreed. They attributed her fatigue to other causes: her damaged leg, her age, her inability to train properly because of her preoccupation with raising money, not to mention the general disappointments in her personal life. Krystyna confided that Wanda appeared less strong and not as powerful as before. Nanga Parbat marked the last time this powerful team of four women would climb together.

Another partnership at the end of its natural life.

CHAPTER EIGHT

THE THIRD MAN

Who is the third who walks always beside you?
When I count, there are only you and I together
But when I look ahead up the white road
There is always another one walking beside you
—T.S. ELIOT, "THE WASTE LAND"

While Jurek concentrated on his race with Messner, Voytek was left alone with his own obsessions, one of which was the West Face of Gasherbrum IV. The 2500-metre West Face is known as the Shining Wall because of a band of marble across the centre of the face that shimmers in the evening light. A starkly elegant triangle of ice and rock, the mountain offers no easy way to the top. Five previous attempts on the West Face had all been turned back by difficulties about halfway up.

Voytek had memorized the wall, deciphered its weaknesses and its traps and concluded that the key to the puzzle was a huge couloir, right of centre on the face. He thought it strange that the previous five parties hadn't used it, since the steep angling gully provided direct access to the heart of the wall. Although the couloir was an obvious catch basin for avalanches from above, Voytek felt that in the right conditions it could be climbed quickly and safely, and that doing so would allow him to bypass some of the rock sections that had defeated previous teams.

He and Jurek had considered tackling the face, but it was Austrian climber Robert Schauer who eventually became Voytek's partner on what would be an epic 11-day effort. Born in Graz, Austria, in 1953, Robert had begun his Himalayan career in 1974 with an ascent of Pumari Chhish (7458 metres), which was followed by Gasherbrum I, a new route on Nanga Parbat, ascents of Everest, Makalu and Broad Peak, and a winter ascent of the Eiger. Robert was clearly qualified for Gasherbrum IV. After discussing the project together with Voytek, the two agreed they would make a good team. They were initially meant to be a party of three, but the second Austrian, Georg Bachler, backed out at the last minute, citing some differences with Robert.

Once at the mountain, Robert and Voytek studied the face from the base, relieved to see that it was relatively free of snow because of the long dry spells earlier that season. The weather continued to look promising, and since they had no access to a weather forecast, they trusted their instincts.

Carrying only their clothing, a rope, a few pieces of climbing equipment, a bivouac sack, some food, fuel and a stove, they raced up the snow couloir, initially climbing unroped. At mid-face, when they reached the steep, luminous marble wall, they hauled out the rope and began belaying each other. It was here that the problems began.

The undulating waves of rock reflected the light in subdued milky hues, revealing a cruel smoothness that offered no weaknesses or cracks into which the climbers could place protection to stop a fall. Voytek searched unsuccessfully for solid belay placements. Their belays were often "psychological" rather than real, for both climbers knew that the pitons they had placed would never hold a fall. Each step up was measured and exact. No quick moves. Always maintain balance. Up and up. Voytek described the terrifying image: "How beautiful, the horrifying long rope, swinging away!"[29] It began to look as if they had wandered into a deadly trap. Voytek was afraid to move up into the unknown, but he was also not yet willing to face the shame of retreat. He struggled to save his dignity by climbing higher and higher, against all reason. He was exhilarated and grateful each time he overcame his fear, but then he would have to push on to the next barrier, only to face the demon once more – it was a kind of psychological terrorism.

After six days of appallingly difficult and dangerous climbing and cold, uncomfortable bivouacs on narrow, exposed ledges, they reached the final slabs and snowfields that led to the summit.

That night, the weather changed. It began to snow. All night long, the snow built up around their bivouac sack, threatening to push them off their airy perch. They waited all the next day for the storm to break, but it continued. Now they were out of food and fuel.

They were at 7800 metres. Retreat was not an option, for they would have needed many more than their 10 remaining pitons to rappel down the massive face they had climbed. They could only wait for the storm to end.

The second day passed. The snow continued to fall. They drifted in and out of a semi-delirious state, as hypoxia and dehydration sucked the life from their spent bodies. Both climbers sensed an ominous, unfriendly spirit from the mountain that seemed to oppose them more each day. Robert became convinced there was a third member in their party, and he blamed that imaginary partner for having slowed them down. As avalanches passed over them, Robert felt the third man trying to push him off the ledge into oblivion.

They were sleep-deprived, hungry, thirsty and extremely stressed. Scores of climbers have felt the presence of a third person in similar situations, but Robert's hallucination was unusual, for his third man was malevolent. In most cases like this the third man appears helpful, functioning as a kind of coping mechanism to evoke a caring companion. The character of Robert's strangely threatening companion probably indicated the severity of his fear.

Voytek reacted to their situation by conducting odd experiments: he would pinch his thigh to see if he could still feel pain. In his semi-coherent state he was thinking that, within a couple of days, that thigh – that piece of human flesh – could easily become a piece of ice. With his little experiment he was mentally preparing himself for the possibility of turning into a lifeless block of ice on that very spot. As Johnny Cash sang, "I hurt myself today … to see if I still feel."[30]

But Voytek wasn't giving up. A breakdown wouldn't have solved anything; it would have been a decision to die. Like the protagonist in *Jesus Christ Superstar*, Voytek was *prepared* to die, but he had not yet *decided* to die. Big difference.

As they shivered on their ledge, they considered their options. When Voytek brought up the possibility of retreating down the face, Robert's spirits plummeted and his confidence in his partner began to waver. Up until then, Robert had drawn strength from Voytek, who had been so prudent and practical. After leading through all that terrifying terrain, could he be losing touch with reality? Robert had lost all interest in the summit, yes, but he knew that retreating down the face was also out of the question. They needed to reach the ridge.

Voytek's thoughts began drifting into dangerous territory. He had often contemplated the act of dying and had concluded that the most important thing was to be fully aware of the process. That his life would end was now so self-evident it hardly warranted concern. It was more important to understand the wonder of this fleeting gift – life.

As he mused about the very real possibility of imminent death, he worried about Robert. This moment – this almost sacred experience of being so close to death – was important in a terrible kind of way. Being unaware of it would be a desecration for Robert. Voytek silently debated whether to approach the subject with him, and finally the urge to speak was too strong. He began tentatively, haltingly, his voice raspy with fatigue and cold: "Robert, I ... I ... I'd like to…"

Robert interrupted quietly but firmly, "I know what you're thinking. I'm ready. I'm prepared for this. Don't worry."

That night the temperature dropped. The sky cleared.

The next morning, as the sun began to warm their frozen bodies, they examined and tested their body parts. They flexed their fingers, stretched their aching shoulders, extended their stiffened legs and tried to wiggle their toes inside their rock-hard boots. They crawled out of their snowy coffin and began labouring up through the thigh-deep snow. They had brought food and fuel for a maximum of five bivouacs. They were now on day eight. But as British hard man Doug Scott once said, "You'll never find enlightenment on a full stomach."[31]

When they reached the ridge late that afternoon, the decision was obvious. There was no need for discussion. Even though they were weakened and hallucinating, their judgement was exceptional. They looked across at the apparently easy traverse to the summit, just 25 metres higher, and instead started rappelling down the unclimbed Northwest Ridge. As soon as they started down, the foreboding feeling that had plagued them both for days drifted away, to be replaced by phantom creatures and brilliant mirages.

Each step forward in the deep snow took enormous effort. An awkward thrust originating from their throbbing hips, lift the entire leg, push against the wall of white, try to advance a few centimetres, force the leg down. Try and gain some advantage from gravity pulling, pulling inexorably down. Robert stopped, gasping, leaning on his ice axe. He looked up, saw a raven hovering above him and stared spellbound as he imagined himself the raven soaring without effort, gazing down at this barely living wreck of a man clinging to the mountain.

Then partway down the ridge, Voytek sensed that a third person was back.

Slumped down in the snow, shielding his eyes from the glare, Voytek called, "Robert, I would like to tell you something, but it's very strange."

Robert stopped moving and collapsed over his axe. "I know what you mean," he gasped.

"You sense him, the third person?"

"Yes."

This time, the third man seemed compassionate, and they felt a tremendous boost to their chances for survival. Robert's hallucinations took a pleasant turn as he found himself in a heaving mass of people, all of whom radiated warmth. He meandered down a busy street and into a supermarket, where he sampled the most delicious sausages he had ever tasted. Almost immediately he was transported to an elegant restaurant in his hometown of Graz, dining on a succulent pork roast and exquisite crusty dinner rolls smothered in softened butter. Eating until his stomach ached with pleasure, his eyelids became heavy with drowsiness. The images enhanced his eerie sense of well-being, and he felt he had nothing to fear.

Voytek tilted his head sideways, straining to hear what he thought were the distinct sounds of Barbara Streisand singing a familiar tune. He stopped and shook his head in astonishment. The music disappeared. He straightened up, lifted his ice axe and continued his downward march. The music returned. He could hear a clear melody and a definite beat. He stopped again. The music disappeared once more. He repeated the experiment, fascinated and curious about the melody's source. He reasoned that it couldn't be a hallucination, because he would have heard it the entire time. This was different. When he moved he could hear it, and when he stopped he couldn't. He wondered if it could be the sound of the rope moving across the snow that was producing the music, and of his own footsteps providing the beat.

Lower down the mountain the apparitions ceased, and when the climbers reached their camp they collapsed. Voytek couldn't stop thinking about his Streisand experience and he struggled to fathom what had been happening to him. Although he deduced that it was "the sounds of the human machine breaking down,"[32] he was convinced that there were corners of the brain that could only be released in extremity. Himalayan climbing was an activity that gave him access to those secret, inaccessible places. This was yet another gift from his chosen passion.

❊ ❊ ❊

For years Voytek was devastated that they hadn't reached the summit of Gasherbrum IV. But as time passed, his assessment changed to a feeling of acceptance, even gratitude. "There are times when these undertakings miss the final point and this signals human weakness, which makes them more beautiful," he said. He grew to understand that failure can produce long-term benefits. The shape of life has many curves, and some trend downward. Weakness, sickness, loss, growing old. Failure and humility can help prepare one for those inevitable disappointments.

Voytek later claimed that his greatest reward from the Gasherbrum IV climb was the understanding he gained about death. During those enforced hours of reflection at the bivouac, he maintained a sense of calm and dignity in the face of his mortality that, he felt, prepared him for the rest of his life. But those days of terror almost certainly affected his future style of climbing and his tolerance for risk, because time after time, he would show caution when his climbing partners did not.

❋ ❋ ❋

The international climbing community called their climb the "Climb of the Century." Voytek was skeptical and used other descriptors: "a great joy of creation; a perfect trap; illusory; a thorn." He scoffed about the designation, saying, "Does it make sense to declare a poem of the century? Can you choose a woman of the century?" "Did anybody repeat GIV to confirm our illusion of it?"[33] he queried. No one did until 1995, when a Korean team sieged the face but by a completely different route. Even today many believe that although the 1985 climb may have been equalled, it has probably not been bettered.

But the climbing community's overwhelming admiration of this climb wasn't just meaningless gushing. It signalled a new and more discerning set of performance indicators: summits were not as important as unique objectives and style. Messner weighed in with his opinion and called the Gasherbrum IV climb superb. Doug Scott maintained that the ascent had been made in impeccable alpine style up the most technically difficult rock and ice ever climbed at that altitude. Voytek interpreted this universal acceptance of their climb as having created a "finished work," a sign that alpinism was more an art than a sport. "Only in art does a missing link contribute to the meaning of a piece," he said.

Despite their spectacular performance, Robert and Voytek never climbed together again. Differing memories of their climb even caused a rift for a time. Sadly, the bond they had formed while preparing for the possibility of dying together, high up on the Shining Wall, was not strong enough to withstand the pressures of the lower elevations.

❋ ❋ ❋

Voytek had attained the heights of spirituality and pushed his vision to the limit, but, as it is for so many alpinists, his obsession proved to be too much competition for his personal life. Shortly after he returned from Gasherbrum IV, his wife, Ewa, asked for a divorce. Although they had lived together in Krakow for almost 14 years, she had grown tired of his many absences. She was lonely. She was bored with his obsession. "If you are waking up with climbing dreams in the middle of the night, it is not acceptable to your partner," Voytek admitted with a sad smile.

His problem was not limited to nighttime dreams. There were daylight hours when, in the midst of fantasizing about a particular climb or a route, tiny drops of perspiration would appear on his hands. He called the effect "Magic Pump" – an internal pump that would push drops of liquid out of his body. "I *hate* Magic Pump because it broke my first marriage," he stormed.

His breakup with Ewa would not be the only one in Voytek's life, and theirs was certainly not the only marriage to suffer from the strain of having one partner devoted to alpinism. It was difficult to maintain a stable home life in such circumstances. Voytek believed that a real mountaineer required a full heart, a lot of suffering, a high degree of motivation and deep commitment. He likened mountaineering to other creative disciplines, stressing that to be a serious poet or musician would likewise be hard on a marriage. But he was minimizing the reality that, with mountaineering, the constant trips away only aggravated the tension, as did the very real danger of death.

It wasn't just the absences and his obsession with climbing that created the chasm between Voytek and his life partners. Whenever he returned from the mountains he was a different person, a completely relaxed man. But the change was more fundamental. His inner calm was so distilled by the alpine context that it was not attainable in everyday life, a fact that created distance between Voytek and others. "When you are in very calm state, when you are really at peace with yourself, your surroundings are very different," he explained. "You are serene. You can accept that you will die some day." Slovenian climber Tomaž Humar also believed that each climb changed him at the deepest level. He described it as a growth in his consciousness. Again, a very private matter. Austrian climber and filmmaker Kurt Diemberger described it as "a feeling of contentment that you could never explain in words ... it shows in the eyes." And when Voytek's partners saw that look in his eyes, they knew he was lost to them, at least temporarily.

Voytek didn't need success to achieve this heightened level of calm. He cited many instances – including four attempts on K2 – during which, although he was totally defeated, he learned to appreciate the small, exquisite beauty around him, a feeling that could reach an almost painful magnitude of intensity.

Sometimes that beauty emanated from nature, other times from ideas. Greg Child recalled an evening at K2 base camp in 1987 after weeks of high winds and frustration on the mountain. He had wandered over to Voytek's tent, which was glowing warmly from the light of a single candle. Rather than fuming about the bad luck, Voytek was calmly reading a French text, improving his command of the language and savouring the solitude. Continued success was dangerous, in his opinion. It left no time to enjoy the beauty to be found in a quiet evening alone.

Too many climbers, Polish and otherwise, believed that they were only as successful as their last climb and that their value as human beings as based on that continued success. They were convinced – or pressured into believing – that success was worth any risk, including injury and death. As a result, too many children and partners, parents and siblings were left with the pain of having loved a climbing martyr. Measuring his objectives through different criteria undoubtedly saved Voytek's family from that fate.

CHAPTER NINE

THE ART OF SUFFERING

...there are men who, on the approach of severe pain, hear the very opposite call of command, and never appear more proud, more martial, or more happy than when the storm is brewing; indeed, pain itself provides them with their supreme moments! These are the heroic men...
—FRIEDRICH NIETZSCHE, *THE JOYFUL WISDOM*

When Jurek and Voytek met up again, Jurek suggested another climb together. He knew of a couple of Polish winter expeditions planned for Dhaulagiri and Cho Oyu, both 8000ers. Was Voytek interested? Voytek said that no, he wasn't interested in winter climbs. But Jurek definitely was, particularly two in one season. They would add to his collection.

Jurek's plan was unorthodox in the extreme: two 8000ers in winter, a considerable distance from each other. For that reason, he wasn't totally forthcoming with the leaders of either expedition; he knew that neither team would be terribly happy about sharing his attention and effort. Andrzej Zawada, leader of the Cho Oyu expedition, harboured some suspicions about Jurek's intentions, but he kept quiet because of his deep respect for Jurek. Adam Bilczewski, leader of the Dhaulagiri expedition, was not so accommodating. There were awkward discussions about who would pay for Jurek's trip, since he hadn't put in his allotted time on the Katowice smokestacks like the other members of the team. He finally discounted Jurek as a serious contender, and when the number of expedition barrels exceeded the available truck space, two barrels were left off – Jurek's barrels.

Jurek didn't create a fuss about the slight, and it did nothing to alter his plans. He was a man of few words, private and self-contained. He wasn't known to be argumentative, but he was definitely not a pushover. Once he decided on a course of action there was no turning him back. If others didn't agree, he pushed on, alone.

His amazing strength, good health and physical fitness allowed him to achieve just about anything he set out to do, regardless of how much help he received from his friends. His record of success in the mountains was so amazing that people just assumed he would achieve his goals without exception. His rare failures were met with disbelief and shock. Even then, he didn't complain. There were occasional angry explosions, but only for a moment. Having Jurek on an expedition brought confidence to every single person on the team. Jurek climbed mountains – all the way to the top. That's just what he did.

✾ ✾ ✾

The Dhaulagiri team headed off without him. But Jurek had his own sources of funding, and it wasn't long before he was in Nepal. He met up with the Cho Oyu team in Kathmandu and disclosed his plan. He would go to Dhaulagiri first, climb it, then rush over to Cho Oyu and try to catch up with the team before their climb was done. Some members of the Polish–Canadian Cho Oyu team, including Jurek's friend Zyga Heinrich, protested that this wasn't fair. All the hard work of putting in the camps and equipping the route would be done by the others, whereas they had been counting on him to help. By arriving late he would just be a burden on the team. After all, it was a *winter* expedition. There would be an enormous amount of work to be done, in conditions of severe cold. Every member counted, and Jurek was one of the strongest.

The debate continued. Finally, there was a vote: it was an even split. Everyone looked at Andrzej, the leader. He stared back at his "Zawada Boys." Each one of them had worked hard to be on this expedition. They had painted smokestacks, trained hard and said goodbye to their wives and children with the full knowledge that they might not return. They deserved a fair shake. Then he looked at Jurek – the amazing überclimber. Jurek's eyes shone with anticipation, his face was unflinching and his body was strong and able. "I've made up my mind," Andrzej declared. "Jurek can go to Dhaulagiri. We'll wait for him at Cho Oyu. It is a grand idea, rather wild. But it might come off." Andrzej could see beyond the scope of *this* climb and *this* team. He knew that Jurek was special. He was a visionary. He was attempting things nobody else had tried. He was setting new standards. *Poland* was setting new standards. Andrzej wouldn't dream of holding him back. It was a classic case of the student surpassing the master, and Andrzej was mature enough to accept – and celebrate – that reality.

Jurek packed up and climbed aboard the first bus to Pokhara, the largest town near Dhaulagiri. It was December 20. He marched over to the ticket office and bought a ticket for a short flight on a 20-seat Fokker to take him to Morfa, a village even closer to Dhaulagiri. But the conditions had to be perfect for the Fokker to lift off.

Two days passed. No flights. On the third day a few passengers piled into the plane, ready to go. That flight, too, was cancelled. By the 24th, Jurek's spirits began to sink. There he was, stuck in Pokhara in a cheap, cold, bare room, no friends around, bad weather, and it was Christmas Eve, the most important night of the year for his family. His thoughts turned to home, to Celina, to his two sons and the warmth and light and love of the family celebration that he knew was taking place without him. He could almost taste the delicious traditional prune soup. There would be Christmas goodies and gifts. Alone, he lit a candle, boiled up a packet of soup, opened a can of sardines, read a passage from his Bible and ate a consecrated wafer, as his faith dictated.

Christmas morning found him back at the Pokhara airport, seated on the plane. Another cancellation. It was obvious that his time-saving plan had seriously backfired. He could have walked the entire distance to Dhaulagiri in those five days.

On Boxing Day he returned to the airport and the ritual was repeated once more. But this time they took off. The little plane headed straight up the long, narrow valley, gaining elevation and bucking headwinds the entire way. As it tossed and heaved like a frisky bronco, Jurek prayed.

At Morfa he found a young porter to go with him to base camp, but at twice the summer rate. Jurek was happy to pay because the porter seemed fit. He claimed to know the route, and he even offered to cook. Winter travel would be tough and their route crossed two passes that were higher than 5000 metres. The situation deteriorated almost at once, however. The porter did *not* know the way, could barely make tea and lagged behind Jurek, even though Jurek was breaking the trail and carrying most of the load. The porter had become a liability.

They reached base camp after four days. Jurek sent his "guide" back down to the village and joined up with his team, which by now had only managed to set up Camp II. There was still a lot of work to be done. The climbers had been at altitude for three weeks, so Jurek's first concern was his lack of acclimatization. He not only had to keep up with them, he had to contribute to the effort of setting up camps and fixing lines.

He monitored his body closely, careful not to go too high too quickly. For the first couple of days, his pulse hovered at 70, his normal sea-level rate. As the days passed and he climbed progressively higher, it dropped, finally bottoming out at around 48. Most people experienced the opposite, but Jurek's body seemed custom-designed for altitude; it became increasingly efficient the higher he went. It was as if the mountains provided him a level of calmness from which he could extract his highest level of performance.

Up and down the mountain they went, long days of wading through waist-deep snow with the constant threat of avalanches wearing them down. They set up Camp IV at 7000 metres, hoping it would be their last before attempting the peak. Andrzej Czok, Janusz Skorek and Jurek started off the next day, but by noon they had only reached 8000 metres. They knew they wouldn't make the summit that day, so they descended all the way to base camp.

The winter storms continued, with snow falling most days. Although their route up the Northeast Ridge was not technically difficult, and their camps were now established, the huge volume of snow buried both their tracks and their tents. Visibility rarely exceeded 15 metres. At night the bitterly cold winds destroyed their camps, carrying gear as far as 500 metres and stripping the tents from the poles, leaving the stunned climbers exposed to the elements, huddled in their sleeping bags.

Bilczewski, the leader, selected two summit teams, with Jurek on the second. The first team got no higher than Camp IV. Jurek and Andrzej Czok were poised at Camp II, so they now began to move higher up the mountain in anticipation of their summit attempt. When they reached Camp III it was completely buried by snow, so they kept on climbing, arriving late at Camp IV in bitterly cold temperatures. From their previous experience, they knew they had to move Camp IV higher in order to make a serious bid for the top. But the next morning an avalanche landed on their tent, threatening to crush it – and them. They burst out of the flattened tent in a panic, gasping for air. Amazingly, the tent poles were only bent, not broken, so after digging out the tent, straightening the poles and packing up, they moved everything up to 7700 metres. Now on a ridge and subject to the full force of the wind, they were cold and tired but poised for the summit, and that was all that mattered.

Andrzej was strangely quiet in the crowded tent. He turned away from Jurek and massaged his legs and feet, vainly trying to rub some life back into them. They had begun to freeze, but he showed no sign of turning back.

The next morning they crawled out and started up. Snow continued to fall. Each time they reached a summit, another loomed just a bit higher. They inched along the summit ridge, peering into the murky half-light. Then, out of the fog, the ridge reared up steeply, taking them completely by surprise. Now they had to concentrate. They couldn't stop to set up a proper belay, for they would have frozen in place. Instead, they placed running belays and climbed together. This method was not as secure, and it presumed no falls, but it seemed the only option.

They arrived at another high point and discovered a bamboo cane. A bit confused, they looked around, but there was nothing higher: they were on the summit. They barely spoke. Ice encrusted their faces. Jurek took a few quick pictures and they headed down immediately, not even bothering to call base camp on the radio until 4 p.m.

Winter days are short. Within moments it was dark and Jurek and Andrzej were lost on the endless ridge. Wandering in circles, they realized they were in danger of stumbling onto treacherously steep terrain, so they stopped. A bivouac in winter at over 8000 metres is a frightening prospect, but they had no choice. They dug a small hole in the featherlight snow and sank down onto their packs. It was −40° Celsius. They had nothing to eat or drink. Jurek concentrated on one thing only: staying awake. Occasionally he would slip into a dreamlike state, only to wake with horror a few minutes later, thinking that hours had passed and he must be frozen in place. The night dragged on. They beat on each other to keep blood moving to their arms and legs. They spoke quietly, giving each other encouragement and hope. They focused on breathing, on living.

Dawn crept over them. They unfolded their frozen arms and legs from their crouched position and began to move. In half an hour they reached the tent, where they radioed in again, to the immense relief of base camp. Someone asked about their physical condition, at which point Andrzej admitted that he could feel absolutely nothing in his feet.

They spent the next few hours brewing tea and rubbing Andrzej's feet. It was 2 p.m. before they left the tent, yet they were confident it would be easy going ahead, with a straightforward descent to Camp II or lower. But they had miscalculated how tired they were. Their downward progress was so slow that it looked unlikely they would even make it as far as Camp III. Another bivouac loomed.

Jurek sat down in near defeat. Each subsequent high-altitude bivouac was becoming more difficult for him. He sensed that he only had a few more winter bivouacs left in him; he dared not carelessly spend all of this priceless currency called survival. At that moment, Andrzej disappeared from view. Jurek forced himself to get up and follow Andrzej's tracks. Then they vanished.

Jurek panicked. He began to traverse over to where he thought Camp III should be. He could see nothing. He shouted. No response. He backtracked to the ridge and shouted again. Completely confused about the route and his location on the mountain, he started down the ridge, all the while convinced he was going the wrong way. But which way was right? And where was Andrzej?

When darkness fell Jurek was still on the ridge, plunging blindly down. That's when he realized he would be faced with another night in the open. He was still confident that he could last the night, even though he was completely shattered. But he wanted warmth; he so badly wanted a warm drink. His confidence wavered. Maybe this night would end badly – he could die. At that moment the ground dropped out from under him and he was falling. He slammed into the ice with his axe, slowed his fall and ground to a stop. He knew it was time to stop moving, so he dug a small niche in the slope to escape the wind and opened his pack to retrieve his headlamp. It fell. "I sat down on my rucksack and the great battle for survival began all over again."[34]

That night he hallucinated wildly. He was in a well-lit village 4000 metres lower, drinking and eating, warm and safe. In and out of consciousness, he spent the night sitting upright, stiffly, so as not to drop anything else. The wind tore at his body, draining what little warmth remained. He slipped into a stupor.

A vision of his favourite alpine hut in the Morskie Oko valley drifted by. Six guys sitting around the table, the soft glow of a candle, a big pot of tea. Talking, laughing, telling tales. Late in the evening, they lower their voices. Someone asks, "Have you touched the looking glass yet? Have you taken a peek?" Jurek looks sideways to see the reaction. Some look blank, not understanding the question. But a few exchange knowing glances with Jurek before looking down. They have taken a peek. So has Jurek. They know what it feels like to approach the thin red line. And they know they'll go back, to repeat the experience of the greatest possible adrenaline rush. He pours another imaginary cup of tea, warming his cold hands.

At dawn, Jurek was still alive.

He staggered down to Camp II and called out in a hoarse voice. His teammates burst out of the tents, relieved to see him. Andrzej was there, too, safe, except for his feet and fingers. They packed up and headed for Camp I, happy to be together and confident in their plan for the day.

They didn't reach Camp I. The snow was so deep and the going so slow that they were forced to bivouac one more time, Jurek's third in as many days. But with a stove, slightly warmer temperatures, thicker air and some soup packets, the experience didn't feel quite as cruel as the others.

They finally reached the security and comfort of base camp in the late afternoon of the following day.

Andrzej's feet and hands were a mess, badly frozen. The team mobilized quickly to evacuate him to lower ground where he could get proper medical attention. They ate one last meal together and headed down. All except Jurek. He had another mountain to climb, and the shortest distance to it was not down with his team but back over the French Col.

It had been snowing continuously for the past few weeks, so he wasn't surprised to encounter chest-deep snow. Despite enormous effort, he couldn't make much headway, and he began to seriously doubt that he would make it through. One possibility was to turn around, go back over the pass, join his team, go to Kathmandu and travel to Cho Oyu the long way. But the days were passing and the Cho Oyu team wouldn't be there much longer. If he was going to catch up with them he'd have to hurry. It was now January 25. The Cho Oyu permit ended on February 15.

He flailed in the deep snow, creating a kind of tunnel, one metre at a time. It was a mindless, wretched fight that at times brought him to the edge of tears. After an entire day's effort he looked up and could still see his last bivouac site.

Each night he examined his feet, which were deteriorating at an alarming rate. They had become slightly frostbitten on the Dhaulagiri descent and now they were blistering. The blisters grew each day. They became infected, oozing foul-smelling pus. They had begun to rot. He cleaned them as best he could, wrapped them up in bandages and carried on.

When he reached the village of Morfa, he stumbled into the house where he had stayed on the way in. The family looked at this wretched apparition in disbelief but took him in and fed and housed him. Jurek felt as if he had arrived in paradise. He couldn't imagine anybody in the whole world happier than he was at that moment.

His happiness evaporated, however, when he learned there wouldn't be a flight out for three days. No option but to walk on his oozing, blistered feet. He found a porter with whom he made the seven-day trek to Pokhara in only three days. Jurek grabbed a taxi at the trailhead and arrived at the station just as a bus was revving up its motor to depart for Kathmandu. He jumped on board and was in Kathmandu by 10 p.m. He raced over to the trekking agency in charge of the Cho Oyu expedition and radioed the team.

"Polish Cho Oyu expedition. Polish Cho Oyu expedition. Come in, please."

"Come in. I hear you. Catch a plane immediately. We are waiting for you. Over."

Jurek bought a ticket for Lukla for the following day and then waited, frustrated, as two days' flights were cancelled. He got out on the third day. The pace quickened. He hired a porter who agreed to walk three stages in one day. Jurek's feet were still numb and oozing yellow pus, but on the second day they walked three more stages. By the third day the porter had had enough and went on strike. At that moment, a runner appeared from the Polish base camp. He picked up the porter's pack and carried on while Jurek scrambled to keep up. At 2 p.m. on February 8 they arrived at the Cho Oyu base camp.

The expedition was in full swing. Despite Andrzej's initial assessment of the 2800-metre face as "diabolically dangerous," two-man teams had fought valiantly for weeks against the cold, the difficulties and the dangers. Now all the camps were in on a new route on the Southeast Pillar, and climbers were at Camp IV, ready for the first summit bid. Ignoring his feet, Jurek repacked his pack, changed his socks and readied himself for an early-morning departure for Camp I.

He was joined by Zyga Heinrich, a tough, no-nonsense Polish climber who, like Jurek, was not averse to suffering. Jurek and Zyga reached Camp I with no problems. The next day was more difficult as they wove their way around teetering séracs, struggling to free the fixed lines buried beneath the collapsing towers of ice. They crawled up the mountain and waited a day as the first summit team made their attempt.

While Jurek and Zyga huddled high on the mountain, the atmosphere at base camp was electric. With their binoculars, the base camp team could see the wind howling on the summit. Two tiny dots crept across the upper icefield, just below the top. One disappeared, and then the other. Andrzej Zawada grabbed the radio. "Hello, do you hear me?" He heard only a crackling roar, the sound of the wind. "Are you on top?" The answer finally came. "I don't know. I don't know, but there is nowhere higher to go!" The two Maciejs – Pawlikowski and Berbeka – were on the summit, lying flat for fear of being blown down the face. Andrzej could not contain himself. "What joy! Such a climb, and in the winter!"

Now it was Zyga and Jurek's turn. Four days after arriving at base camp, Jurek was faced with a thousand-metre vertical climb, some of it difficult and technical, in order to reach Camp IV. To add to the danger, some of the fixed ropes that the team had previously placed were now missing because they had been needed higher up the mountain. Due to the great elevation gain, the difficulty of the route and the shortness of the winter day, Zyga and Jurek ended up at the most difficult section when darkness fell.

Once again, Jurek dropped his headlamp.

For the last 160 metres, Jurek climbed by Braille. Methodically, he drove each ice axe as firmly and efficiently as possible into the hard, steep ice, listening for the recognizable *thunk* that signifies a good placement. When both axes were securely in place, he would move one cramponed foot up, slam it into the ice, test it for stability, then move the other foot. Over and over again, he would initiate the movements, ensuring that each point of contact was sure. There was no room for a mistake.

Jurek was belaying when Zyga fell, penduluming across the steep, icy face. Jurek held him, but it took some time for Zyga to get back on his feet and continue up. Jurek had no idea what had transpired, only that their progress had ground to a horrifying halt. "What happened?" he demanded when Zyga staggered up. "I came off on the traverse," Zyga gasped. "I've had enough."

There was now no question of continuing on to the relative comfort of the tent at Camp IV; they needed to stop and set up some kind of shelter. They hauled out the bivy sheet, dug out a small indentation in the snow, sat on their packs, rolled up together and waited. The winter temperature dropped and the wind tore at their flimsy tarp, chilling them dangerously.

Morning revealed a cruel sight. The tent was just 60 metres away.

They crawled out of the frozen snowhole and staggered to the shelter, where they crept in, collapsed in a heap and brewed some tea. Just a short rest, they thought. Maybe an hour, and then we will go to the summit.

An hour passed. Then another. They drifted off in the warmth of the sleeping bags. Drank more tea. The day passed, as did the night.

They awoke early on the morning of February 15, the last day of their climbing permit. There was no discussion. The only direction was up. After several hours it was clear that, despite Jurek's confidence in his acclimatization and his strength, he was actually climbing quite slowly. Zyga too was having problems. It was 4 p.m. and they were nowhere near the summit.

"What should we do?" Jurek asked. "If we reach the summit before sunset, that will be great, but we will certainly face a descent in the dark, plus, the possibility exists that we will need to bivouac again." He didn't typically go down until he reached his goal, so it was a strangely worded question, almost an open invitation for Zyga to say, "It's too late, it's too dangerous, let's go down." Jurek knew that Zyga was a more conservative climber and had often chosen life over summits; his answer would almost surely be to go down.

Wanda Rutkiewicz, as a young girl, riding on a bicycle with her father and older brother.

The young Wanda Rutkiewicz tries out the sport of climbing.

Portrait of the young Wanda Rutkiewicz, showing signs of strength and perseverance.

Andrzej Zawada and Anna Milewska.

Polish team on their way to the Karakoram.

Climbers on summit of Kunyang Chhish, August 26, 1971. From the left: Andrzej Heinrich, Jan Stryczynski, Ryszard Szafirski.

Alison Chadwick and Wanda Rutkiewicz in the Tatras upon their return from the Hindu Kush in 1972.

Alison Chadwick-Onyskiewicz, Wanda Rutkiewicz and K. Zdzitowiecki on the summit of Gasherbrum III.

Gasherbrums II and III.

Polish climbers making a living on the Katowice smokestacks.

The Lhotse 1974 team gathers in Warsaw. Andrzej Zawada, expedition leader, is on the left. Voytek Kurtyka, looking seriously concerned, second from right.

Andrzej Zawada, leader of the Lhotse fall/winter expedition in 1974.

Voytek Kurtyka (1974).

The young Jerzy Kukuczka discovers rock climbing.

The young British climber Alex MacIntyre.

Jerzy Kukuczka negotiating with Straż Graniczna (border patrol) at the Polish–Slovakian frontier in the Tatras Mountains.

Voytek Kurtyka, Krzysztof Żurek, John Porter and Alex MacIntyre at the Warsaw airport on their return from Changabang.

Zyga Heinrich, Jerzy Kukuczka and Sławomir Łobodziński in an icecave at 7900 metres during the ascent of the South Face of Nanga Parbat, 1985.

Jerzy Kukuczka, Zyga Heinrich and Sławomir Łobodziński approaching the summit of Nanga Parbat, 1985.

Celina seeing Jerzy Kukuczka off on his Alaskan expedition.

Wanda Rutkiewicz summits Everest, the first European woman and first Polish climber to do so.

Wanda Rutkiewicz meets the Pope following her Everest climb and on his first visit to Poland after becoming Pope.

Bogdan Jankowski and his communications centre at Everest winter basecamp.

Krzysztof Wielicki and Leszek Cichy in Everest base camp, two days after having made the first winter ascent, February 17, 1980.

Voytek Kurtyka, Jerzy Kukuczka and Alex MacIntyre at Makalu, 1981.

Expedition truck in Warsaw, prepared to leave for K2 in 1982.

Wanda Rutkiewicz at K2 in 1982, still on crutches.

Voytek Kurtyka and Jerzy Kukuczka in K2 base camp, 1982.

One of the magic teams of the Golden Age of Polish Himalayan climbing: Jerzy Kukuczka and Artur Hajzer.

Voytek Kurtyka on Gasherbrum II, East Summit.

Voytek Kurtyka getting in some last-minute training in Kathmandu (or perhaps it's just the exuberance of youth).

West Face of Gasherbrum with the Kurtyka/Schauer route.

Andrzej Czok and Jerzy Kukuczka starting on their summit attempt on Dhaulagiri in winter.

Fixed ropes below Camp 2 on the Cho Oyu winter expedition.

Rappelling steep ice section from Camp 2 on the South Face of Lhotse.

Climbing the Messner line above Camp 1 on the South Face of Lhotse, 1987.

Artur Hajzer at South Face of Lhotse base camp, smoking because there was "too much oxygen at base camp"!

Climbing alpine-style on the South Face of Lhotse at around 6500 metres.

The route on the Cho Oyu winter expedition.

Krzysztof Wielicki and Jerzy Kukuczka resting after their descent from the summit of Kangchenjunga – in winter.

Wanda Rutkiewicz at K2 base camp.

K2, with the Magic Line Route, 1986.

Przemyslaw Piasecki climbing in a whiteout on K2, 1986.

The slender peak of Manaslu East.

Jerzy Kukuczka on the summit of Shishapangma.

Jerzy Kukuczka celebrating his 14th 8000er: Shishapangma.

1987 Polish route on the South Face of Lhotse, showing camps and high point reached just below the summit.

IN MEMORIAM
RAFAŁ CHOŁDA
25.X.1985
CZESŁAW JAKIEL
15.IX.1987
JERZY KUKUCZKA
24.X.1989

Memorial plaque at the base of the South Face of Lhotse, commemorating three Polish climbers who lost their lives on the face.

AUTHOR: WITOLD SAS-NOWOSIELSKI

Left: Alpinist of 45th Anniversary former Polish People's Republic

1. Helmet: looks like everybody else's. (Coal miner's helmet; KWK Kleofas is the name of a coal mine factory in Katowice.)
2. Welder's glasses. (Please note that Krzysztof Wielicki used this type of glasses during his winter ascent of Mount Everest.)
3. Nylon shell (anorak) sewn by my cousin Lusie.
4. Backpack, Waciak type. (This was made by leather worker Mr. Waciak from Krakow, who made packs for all the Polish climbers.)
5. Mammut rope, cut during a climb on Les Droites.
6. Reserve (stock) of canned meat or fish for 30 days of climbing.
7. Stubai axe found at the base of the Eiger.
8. Lightweight carabiners and pitons from many sources (usually found abandoned on climbing routes in the Alps).
9. Wool pants made from an old overcoat.
10. One sock, from Mrs. Rubinowska. (She was a climber who hand-knitted woolen socks for all her climber friends.)
11. Second sock, knitted by an ex-girlfriend.
12. Zawraty leather boots, full of water and frostbitten feet.
13. Waterproofing shoe polish, available on the Slovakian side of the Tatras.
14. Crampons. Left one has 10 points and was borrowed from the Club storehouse. Right one with 12 points was found at the base of the Matterhorn.
15. The place by the table. (An important and very specific place in the Morskie Oko mountaineering hut in the Polish Tatras. It held a place of great emotional and spiritual significance for Polish climbers.)

Trango Tower East Face with Kurtyka/Loretan route.

Voytek Kurtyka and Erhard Loretan at base of Trango Tower.

Voytek Kurtyka and Erhard Loretan on Trango Tower.

Voytek Kurtyka on Trango Tower.

Members of Krzysztof Wielicki's Gasherbrum expedition: Carlos Carsolio, Ed Viesturs, Krzysztof Wielicki and Jacek Berbeka.

Krysztof Wielicki on top of Gasherbrum I.

Approach march to K2

North Face of K2.

From the summit of Kangchenjunga after a storm.

Krzysztof Wielicki, greeted by Manam, after his solo climb of Nanga Parbat, his 14th 8000er.

Darek Załuski climbing the most difficult section during the 1997/98 winter attempt of Nanga Parbat. This was the last expedition led by Andrzej Zawada.

Sculpture of Jerzy Kukuczka at Reinhold Messner's mountain museum in Italy.

Voytek Kurtyka, 2003.

"We are too close to the summit … We go as long as we can," Zyga rasped.

Jurek was astonished. Wow, is this Zyga? What just happened here? He turned around and kept plodding up, sure that they would need another bivouac, probably near 8000 metres. He was so used to high-altitude bivouacs by now that they barely caused a second thought.

At 5:15 p.m. they were on the top. The sun's red orb slipped behind the ridge, and the summit plateau was suffused with a warm purple glow. But it was far from warm. The temperature plunged the moment the sun disappeared, and after a few photos they began descending.

The next few days were horrifying. Fatigue, frostbite, the altitude and the cold all took their toll. Jurek fell off a steep sérac, and when Zyga rappelled down to him they decided to stop before they pushed too far. They spent that first night in a bivouac at 7700 metres. It was the coldest night of the entire trip, recorded at base camp as −33° Celsius. Then they took a full day to rehydrate and rest in Camp IV. The next day they barely made it to Camp II. The following day they planned to descend at least as far as Camp I, but their extreme fatigue caused them to start very late. When they finally reached the glacier on which Camp I was located, they saw tiny dots coming toward them. It was their team coming up from base camp to help them down. Relief flooded Zyga and Jurek as they thankfully joined their mates and descended all the way to base camp – once again travelling in the dark.

The next day they broke camp and headed out. Even Jurek could now barely stand upright. His feet, which normally fared quite well in his oversized boots, had deteriorated even more, and within days he was in a hospital in Delhi being treated for frostbite.

Andrzej, a leader sometimes criticized for his obsession with winter and the suffering it brought to his climbers, was proud of what they had done. But this time his greatest joy came from his team's spirit of cooperation rather than their exceptional climbing achievement. Andrzej had led enough expeditions to know that camaraderie didn't always prevail over personal ambition. But on Cho Oyu it had.

Jurek was marooned in Delhi for 10 days, waiting for an Aeroflot flight to Poland. When he called home to Celina to explain, he could hear the boys giggling and playing in the background. The enforced delay gave him plenty of time to think. The race with Messner was real. His doubleheader winter climbs had changed the game entirely. Not only was he within striking distance of Messner, but he was climbing in much better style. All but one of his climbs so far had been a new route or a winter route, sometimes both.

But he was oh, so tired. These days he was almost always tired; now he was forced to acknowledge it. Celina and the boys were so good, so comforting, so cozy. What he really wanted to do was crawl into his bed and sleep, not to think about the Himalaya. It was hard to imagine enduring another 8000-metre bivouac. Thankfully, his toes were still intact, but what about the next time? They were more vulnerable to frostbite now. His body had taken a punishing hit on these last two climbs, and he felt severely depleted. Maybe a rest would be good?

But Messner wasn't resting. Not at all.

❄ ❄ ❄

Despite his need for recuperation, Jurek wasted little time. By May of that year, he was on his way to Nanga Parbat. With a large Polish team, and once again climbing with Zyga, he reached the summit on July 13, 1985, via a dangerous and avalanche-infested new route on the Southeast Pillar. But not without incident. Piotr Kalmus was swept to his death by an avalanche while crossing a couloir near Camp II. The tragedy seemed not to faze Jurek; Nanga Parbat was number nine, and by fall he was on Lhotse, an 8000er he had already climbed.

In the race with Messner, Jurek had decided that his rules of competition would include style: he would ascend the 8000ers either by a new route or during the winter. His previous Lhotse ascent had been via the normal route in the summer of 1979, so he was back to climb it again, despite his fatigue from the previous two years. He came to Nepal a month later than the team, and by the time he reached base camp they were already at 8000 metres on the massive, technically difficult and unclimbed South Face. The greatest problem with this face was that the real difficulties begin at 8000 metres. The first summit team tried a couple of options. No success. Then Jurek headed back up with Rafał Chołda to their camp in the upper cwm. Climbing unroped, Rafał slipped and fell. Another partner dead.

Jurek came down, convinced the climb was over. Most of the team felt the same way, deflated by the tragedy. But they hadn't counted on the energy and ambition of their young, fair-haired teammate, Artur Hajzer.

For days, Artur stumbled around base camp like a drunkard, confused about what to do. He didn't want the expedition to end this way but wasn't prepared to be a tragic hero, either. The problem was that last steep barrier so near the top. Nobody knew precisely how hard it was; but they knew it was hard, and it was undoubtedly high. Finally, Artur came to a decision:

"If anyone feels they can get across the great barrier and still keep going, I will go with them," he said to the team. "I can follow this section, but I can't lead it."[35] There were no volunteers. Most voted to wrap up the expedition.

Then a member of a French expedition expressed his willingness to lead the difficult top section if Artur would go with him. Artur approached his expedition leader, Janusz Majer, who agreed there might still be a chance. Jurek was still high up on the mountain, and Artur thought he might want to join them on this final summit attempt.

But after 60 days of the expedition, even Artur was worn down. Like the others, his lips were swollen, his face was burnt, his eyes were bloodshot and he was skinny and sore, the picture of deprivation and despair. Still, he felt it would be a sin not to try it. There were six stocked camps and a kilometre of fixed line, including 100 metres on the great barrier near the top. The weather was good and there remained only 200 metres of climbing in unknown territory to the summit.

Of course, a possible price was their lives. What was it that pushed them toward the top? They were well beyond the nationalistic pressures of the early Polish expeditions. Even the financial pressures had eased. If they failed they could almost certainly return another year. No, this last effort was fuelled by personal ambition, particularly that of Artur.

They headed up one more time, but it was ultimately Jurek who ordered them down. Artur did what he was told, based on his immense respect for Jurek, but he never completely agreed with the call. Jurek later admitted that his extreme exhaustion probably influenced his decision to call off the climb.

❄ ❄ ❄

What Jurek really needed was a year off, a full 12 months with Celina and the boys. He was blessed to have a partner who accepted his obsession with the mountains and who was raising their family almost completely on her own. When Jurek had first expressed his interest in the two winter climbs, Celina was pregnant with their second child, Wojtek. Jurek had just returned from Pakistan in September of 1984 and had proposed to leave in November and be away for most of the winter. Many families would have rejected such a proposal, but Celina's and Jurek's parents rallied together to give her the support she needed and Jurek the space he so desired to achieve his goals. Wojtek was born on October 26, 1985, amidst the final stages of Jurek's preparations to leave.

Despite the support system, Celina's life wasn't easy during this time. She had stopped working outside the home in order to raise their children. For her, family was number one. She praised Jurek in his role as a father but added, "When he was here, that is." When Jurek was at home he embraced family life, played with his kids, consulted with Celina about how to raise them and how to look after their house, make repairs and maintain it. But for the most part she functioned as a single mother, a role that the patient, loving Celina seemed to accept.

There was only one topic that never arose between them: Jurek's climbing. Celina sometimes learned about his plans from offhand remarks by his friends, or from newspaper articles. Even his dream of climbing all 14 of the 8000-metre peaks never came up in conversation. His life seemed divided into two separate worlds: his climbing and his family. She occasionally toyed with the idea that he might give up climbing to be with them, but she knew this was impossible. Climbing was his life. The longevity of their marriage was in great part due to Celina's acceptance of Jurek's double existence. Many other climbing partnerships were incapable of surviving the strain – as Wanda, Voytek, Krzysztof and others had learned. Still, a little time at home was what Jurek needed more than anything.

❄ ❄ ❄

But the race with Messner was still on, and by late October of 1985 Jurek travelled from Lhotse to Kathmandu to meet up with the advance party for a Polish winter attempt on Kangchenjunga. Jurek was listed as an expedition member, but he was almost sick with dread and confusion. Was this not the life he had wanted? Living and climbing in the greatest mountains on Earth? Why then did he miss his family so? Why did he long, almost painfully, for the comforts of home?

Instead of joining the team directly, he hopped on a plane and retreated to his log cabin at Istebna, not far from Katowice, with a view of the soft green folds of the nearby hills. He ate, slept and drank endless cups of tea. He played with the boys, talked with Celina and revelled in the joys of domesticity. Their home overflowed with climbing friends who came to eat and drink and to share climbing stories far into the night.

But he knew he eventually had to leave the retreat, and on December 12 he left again for Kathmandu. The Kangchenjunga team included some of Poland's best: Artur Hajzer, Krzysztof Wielicki, Andrzej Czok and others. Their objective was the normal route on the Southwest Face. Jurek felt it was completely feasible, even in winter. After his Istebna holiday he felt rested and at one again with the mountains. His feet had healed and his confidence was high. If he got up this peak he would be only two mountains behind Messner. Besides, Kangchenjunga had a long and noble Polish history: first ascent of the South Summit, first ascent of the Central Summit, new route on Yalung Kang. A successful winter ascent would complete the circle.

Inevitably, on a team crammed with climbing stars, there was competition. Any number of them could be a summit contender, and all were ambitious. Finally it was time to select the summit teams. All the climbers met in the mess tent, nervous and excited. The negotiations went late into the night before the teams were selected. Artur Hajzer was on one of them, along with his climbing partner, Bogusław Probulski. It all came to nothing when, the next morning, Probulski was gone from camp. "Got away – solo – aiming for the summit," Artur exclaimed. "My partner ran away from me and the rest of the team."

After that inglorious start, two other summit teams began working their way up the mountain: Jurek and Krzysztof Wielicki, and Andrzej Czok and Przemek Piasecki. As they climbed upward, it was impossible to ignore Andrzej's persistent cough, a result of the altitude and cold. It seemed surprising, considering his natural aptitude for high altitude and his astonishing strength. His record was impressive: 8000 metres on K2 by a new route, Lhotse without oxygen, a new route on Everest, the West Face of Makalu, and Dhaulagiri. Kangchenjunga would be his fifth 8000er in the winter. But Andrzej's cough grew worse the higher they went; the dry, frigid air was taking its toll. At Camp IV it became painfully obvious that Andrzej would have to descend. Only Jurek and Krzysztof would continue up.

They set off at 5:45 a.m. on January 11 with 800 metres to go, plodding along in the thin, cold air. Soon they lost feeling in their legs. At 10 a.m. the sun hit them and warmed their bodies, stimulating a bit of sensation in their extremities. Each climber moved alone, unroped, at his own pace. Since the terrain was not too steep, there was no need to belay. Krzysztof tagged the summit first, turned around and started down immediately. Jurek met him just below the summit, where they exchanged not one word. Their minds were dulled. They were robots. After a few photos, Jurek too turned down. They trudged down to the camp and radioed in their success to base camp. The response was strangely muted, for, much lower down the mountain, Andrzej was gravely ill.

Halfway between Camps IV and III, Andrzej had become so weak that he could hardly walk. They had practically lowered him to Camp III.

Crammed into one big tent, they spent the night cooking up fluids for the healthy climbers on one side of the tent, and administering diuretics to Andrzej on the other side. His condition worsened by the minute. At one eerily quiet point they looked over to where Andrzej was resting. He had stopped breathing. All attempts at resuscitation were unsuccessful.

In complete shock, the expedition members buried him in a crevasse near Camp III. Jurek stood a long time gazing down into Andrzej's final resting place, tears in his eyes. Deeply religious, he pleaded, "Why has God taken away such a good person?"

When they arrived back in Kathmandu at their regular haunt, the Tukche Peak Hotel, they were a subdued group, deep in mourning. Yes, they had climbed Kangchenjunga, in winter, but Czok had been the price. That cost was much too high. This was Jurek's third expedition in a row that had ended in tragedy. The Polish obsession with firsts, races and winter climbs was resulting in an astonishing number of deaths. Poland's dominance was beginning to look more like a death spiral. Jurek forced himself to ignore the magnitude of what was happening around him. It was the only way to keep going. He didn't have the luxury to pause and reflect.

CHAPTER TEN

MOUNTAIN OF MISERY

Landscapes are culture before they are nature, constructs of the
imagination projected onto wood and water and rock.
—SIMON SCHAMA, *LANDSCAPE AND MEMORY*

Everyone I know
Goes away in the end
—TRENT REZNOR, "HURT"

The year 1986 was a highly unusual one on K2. Pakistan had recently discovered the economic potential of the mountain and had issued an unprecedented nine expedition permits. There were climbers crawling all over the peak: a Polish team on the South Pillar known as the Magic Line; an international team that eventually moved to the Abruzzi Ridge; a South Korean team on the Abruzzi Ridge; a British team on the Northwest Ridge; and more. Wanda's three climbing partners from Nanga Parbat were all there with the Polish team led by Janusz Majer. Wanda was not among them.

She had returned to Poland from Nanga Parbat victorious, full of confidence and financially secure thanks to the success of her recent films. An unpleasant surprise awaited her when the Polish Alpine Association accused her of embezzling expedition funds. She eventually cleared up the matter, but she declared she had never been so unjustly treated in her life. She immediately bought a spot on a French K2 expedition, where she would compete against, not join, her compatriots.

The three Polish women on the Magic Line team were convinced that Wanda's decision to climb with the French was strategic: the latter were scheduled to be on the mountain before the Poles, giving Wanda a distinct advantage in becoming the first woman on top. Anna Czerwińska felt that Wanda had completely abandoned the idea of Polish women's mountaineering. "She simply stopped. She had the perspective of climbing K2 and she adopted the tactics of trying to be the first."

Base camp soon blossomed into a village of brightly coloured tents, with climbers from around the world, all with a single objective: to reach the 8611-metre summit of K2. The South Korean effort was the richest, with miles of fixed lines, an army of high-altitude porters and lots of bottled oxygen. With 16 different types of Korean tea on the menu and a wide selection of films, their mess tent quickly became a popular hub.

Wanda felt comfortable at K2 base camp. She described the feeling in a postcard to her friend Ewa.

> Dear Ewa,
> My best wishes and kisses through this card. We are at the head of the Baltoro Glacier … everyone is getting along well although I do feel a little isolated because I don't speak French. There are lots of expeditions and lots of friends here. I feel like I'm at home. The porters recognize me and greet me like a local. They always shout "abi Wanda good".
> I don't really know what it means but I think it's something good.
> Don't forget about me. Kisses and best wishes for my closest friends and family. Wanda.

Despite their original plans, climbers moved around the mountain, changing routes at will, depending on conditions, weather, their acclimatization and their skills. This was all illegal, of course, since climbers who apply for and are allotted a specific route are expected to stick to it. But it seemed that nobody was enforcing the rules, and this soon added to the confusion – and crowding – on certain parts of the mountain.

Wanda's team of four consisted of herself, Michel Parmentier and the French climbing couple Liliane and Maurice Barrard. The tall, powerfully built and mustachioed Maurice, with his long grey hair, and his bewitchingly petite, dark-haired wife, made a charming pair. Wanda admired and even envied the Barrards, referring to them as a perfect couple.

She was less enamoured of Michel. Everything about him irritated Wanda: his unruly brown curls, his hazel eyes and strong cigarettes, his habit of excluding her by speaking French with the Barrards, his arrogant self-confidence. Michel wasn't all that fond of Wanda, either. As a French journalist, he harboured plans to write the story of the first woman up K2, and that woman was meant to be a French woman – Liliane – not Wanda. The close quarters of their shared tent only magnified the differences between Wanda and Michel.

Since this was Wanda's third attempt at the peak, she was already familiar with the route up to 7350 metres. But they were the first climbers on the mountain this season, so they didn't have the benefit of any camps, broken trail or trustworthy fixed ropes from other expeditions. Their objective was the Abruzzi Ridge, using lightweight tactics with no supplemental oxygen. They also planned to do it in record time: five days round trip. Their strategy was bold. They decided not to equip the traditional high-altitude camp locations with tents and sleeping bags. Instead, they would set up food and fuel caches along the way. They would carry ultralight tents and sleeping bags so they could bivouac wherever they needed to, depending on the weather, their energy and the time of day. This would give them more flexibility as they moved upward, but it also left them vulnerable to the mountain's notorious storms. They could easily become stranded far from their caches. This style of climbing was new to Wanda, and she found it interesting. Although she understood the risks, she was not apprehensive; rather, she was confident that what Liliane could do, she could do too.

Kurt Diemberger, who was at base camp with his British climbing partner Julie Tullis, recognized, perhaps more clearly than Wanda, the boldness of the French team's approach, particularly since they were first on the mountain. In his book *The Endless Knot*, he wrote: "Nobody attempting a 'lightning dash' later in the season should compare his climbing time with that of earlier ascents when the route is in a very different state." His comments may have been a veiled reference to French climber Benoît Chamoux, who later that summer would race up the mountain in just 23 hours. Or perhaps it was just an indisputable statement of fact that the nature of the mountain, with its fixed ropes and established camps, was fundamentally different for those who came later in the season.

> Dear Ewa,
> Maurice and Liliane are okay … they are an example of a truly rare climbing marriage. At the same time they are very closed and they function best when they are together…. She is always with Maurice, where I am always stuck with Michel. He is the biggest egotist and egocentric person that I've met … a complete narcissist only interested in his own pleasure. He always gives himself the freedom of choice and decisions. This means that it curbs my own freedom. Yesterday he told me 'why are you even here with us French and not with your friends the Poles over there? I don't need you at all. But you need me and you're worse for that'. After that I sort of started to get ready for a solo attempt of K2. Wanda.

While her partners moved up the mountain, Wanda stayed in base camp, suffering from a bout of high fever and tonsillitis. After several days of rest she finally felt ready to join them, and just three weeks after arriving in base camp they began their summit attempt. It was June 18. Climbing steadily up the Abruzzi Ridge, they spent the first night at Camp I. They skipped Camp II and chose instead to bivouac at 7100 metres on the ridge of the Black Pyramid. Here they cached some of their climbing equipment in order to lighten their packs. They continued up, skipped the usual Camp III situated at 7350 metres and moved higher to bivouac at 7700 metres. Wanda described the site: "It was under the big barrier of the overhanging séracs in a conveniently level patch of snow, which was only a little dangerous."[36]

It was then that their lightweight strategy caught up with them. When Wanda and the Barrards reached a collapsed snow bridge across a crevasse not far above their bivouac site, they decided it was time to rope up. But Michel had forged on ahead with the rope still stowed in his pack because the snow bridge had been intact when he crossed it. In fact, it was his weight that had broken it just as he leapt to safer ground. The three remaining climbers were forced to take a dangerous and exhausting detour to bypass the slot. The top of their detour ended in a difficult overhang about three metres high. They got up it, but not without an enormous outlay of time and energy. Technical climbing becomes an entirely different experience at just under 8000 metres, and their efforts utterly depleted them.

That day they reached only 7900 metres before they were forced to bivouac again. The time-consuming detour around the snow bridge had forced one more bivouac at extreme altitude – a fatal error, as it would turn out.

By this time, the tension between Wanda and Michel was so toxic that she had resorted to using a small borrowed tent to avoid sleeping next to the Frenchman. She couldn't stand the sight of him or the smell of his smoker's breath. "Three tents for four people sounds a bit much," she admitted, "but the extra weight in my sack was the price of independence."[37]

They eventually abandoned the rope altogether. This exemplified, perhaps more than anything, the superb condition and skill level of the four climbers. To approach the steep and often icy upper slopes of K2 without a rope required unwavering confidence. Wanda later commented, "It would have been wonderful to find some fixed ropes up there, but who's going to drag ropes up to that sort of altitude?"[38] She could not have imagined the scene more than 20 years later when, despite a spider's web of fixed ropes, 11 people died on the upper reaches of K2.

Wanda and her teammates were now in the "death zone," where the body steadily deteriorates. Their biggest problem was snow, very deep snow. Placing one foot in front of the other on wind-firm, drifted snow is hard enough at altitude, but lifting one's leg out of each snowy hole only to plunge even deeper into the next, leaning on one's ice axe and gasping for breath, is agonizing work. The enormous effort shatters the climber out front breaking trail, and the ones behind become progressively colder as the pace inevitably bogs down. They took turns at first, but Michel proved strongest, so he eventually took over the arduous job.

He found a small rock platform at 8300 metres where they could bivouac one last time. They now had just one stove, one two-person tent and no sleeping bags. It was their third night above 7500 metres.

Below them stretched the full expanse of the mountain: the overhanging wall of ice under which they had climbed (known as the Bottleneck), the Shoulder, the Black Pyramid, House's Chimney and the lower slopes leading to the Godwin Austen Glacier. The technical difficulties were below them, and they were now very close to the summit.

Wanda was pressed up against Michel as they were forced to spoon in the tiny tent. She recoiled at his touch, despite his warmth. Her mind raced, reviewing again and again what might happen the next day – summit day. She felt strong – maybe not as strong as Michel, but she still had some reserve.

They awoke early on the morning of June 23. The day was splendid: sunny, cloudless and still. Wanda, who was last to leave the tent, caught up with the others just as they were stopping for a short soup break. She was surprised at this unusual behaviour, this lounging about, cooking so near the summit. Could she be hallucinating? But she wasn't; the three French climbers had settled in for a hot lunch. Wanda smiled at the Gallic obsession with food, declined the invitation, and continued on alone. The others seemed not to notice.

At age 43 she was as strong and confident as she had ever been on a high mountain, physically at the peak of her powers. By 10:15 a.m. she was on the top, becoming the first Pole and the first woman to climb K2. She laughed. She cried. She knelt and prayed. "At that moment I felt I had a gift of infinite time.... I felt no triumph, but I did feel that God was near me...."[39]

Then she wrote her name, along with Liliane Barrard's, on a piece of paper that claimed the first women's ascent. She wrapped it up in a plastic bag and placed it under a stone a short distance below the main summit.

Liliane had still not arrived, so it might have been a little premature, and perhaps overly generous. But she was very clear about noting her own arrival time – 10:15 a.m. – and after Liliane's name she left a blank.

Wanda sat down on the summit and waited. And waited. The sparkling clear day was extremely cold, so, in order to stay warm, she climbed a short way down the northeast side and collected a few stones as souvenirs. Back to the top and more waiting. She began a mental list of the friends she might give her precious K2 stones to; there were lots of possibilities, but number one on her list was Charlie Houston, the American who had tried so hard in 1938 and 1953. She liked Charlie and felt that he had deserved the first ascent, not the Italians. He had certainly earned a rock from the summit.

As the cold began creeping into her extremities she realized she would have to start descending. No sooner had she started down the South Face than she saw her partners labouring up in her tracks, so she went back up. They finally joined her on the summit at around 11 a.m. for an emotional round of hugs.

At noon, cold and tired, the four began their descent, the most dangerous part of any climb. Pressing ahead, Wanda reached their bivouac site at 8300 metres and stopped for a brief rest. When the flagging Maurice Barrard arrived, he stated they would have to spend the night. Wanda uncharacteristically agreed, although she knew another night that high on the mountain would mean further deterioration of their bodies. She may have wanted to stay with her team, or maybe it was the gauze of altitude that was clouding her judgement. She later wrote about this critical moment: "I was surprised, but not unhappy. 'I don't need to go down today', I thought. I was tired, but not exhausted…. I was not worried. But I should have been…. I didn't know in the sunshine that death was following us down."[40]

Once again they crammed into the two-person tent with no sleeping bags. After a restless, cold and uncomfortable night, they awoke even more fatigued. Wanda had taken two and a half sleeping tablets and was still dizzy the next morning. Michel was impatient to head down. The Barrards were very quiet.

Still climbing without a rope, each of them now had to make their way down two of the most dangerous sections of the mountain. They inched their way across the icy, downward-sloping, 50-degree traverse, knowing the consequences of a fall would be fatal. Wanda concentrated on keeping her balance as she tried to fight off the lingering effects of the pills. Michel was moving faster and was first to reach the top of the Bottleneck, a narrow gully of even steeper ice, loose rock and unconsolidated snow.

At that moment, out of the corner of her eye, Wanda saw Michel falling, tumbling faster and faster down the chute, only to emerge unscathed from a snowdrift near the bottom. He didn't look back, just dusted himself off and kept going. After the shock and adrenaline had subsided, Wanda refocused and went back to the task at hand. She cautioned herself with each placement of her boot: "Careful, Wanda, careful! No one can help you here, no one can get you down … you are alone."

Her concentration was so intense that she forgot about the Barrards. But she knew they had each other, whereas she was on her own. When she neared the bottom of the gully, she stopped to catch her breath and looked back to see the couple moving slowly near the top of the Bottleneck. Maurice was above Liliane, and Wanda was relieved because, although the Bottleneck was steep, it wasn't icy; there was plenty of soft snow.

As she continued down, a bank of clouds moved in, surrounding the mountain and obscuring the crevasse-riddled snowfield in front of her. Navigating this minefield of slots was dangerous in good visibility; now it was almost suicidal. Yet she felt strangely calm and euphoric: "My sense of invulnerability was a danger, but it was also allowing me to function without physical inhibition and preserving me from panic. It saved my life by letting me climb to the utmost of my skills and permitting my luck to hold." [41] Wanda was in fact – perhaps unconsciously – drawing on her many years of experience in conditions such as these. Despite her addled mind, her muscle memory was strong, her instincts reliable. It was her cumulative knowledge – not just luck – that got her through that day, high on K2, without a rope.

She caught up with Michel at 7700 metres. That night, buffeted by the wind and snow lashing at their tent, the two got very little rest. The next morning he told her he would wait for the Barrards, but since they were running out of gas, he urged Wanda to continue down with some Basque and Italian climbers camped nearby. She agreed and set out.

Snow began to fall. Thick fog enveloped them. Worn out from the climb and too many nights above 8000 metres, Wanda couldn't keep up with the others and was soon left alone on the mountain. She struggled to see their tracks, but the wind quickly drifted them in with fresh snow. By this time she had lost her gloves and was using her reserve pair, which were too thin for the frigid temperatures.

Then, in the distance, she spied two strokes of darkness against the white – ski poles! And just below them, the fixed ropes. In her intense relief at reaching the security of the fixed lines, and in a befuddled state of mind, she thought the Basques must have left the poles for her. She took them and slogged on down, clinging to the ropes in order to avoid being blown off the mountain by the storm, which had whipped itself into a raging gale. She stopped. A terrible possibility had occurred to her.

What if the poles had not been left for her use but to signal the beginning of the fixed lines for those descending above her? They would now be in a much more dangerous situation. Yet she knew she was too far gone to retrace her steps and undo the damage; she had to go down to survive. She concentrated on the repetitious yet life-saving movements of clipping her carabiner into the fixed rope, sliding the carabiner down, reclipping at the next rope, never losing her concentration. She later described that desperate descent as her worst day on K2.

It was evening before Wanda reached her tent at the foot of the Black Pyramid. She collapsed in a heap and slept. There she waited, another day and another night. She forced herself to heat some water and eat a little. Each small movement hurt. Her frostbitten hands struggled with the most basic tasks: zipping her jacket, lighting the stove, opening the soup packets, balancing the precious liquid. Still her teammates did not arrive.

She strained to recall her last glimpse of Maurice and Liliane, inching their way down the Bottleneck. Was there some clue in their position on the slope? Had she missed something? And where was Michel? She was sure they had spoken at 7700 metres, but maybe not. She was no longer certain. She felt terribly alone. Would she be the only one of her team to make it down alive? Drifting in and out of consciousness, Wanda lost track of who was on the mountain and where. Everything that was still alive inside of her screamed *get off this mountain while you still can!*

She stuffed the pathetic remains of her climb into the pack: her stove, the empty fuel bottle, the pot encrusted with soup remnants and finally her soggy sleeping bag. She crawled out of the tent to continue the interminable descent and saw a figure below her. It was Benoît Chamoux on his way up to help Michel, who had radioed that he was on the fixed lines but in desperate need of assistance. Benoît explained that in the whiteout conditions, Michel had had a difficult time locating the fixed lines, and it was Benoît who had talked him down the upper part of the mountain, metre by metre. She wondered about those ski poles: would they have made a difference?

Still no word from the Barrards.

At this point two Polish climbers on their way up to help her appeared. Wanda's stoicism finally crumbled and she gave in to her emotions, weeping quietly as she clung to them. After all the loneliness and bitterness and competitiveness, someone cared about her.

By now Wanda's face was frozen, as were her hands and feet. When British filmmaker Jim Curran watched her hobble into base camp, he was horrified at the change in her appearance. Radiant before the climb, she seemed to have aged 10 years in 10 days. "Her face seemed to have caved in," he said.

❄ ❄ ❄

While the drama with Wanda's team was unfolding, the rest of the mountain hummed with activity, too. The Polish team led by Janusz Majer was on the Magic Line, a route that many called K2's "last great problem." Another team on the Sickle Couloir route on the South Face included Jurek and Tadek Piotrowski. It was a sign of the strength and depth of the Polish climbing community that they had put three separate teams simultaneously on three different routes on what was widely considered to be the hardest high-altitude mountain on Earth.[42] Regardless of whether they summited, the Poles dominated K2 that year.

It was Tadek, one of Poland's most accomplished climbers, famous for his icy-river training swims, who had secured a couple of spots for himself and Jurek on the international K2 expedition led by Karl Herrligkoffer. This was the first international expedition Jurek had joined, and the contrast in economics was painful. Unplanned expenses popped up frequently: tips, special favours, forgotten tariffs. Although this was not a problem for the Europeans, the Poles were close to panic. They were proven masters at spending inordinate amounts of time in the Himalaya, but one of their secrets was frugality.

When Karl handed out brand new Adidas shoes and soft woolly socks to the porters, Jurek looked on in envy. The entire atmosphere was mildly irritating, including the attitude that he sensed from some of the team members. There were a number of Swiss guides along. Jurek scoffed about one of them, describing him as "thin as a racehound, who all his life does nothing but run about in the Alps." There was nothing basically wrong with Jurek's body shape, but when one of the guides stared pointedly at his slightly paunchy belly and commented that he didn't look much like a mountaineer, Jurek was insulted. "We can have a chat at 8000 metres," he muttered to himself, and walked away.

The Western European climbers became agitated when Karl threw his support behind the Poles' wish to try a new route on the South Face of the mountain. "You two will be playing the first violin here … Whatever you need, you will get," he declared, much to the horror of the rest of the team. The Swiss and German climbers had no interest in anything but the normal route up either K2 or Broad Peak. A dangerous new route was not on their agenda, for they had their professions and a comfortable life back home. For Jurek and Tadek, there was nothing more important in the world than to climb this mountain by a new and difficult route. Their obvious differences prompted Jurek to observe that Western climbers were much like Western cars: better on good roads, but the old Polish models keep going, even when the road gets rough.

Karl wasn't planning to be on the mountain at all, as this, his 24th expedition, was merely a celebration of his 70th birthday. His health was questionable, so before long he called in a helicopter to whisk him away from base camp to lower, more comfortable ground. At that point, the team split up and the less ambitious members headed off to what they thought was easier terrain.

Jurek and Tadek began working their way up the South Face, some of which was familiar ground to Jurek, since he had been up to 6400 metres on the face in 1982 with Voytek. At the first camp they had four climbers with them. At the next camp, two. Finally, only Tadek and Jurek remained on the route. They fixed lines as high as they could and then retreated to base camp to wait out a snowstorm. They were acclimatized and ready to try for the summit. Everything depended on the weather.

They waited 10 days. At the end of June the sun reappeared. They waited another two days for the masses of new snow to settle on the icy skin of the South Face, and then they were off. Day one: 6400 metres. Day two: 6950 metres. Day three: 7400 metres. Day four: 7800 metres. Day five: 8200 metres.

The next morning they left their tent with just two 30-metre lengths of rope, three pitons, one ice screw and their ice axes, planning to reach the summit and return to their camp at 8200 metres. But in front of them rose a hundred-metre barrier of almost vertical rock covered in loose unconsolidated snow. The entire day slipped by before they were able to surmount that difficult stretch of technical ground, on which every move was agonizingly difficult. They gained height one centimetre at a time, fighting for every step. Jurek admitted that it was the hardest climbing he had ever done at this altitude. It was their many years of climbing mixed rock and snow in the cold Tatras winters that undoubtedly got them through this crux on K2. By the time they reached the top of the most difficult section, it was too late to continue. It began to snow.

They rappelled back to their bivouac site for the night. No sooner had they begun to cook than they dropped their last spare gas cylinder thousands of metres below them. Now they were in trouble. No gas meant no cooked food and, more worryingly, no fluid. They had just spent a physically and psychologically demanding day at over 8000 metres, and now they were facing a bivouac with no water. Parched with thirst, they survived the night but realized they would have to revise their plan. Instead of climbing to the summit and descending their South Face route, they would have to descend as quickly as possible from the summit down the normal route on the Abruzzi Ridge, where they would hopefully find a fully equipped camp. This was their only option, but it was risky because neither of them knew this other route.

By 2 p.m. the next day they had surmounted the barrier and were on easier ground along the ridge. As the day wore on, the snowfall intensified and visibility decreased. But there were occasional footsteps discernible in the snow from previous ascents up the normal route; they were confident they were in the right place. They continued, feeling their way up the ridge. At 6 p.m. it began to get dark. Jurek was sure they must be near the summit.

He reached a sérac and stopped briefly, leaning heavily on his ice axe to catch his breath. As he stared mindlessly down at the snow, he almost fell over from shock: there were two French instant-soup wrappers abandoned from some previous climbers. He guessed that they must have belonged to Wanda's team, and he knew from her description that they had bivouacked just below a sérac at around 8300 metres. These soup wrappers had to be from that bivouac. He almost threw up in disappointment. If that was the case, they were still a long way from the summit. As he stared down at the wretched wrappers, Tadek arrived.

"Look at these stupid wrappers. I think we are at Wanda's bivouac site. It's lower than I thought – only 8300 metres."

"Who knows," Tadek replied in a weary dejected voice. "It's so foggy it's impossible to know where we are. We could just stop here and go on tomorrow."

"No no, we can't do that. If we stop here we won't have the energy to go up tomorrow." Jurek was forceful now.

"Well, what should we do, then?"

"Go up. Let's keep going. I'll just go beyond that sérac and see what there is. Maybe I'll recognize something."

"Okay," Tadek mumbled.

They continued on and a short time later Jurek turned and screamed. He could see the summit. It was very near. The soup wrappers were from Wanda's French companions' pre-summit lunch stop, *not* their bivouac spot. Relieved, he took a few more steps to the top then slumped down to the ground, gasping and wheezing. He rummaged in his pack, found his camera and began taking photographs. Shortly after, Tadek appeared, lurching upward through the gloom.

The two hugged, wheezed and coughed, and thumped each other's backs, savouring their hard-won victory at the summit of K2, up the hardest route climbed so far on the mountain. After 15 minutes they realized it would all be meaningless if they perished on the top, so they started down. They downclimbed to a spot where they had stashed some equipment and then settled in for another cold, snowy, high-altitude bivouac – this one at 8300 metres.

It snowed all night. With no wind, the mountain was eerily quiet while the soft, deadly blanket grew steadily thicker. The snow continued the next morning, making it even more difficult to find the way down. Everything looked the same. Although they were descending by an easier route, it was all new ground to them. They searched for signs of the people who had gone before them and found occasional bits of old rope, signalling that they were on a well-travelled route. But they frequently wandered off-route in an exhausted state of confusion, forcing them to retrace their steps again and again.

By nightfall they were nowhere near the Austrian camp, where they had hoped to sleep. Instead, it was another bivouac for Tadek and Jurek – another night of physiological decay. It was their fourth night at extreme altitude, and they no longer had the will to dig out a suitable cave. Instead, they made do with just a slight depression that barely sheltered them from the wind. Even the indestructible Jurek suffered that night. "I could feel and see that we were at our physical limits," he later wrote. "Our bivouac was even worse than the night before. For two days we had not even had a drop of water and our bivouac sacs were worn and full of holes. The night was absolute torture as we shivered in the frigid cold, and snow penetrated every nook and cranny. We got only snatches of sleep."[43]

The snowstorm ended at dawn. They emerged from their sacks slowly, thick with lethargy. Through the murk, it appeared to them that they were on a shoulder just above the Austrian camp; Jurek thought he could see the tents. He went ahead a bit, called back to Tadek that the route was clear and, in a moment of clarity, reminded him to bring the rope on which he had sat throughout the night.

"Yes, yes, go on!" Tadek yelled.

Jurek continued down. He looked up and saw that Tadek was barely moving; his coordination seemed shaky. Jurek stopped to wait and immediately dozed off, leaning on his ice axe. When he awoke, Tadek was just above him. Below them was a short steep slope, and then the way was clear to the tents.

"Let's use the rope for this steep section," Jurek said.

"No, we don't need it. Besides, I left it up there."

Jurek rose from his slumped position, repositioned himself on the slope and continued kicking steps. His thoughts wandered to the warmth and safety of the camp; it was so near he could almost feel it. The slope steepened and the snow hardened to ice. He had to be careful now. Place each axe firmly. Kick each foot confidently. The rope would have been good to have here. No problem. It's a short distance. Concentrate.

He glanced up to see that Tadek was following well now, using the same placements as his. Just then Jurek saw a flash: Tadek's crampon flying off his foot. Jurek shouted a warning. Then the impossible happened: the other crampon flew off. Jurek yelled again. "Hold on!"

Tadek tried. His axe was firmly embedded in the ice, but with his entire weight suddenly on his arms, his boots scraping uselessly on the icy slope, he couldn't hold on. He flew off with lightning speed, screaming.

Jurek was directly below Tadek. Instinctively, he gripped his axes as hard as he could and pressed his body against the slope. One moment before impact was the last he could recall before all reality changed for Jurek. He felt a massive blow to his back as Tadek slammed into him. After a couple of seconds he realized that, by some miracle, he was still attached to the mountain. He lifted his head and looked around. All that was left on the icy face were a few nondescript skid marks and small, pathetic pieces of ice skittering down the slope. After that there was nothing.

In a daze, Jurek downclimbed the slope, which ended in a cliff, searching for any sign of Tadek. "Tadek. Tadek. Answer me. Where are you?" Of course he wasn't there. Jurek leaned over his axes once again and promptly fell asleep. Thousands of metres yawned below him. He awoke with a start and realized he had to move away from this dangerous position. For five and a half hours he inched across the remaining 200-metre traverse to the Austrian tents.

He crawled into one of them and rummaged around in a shocked state, looking for anything to eat or drink. He found a can of fruit and slurped it down. Next he found a stove and some fuel and began melting snow. He drank and slept intermittently and then noticed a radio, which he used to call base camp to inform them of the accident. It didn't seem to be working well, but he thought he heard a garbled response, so he slumped sideways and fell asleep again with the radio pressed to his ear. In a delusional state of denial, he crawled into a sleeping bag on one side of the tent, leaving room for Tadek, who would soon be arriving. He had to be. He had a wife and daughter waiting at home.

Over and over, he saw Tadek flying. Did he know that he was about to die? Jurek would have given anything to go back in time, slow things down, press the reset button.

Twenty hours later Jurek woke with a start. It was now 2 p.m. of the following day. He tried to radio base camp again, but he couldn't reach them. In fact, he had never spoken to them, for there were no batteries in the radio. Jurek had only imagined the voices of response.

❄ ❄ ❄

Meanwhile, Janusz Majer was on the Magic Line route with his team of seven, which included Wanda's previous climbing partners Anna Czerwińska, Krystyna Palmowska and Mrówka Miodowicz-Wolf. Aside from Janusz's team, there were three other expeditions with permission to try the route: an American team, the Italian Quota 8000 Expedition, and famous Italian solo climber Renato Casarotto. The American and Italian expeditions reached only 6800 metres before John Smolich and Alan Pennington were killed in an avalanche on June 21 at the foot of the slope below the Negrotto Col. The Americans gave up their attempt, and the Italians soon abandoned the pillar, too, turning instead to the Abruzzi Ridge, where Wanda and her team were climbing. Renato twice reached 8200 metres on the pillar, but after his third attempt he, too, retreated.

Now it was just the Poles, working in two teams; one consisted of four men, the other of three women. They fixed ropes and established camps up the pillar, and, after two bivouacs above 8000 metres, three of the four men – Wojciech Wróż, Przemek Piasecki and Petr Bozik, a Czech – reached the summit on August 3. Because their route was so difficult, like Jurek and Tadek they decided to descend the Abruzzi Ridge.

It was 1:30 p.m. when Wojciech Wróż fell to his death. Przemek had rappelled the last 50 metres of fixed lines and Petr had followed him. They had waited for Wojciech in order to descend the rest of the way to Camp IV, for this section was without fixed ropes. Suddenly they heard a horrible metallic noise. They feared the worst, but they waited. An hour and a half later, a descending Korean climber appeared and reported that Wojciech was nowhere to be seen. Certain that their partner had fallen to his death, they felt their only option was to carry on to the sad huddle of tents at Camp IV, where they collapsed into British climber Alan Rouse's small tent, which he and Mrówka shared with them. They weren't sure what had happened but thought it likely that Wojciech had fallen while down-climbing a small gap between two sections of fixed ropes. They later learned that the gap had inadvertently been caused by one of the Korean climbers, who had cut the rope in order to bridge another missing section of fixed line.

Janusz, Krystyna and Anna had also started up their route, but their nerves were rattled. "It felt like an unhealthy atmosphere," Anna remembered. "You come back and you learn that somebody has died. A bit later, you learn that somebody else is dead. We were beginning to lose our minds."[44] Although they were fighting a losing battle of emotional trench warfare, they weren't yet ready to give in.

The three had moved up steadily in good weather; each day, one camp higher. "The mountain was luring us – into a trap," Anna recalled. They were bivouacked at 8200 metres, ready to go for the summit the next day. Early on the morning of August 4, they received the shocking news of Wojciech's fall. Janusz sat down on the snow, put his head in his hands and wailed, "I've had it, this is too fucking much."

Their decision was unanimous. They packed up and started down. Almost immediately the mist moved in. Snow began to fall. This sudden change in weather occurred on the very same day that a large group of Abruzzi Ridge climbers started their summit attempts. The following day the weather deteriorated in earnest, with hurricane winds so strong they forced the old fixed ropes to stand out horizontally, covered with two-centimetre-long icicles. Janusz and the women fled the mountain, fighting for their lives in the storm and evacuating all their camps on the way down to base camp.

The mountain took no notice of them, preoccupied with those on the Abruzzi Ridge, where the struggle was just beginning. "The mountain released us," Anna said. "I remember the click of my [headlamp] light.... So many people had died. And still the stupid battery worked. I was really shaken by that realization."[45] For the first 24 hours at base camp they rehydrated, ate and dried out. Then it dawned on them – where was the team on the Abruzzi Ridge? Why hadn't they heard anything? Their partner, Mrówka, was there, having abandoned the pillar after declaring it too dangerous. She had instead moved over to the Abruzzi Ridge, to climb with Alan Rouse on a route she thought would be safer.

❈ ❈ ❈

Jurek crawled out of the Austrian tent and, over the next two days, dropped down the fixed lines to base camp. Tadek had become the fifth victim on K2 that year. Wanda had always said Jurek could live for days on a diet of Himalayan rocks and come out fit at the other end. But not Tadek. This was Jurek's fourth consecutive expedition on which he had lost a partner.

Their new route on K2 was exceptional, climbed in a style that brought an entirely new dimension to Himalayan climbing. But Jurek felt no joy at having climbed the magnificent face. His experiences on the mountain were too tragic and the price of success too high. Janusz's Magic Line was another landmark for the mountain, yet he too felt that their loss of life had nullified the joy of their success. Both climbs were overlooked for years, overshadowed by all the tragedies on K2 that year.

❈ ❈ ❈

Everyone on the mountain was vulnerable to the weather, and the storm on K2 had intensified. The situation became desperate as one fatality followed another. Renato Casarotto fell into a crevasse on his way down alone from the Magic Line. He was rescued, but he died shortly after. Now it was impossible to ignore another harsh reality: the Barrards were not coming back. Shortly after, Liliane's body emerged on the lower glacier, brought down by the continuous barrage of avalanches.

Then, at 7900 metres on the Abruzzi Ridge, the situation deteriorated into complete chaos as seven climbers converged at Camp IV, some on their way up, others on their way down. There weren't enough tents or sleeping bags for the climbers, all at the edge of their limits. There, amidst the wreckage of the camp and farther down the Abruzzi Ridge, five more perished: Julie Tullis, Hannes Wieser, Alfred Imitzer, Alan Rouse and Mrówka. Only two survived: Kurt Diemberger and Willi Bauer. When Balti porter Mohammad Ali was killed by rockfall, the total number of dead on K2 topped out at an astonishing 13.

What went wrong? Who, if anyone, was responsible for the multiple tragedies on the mountain? The one common theme was that each climber,

150

like Wanda and her little team, had stayed in the "death zone" too long, had not left any room for error. "It seems absolutely clear that, on no account, should you climb with the thought that all that matters is getting to the top, the rest be damned," Janusz later sadly commented.

For those few who were left, emotions ran high. Kurt was shattered at having lost Julie, his mountain soulmate. Michel felt responsible for the Barrards. Renato's widow was heartbroken. Jim had been in base camp the entire time, trying to understand and absorb the unfolding tragedy, all the while filming the wasted survivors who wandered listlessly from tent to tent, quietly sharing their stories. The thin fabric walls could not hide the coughing and sobbing. Wanda turned inward, unwilling to reveal the depth of her sorrow. Grief merged with guilt, which led to remorse. There seemed little reason to celebrate.

To the astonishment of those left at base camp, despite her frostbite, weariness and sadness, Wanda began preparing for an immediate ascent of nearby Broad Peak. Considering what was going on and what she had just endured, she seemed completely out of touch with reality. She bordered on irrational and would speak only of 8000-metre peaks. She confessed she felt no pleasure about reaching the summit of K2; she had lost too many friends on the mountain. Yet here she was, preparing for another epic on Broad Peak. Her strength and determination were admirable, but it was sad that she seemed incapable of savouring her success on K2. In fact, she seemed just like many other top-level, complex and compulsive climbers, unable to remain fulfilled for long, always driven to seek out the next challenge.

This attempt was more likely a kind of self-medication, however. As she wrote in her journal: "Certain kinds of events only get to me much later … my reaction to aggression, disaster or tragedy is delayed. There are events that I have lived but still can't fully accept."

Battered and broken, Wanda headed to nearby Broad Peak to attempt a solo alpine-style ascent. She didn't even make it to the first high camp before turning back.

❄ ❄ ❄

Prior to 1986, 12 people had died climbing K2. Now, within one season, the number had more than doubled. Wanda had been on enough mountains to recognize the strange atmosphere that had emerged on the Abruzzi Ridge. There were too many teams that were not really teams, just a hodge-podge collection of independent climbers, patched together in a last-ditch effort to get up the mountain. Even though twos and threes eventually formed within that larger group, there was very little loyalty when the situation fell apart. Many were on the Abruzzi Ridge because it was supposedly an easier alternative to their already failed attempts on more difficult lines. This led to a dangerous level of complacency about the route.

The Abruzzi Ridge climbers were not the only ones involved in this tragic sequence of events. Climbers who were descending the ridge after having climbed routes on other sides of the mountain also contributed to the crowding at Camp IV. Their arrivals were unplanned and likely added to the stress.

With dozens of climbers on the mountain, there were several series of decisions that were made, seemingly with good judgement yet without knowledge of what would come next. The apparently acceptable levels of danger and risk deteriorated into situations of extreme survival. But were those levels of risk truly acceptable? Acceptable to whom? Jurek had felt sure that things were still under control until the moment Tadek hurtled into him. Janusz lost his taste for risk only upon hearing of his teammate's death. And even after the carnage, Wanda seemed willing to assume yet more risk on Broad Peak.

Wanda didn't venture onto the slippery slope of laying blame for the deaths on K2, but there was one element that nagged her: Kurt's slow climbing pace. She felt that, through a complicated series of events, his and Julie's slowness had ultimately created a domino effect on a number of the other climbers. And because Kurt had been unable or unwilling to save her close friend Mrówka on the descent, she couldn't let go of her feelings of resentment. Yet it's possible her anger with Kurt was fuelled more by a private admission that she might have acted in the same way. Or was due to misplaced blame because it was *she* who had suggested the change of route for Mrówka in the first place.

❅ ❅ ❅

When Jurek returned to Poland after K2, Artur came to Warsaw to meet him. They greeted each other with restraint. Artur didn't ask Jurek about Tadek, and Jurek didn't say a word about the climb. As Artur manoeuvred the car onto the highway heading south toward Katowice, he mentioned that preparations were proceeding for their trip to Manaslu. Jurek nodded, staring straight ahead. "Are the barrels packed?" he asked.

"Yes," Artur replied. "We are leaving in three weeks." He waited for Jurek to respond.

Jurek was quiet for a bit and then nodded. "Good. I'll be ready."

CHAPTER ELEVEN

FORGED IN STEEL

There are two ways of fighting – you must be a fox and a lion.
—ADAM MICKIEWICZ, *KONRAD WALLENROD*

It was now very clear that Polish climbers were special. They were tough, tenacious and supremely focused on their goals. As Reinhold Messner coined it, they were "hungry, and very, very strong."

Mexican climber Carlos Carsolio, who had first-hand experience climbing with the Poles, was sure that their success was a result of their tough childhoods. "When you are too pampered, you lose the power of patience and suffering," he said. "The Austrians and Germans were very strong too, but only that generation just after the war." Carlos had also climbed with the Slovenians, including the famous Stane Belak-Šrauf, who, while leading a difficult pitch in the Julian Alps, came to the end of his rope without having reached a suitable spot to belay. The story has his partner calling up, "Šrauf, the rope is finished," and Šrauf yelling back, "*I* am the one who says when the rope is finished." He continued on, forcing his partner to simulclimb until a suitable belay could be set up. Carlos laughed at the famous story, adding, "This attitude exemplified Šrauf, the Slovenians, the Poles and particularly Jurek." No mention of the more pampered Western Europeans, the Americans or the English.

American climbing editor Christian Beckwith believed that Polish climbing was synonymous with "exquisite" suffering, that their ability to push through that punishing state toward the accomplishment of their goals defined an "alpine transcendence." Messner agreed that high-altitude climbing was all about suffering, but he was more pragmatic in his description: "I don't believe anyone who says there is a lot of pleasure in climbing the big peaks."

European expeditions arrived in the Himalaya with better equipment and superb training, but it was the Poles who stayed on and on, often outperforming their European counterparts. Not without cost. There were the abandoned families back home, the frostbite, the injuries and the ever-increasing death toll.

One theory, held mostly by foreigners, was that Polish climbers suffered from a deep feeling of inferiority and had something to prove. They had fought and lost countless wars over the centuries. They were poor. They were largely invisible outside their borders. To foreigners, Poland was somewhere "over there" – in Eastern Europe. Their equipment and clothing were inferior, and they had little cash to hire porters and trucks or to buy foreign food. They had to try harder just to keep up with their foreign peers, and in doing so, they surpassed them.

It was an interesting theory, but most Polish climbers rejected it outright. They believed their fortitude and sense of pride came not from inferiority but from the opposite – their aristocratic Polish tradition of nobility and bravery; centuries of castles and swords; soldiers marching through the forests, defending Poland from marauding plunderers – and from generations of oppression by Germans and Russians. "Living between the hammer and the anvil," Voytek Kurtyka called it. Fighting for independence. A continuous state of awareness. Readiness. Courage. Strength. But now the castles and marauders were gone, replaced by the mountains. Swords had become ice axes. It is hard to discount the similarity between the Poles' performance in the mountains and their conduct in war.

There are many vivid examples of celebrated national heroes in Polish art and literature that give life to the tragedy and joy of their noble history. The burning hatred and heroic deeds that feature in the epic poems of 18th-century writer Adam Mickiewicz made a tremendous impression upon his countrymen. He and other writers created larger-than-life figures whose pride and suffering influenced subsequent generations and the Polish philosophy of life. Centuries of battles featured images of winged Hussars, noble steeds storming through icy rivers and across dusty plains, flags billowing, swords poised, blood flowing freely in the bleak birch forests. The images suggested bravery. Enough to fight wars, generation after generation. Enough to break free from the iron grip of Communism – before the Czechs and before the East Germans. Enough to climb the highest mountains on Earth.

Voytek likened this special brand of Polish toughness to the Japanese Samurai tradition, which dictated that if a man was overpowered, a force stronger than him existed. And that proved he was weak, which in turn led to a tragic loss of dignity and honour. The risk of this mindset was that it could lead to bushido, or the "Path of the Sword." Bushido grew out of the ancient feudal bond that insisted upon unwavering loyalty on the part of the vassal. It borrowed heavily from Zen Buddhism and Confucianism. In its fullest expression, the code emphasized loyalty to one's superior, personal honour and the virtues of austerity, self-sacrifice and indifference to pain, if necessary to the point of death. It's doubtful that many individual climbers were aware of bushido, but they nevertheless provided living proof of this tradition throughout their climbing history, sometimes all the way to martyrdom.

Another role model who influenced the fortitude of some Polish climbers was Jesus Christ: his was a life of bravery, certainly, but also one of self-sacrifice. The Polish tendency to emulate Christ goes back to the 18th century, when Poland was overrun and partitioned by its neighbours. The deeply Catholic and poverty-stricken Poles collectively identified themselves with messianic suffering. They believed that, although Poland was being crucified by its neighbours, they were destined to return to glory, just as Christ had. When the Allies failed to support them during World War II, they carried the analogy further to include the Judas story of betrayal. But their faith was strong, and they maintained that just as Christ had brought redemption to mankind, Poland would bring redemption to Europe.

Adam Mickiewicz depicted Poland as the "Christ of all Nations" in his most famous play, *Dziady*. He wrote, "Verily I say unto you, it is not for you to learn civilization from foreigners, but it is you who are to teach them civilization.... You are among the foreigners like the Apostle among the idolaters." Although the influence of the Catholic Church eventually waned, many continued to see themselves as a "martyr nation," and Christ was, after all, the ultimate martyr.

But there were also more practical reasons for Polish toughness. The Poles had started late in the Himalayan arena and had a lot of catching up to do in order to assure themselves a place in mountaineering history. They undertook ventures with no margin for error. The growing death toll proved this to be a risky strategy.

The pressure on Polish climbers was enormous. It was hard to find money, to free up a passport and obtain the proper visas. The paperwork was endless. And what, a cloud in the sky? They were supposed to turn back? Five hundred metres from the summit? Not likely. When they finally overcame all the bureaucratic obstacles, the financial gyrations and the travel, decisions about turning back without success were not made lightly. By contrast, members of Western expeditions could more easily return any time they wished.

When a group of French climbers failed on a summit, they would gather in base camp, joke a little, drink some wine and laugh. Polish climbers would drink too, but their beverages would be of a stronger variety, and in their hearts would be bitterness – the anguish of collective failure. Like the Japanese, their heads would droop in shame. Artur Hajzer stated it bluntly: "Unfortunately we Poles prefer to be a dead hero than a live loser."

There was a flip side to this toughness, this "art of suffering," as Voytek coined it. To survive in intense cold, with little food or water and barely contained fear, all the while giving one's physical all, requires a ferocious stolidness. In Himalayan climbing, this is seen as an attribute. It's referred to with admiration as being "hard-core." Inner strength is admirable, but what does it look like from the outside? Often, selfish callousness. It is easier to concentrate on one's own battle with exhaustion and terror than empathize with a less able partner. A kind of inner deafness, a loss of sight and even a hardening of the heart are sad but frequent by-products of survival in the mountains.

Krzysztof Wielicki, the quintessential warrior, acknowledged that the level of egocentricity in alpinists was high, and he was well aware of the repercussions. "If you want to climb, there is a cost," he said. "Usually the cost is the family. I have to say sorry, sorry, sorry. They suffer at home and we suffer on the mountain." But for him and others, this life of suffering seemed to elicit a perverse satisfaction. "To experience pleasure when you have everything against you, you must have some kind of warrior philosophy," Krzysztof explained. "It is more appealing. It is more exciting."

As so many of the most entrepreneurial Polish climbers proved, another practical factor in the astonishing level of Polish toughness in the mountains was simple economics. Polish climbers proved to be a creative lot, and they devised a system *within* the system – a strategy that liberated them. They discovered a way to travel outside their borders, to experience new cultures and languages, to follow their passion for climbing and make a living at it. They discovered how to be free!

Krzysztof was a good example. He started working as soon as he finished university at the age of 20, then he married and immediately started a family. But he soon realized the futility of working. "Communist time was so nice for us because we didn't have to work … Two months with the painting jobs and it was enough; then we can go for six months to the Himalaya." Together with university professors, doctors and engineers, Krzysztof painted towers and smokestacks – and climbed. "I painted almost the whole of Silesia … the Katowice steelworks, mines, buildings, conveyor belts, chimneys of heat-generating plants, water towers … from Trzebnia to Zabrze," he claimed. "Time had no value back then. We did what we wanted: we met at the mountaineers' club, we dreamt, we made plans, and then set out to the mountains! As grown-ups, we were at a permanent party, having quit our professions, not knowing that in a few years' time capitalism would also come to us." Leszek Cichy agreed that their strategy was spectacularly successful: "We sold equipment; we smuggled equipment; it was perfect!" This, from a university professor.

This exuberance of creative expression wasn't limited to climbers. There was an abundance of artists and writers who thrived creatively during those severely repressed years in Poland. The censorship industry, rather than stifle, seemed to actually stimulate the artistic community. Like the climbers, artists became stronger through oppression; their most creative work came out of the darkest days. When repression collapsed, they collapsed too. They had no idea how to communicate without being rebels. When their world opened, they dried up.

Leszek attributed Poland's great record in the mountains to a much more banal reason: sheer numbers. "There was a veritable army of climbers," he said. "It was inevitable that some would rise to the top." He pointed out that, for more than a decade, there were 10 to 15 Polish expeditions mounted each year to the Himalaya. Those climbers who rose to the top became famous, but there were hundreds more who didn't, despite their phenomenal climbs. A former climbing partner of Voytek, Ludwik Wilczyński, described the situation: "While Zawada was working in the lounges of Polish and international alpinism, and Kurtyka, the community's metaphysical think-tank, walked alone on the roof, the cellars were occupied by filthily dressed outsiders who, singing the no-passport-and-no-job blues and drinking low-quality spirits, gave us all the satisfaction of self-fulfillment and feeling of independence."[46] Down in those cellars were climbers like Druciarz Rudnicki, Adam Zyzak, Wojciech Wróż, Genek Chrobak and Andrzej Heinrich and Andrzej Czok, virtually unknown outside their country.

However, Poland's performance in the mountains was much more than just a matter of volume. The distinctive Polish combination of ambition, economics, politics, history and tradition – it all added up. The results were unbeatable.

❄ ❄ ❄

Almost immediately after Jurek returned from K2 in 1986, and with little time to recover, he and Artur were immersed in preparing for their Manaslu expedition later that fall. Artur joked, "Logically, I shouldn't be going with you; all around you people seem to die." He said it half in jest, but there was some truth to his remark. Artur discounted any lingering concerns as he plunged into the final days of packing for the expedition, which included himself, Jurek, Voytek and Ryszard Warecki, who was planning to film the climb. Carlos Carsolio was also invited, in part for the foreign currency that he would bring to the expedition. Having a foreigner along was like "winning the lottery" for Polish climbers, Artur explained. He and Carlos were the students on this climb, under the tutelage of the masters, Voytek and Jurek.

For years, Voytek had been Jurek's preferred climbing partner. When that partnership faltered, Jurek had moved from one partner to another, taking advantage of whatever situation arose. He sensed a close bond with Artur, despite the 14-year age difference. Artur was now as active in the Himalaya as Jurek, with two or three expeditions per year. "In that time, nobody had jobs," Artur explained. "There were no careers; I was like a professional climber."

The team was planning a new route on the Northeast Face of the main peak of Manaslu, as well as an unofficial, unpermitted climb of Manaslu East, a slender pinnacle that, at almost 8000 metres, was Nepal's highest unclimbed summit. The climbers were in base camp, lounging in the mess tent, when word arrived that Messner had climbed Makalu, his second-last of the 14 8000ers. Only one to go. Jurek had three mountains left to climb, so it now seemed likely that Messner would win the race. The others watched Jurek closely. How badly did he want this? Would this announcement threaten the Manaslu climb?

Jurek rose from his seat and left the tent. It looked like the race was over. Looking up at the East Face of Manaslu, he gave himself a little pep talk: "That's it. Tomorrow we go up there, Mr. Kukuczka."

He walked back in and, after a moment of silence, glared at Artur and broke the tension with a joke: "Look what you've done. They're climbing over there and because of you we're still sitting in base camp, warming our asses. We leave tomorrow."

His determination wasn't shared by Voytek. The warm, wet weather of the preceding weeks had loaded the slopes with tons of unstable snow poised to avalanche at the smallest trigger. Even though the weather had cleared, the route was unquestionably dangerous. They were at around 6000 metres on the mountain when the main discussion occurred.

"Stop, guys." Voytek began. "I'm not going on. It's too dangerous. I'm going back."

"Voytek, we have accepted the risk from the word go," Jurek responded. "We knew it would be like this."

A heavily laden, 200-metre-high snowfield lay above them; if they could climb this slope without triggering an avalanche, they would arrive on the much safer ridge. But Jurek and Voytek assessed the level of risk different-ly. They were both assertive and clear in their arguments, and they couldn't agree. Frustrated, Jurek suggested a vote.

"I'm going down. This is senseless," Voytek said, his voice flat and final. One vote for down.

Artur chimed in, "I'm the youngest here. It's true the risk is high, but I would prefer to go up." One vote for up, one vote for down.

It was assumed that Jurek would vote for up, so now all eyes turned to Carlos. The air hummed with tension. Carlos agreed with Voytek that the risk was too great, yet in a serious and measured voice he said, "As Mexico's economy is deteriorating rapidly, it is my firm belief that this is going to be my last expedition to the Himalaya. For that reason I'm going on and I'll do everything in my power to get to that summit." Despite the gravity of the situation, everyone broke out laughing.

They headed down to base camp to regroup and try again. Voytek fol-lowed through on his decision and left the expedition. There were no hard feelings between him and Jurek, just a difference in climbing philosophy. The rest waited as another spell of bad weather rolled through. Then, one morning while they were relaxing after breakfast in the mess tent, the radio crackled to life once again. "Yesterday, the outstanding mountaineer Reinhold Messner reached the summit of Lhotse. In so doing he has become the first person to reach the top of the 14 highest mountains in the world."

Nobody said a word. Jurek's eyes flickered about the tent, searching for a safe landing. Finally Artur broke the silence. "So, there's no need for us to hurry anymore. We can climb this mountain gently."

Voytek's assessment of the climbing race seemed to be reflected in Himalayan historian Elizabeth Hawley's report on Messner's triumph. "Himalayan mountaineering is not ordinarily considered to be a highly competitive sport," she wrote. "But last autumn's climbing season in the Nepalese Himalaya had much of the drama of a World Cup Final when the race to be first to conquer all of the world's 8000-metre mountains was fi-nally won by Italy's Reinhold Messner by the relatively narrow margin of 14 to 11. By the end of the season the runner up, Jerzy Kukuczka of Poland, had increased his own score from 11 to 12." Although she was clearly ham-ming it up for the benefit of her report, there was an element of truth to her observations.

Carlos, who was now suffering from frostbite and a hand injury, chose to stay back when Artur and Jurek headed up. But they were turned back at 7400 metres. Defeated and deflated, they returned to base camp. They had been on this mountain for weeks now, endangered by the ferocious winds, avalanches and increasingly lower temperatures as October ground to its bitter end. The mountains were empty of climbers. All the autumn expeditions were back in Kathmandu, celebrating either success or defeat.

Jurek wanted one more try. He tossed out an idea for Artur to consider. "Let's tackle it alpine-style by a different route." Not only Artur but also the now somewhat recovered Carlos chimed in with enthusiasm. So on November 5, the trio headed up with one tent and their climbing gear onto the unclimbed Northeast Face of Manaslu. Six days later, Artur and Jurek were on the summit, while Carlos huddled in the last camp, attending to his frostbitten hands.

Frostbite was so common, particularly during late-season expeditions, that climbers almost grew to expect it. Krzysztof once joked, "The fingers are not all equally important. The big one is very important, and maybe the littlest one. But the ones in the middle, not so important. Chop chop."

Jurek's reaction to having lost the race was curious. At some level he must have been devastated. It wasn't just he who had suffered cruelly in this game: his climbing partners had suffered with him. Several had died. Surely there must have been a part of Jurek that regretted the sacrifices and wondered if it had been worth it. Yet he seemed to move past this disappointment too easily. Had the race been all that important to him? The magnitude of his ambition would suggest that it had. But Jurek was more complicated than that. It's true he had lost the race with Messner. But he had modified the rules of the game as he went and, in his mind, and the minds of many knowledgeable alpinists, his version of the race was on a higher level than Messner's because of the way he climbed. As long as he continued to climb these giants by new routes or in winter, he could still be a winner.

Or maybe Jurek had fooled everyone with this competition: perhaps the race had just been a tool for him, a funding and marketing strategy that provided him a way to keep doing what he loved – return to the mountains, again and again.

CHAPTER TWELVE

HIMALAYAN ROSARY

Tell me, what is it you plan to do
With your one wild and precious life?
— MARY OLIVER, *THE SUMMER DAY*

By the end of 1986 there was no country in the world that dominated Himalayan climbing the way Poland did. There were individuals from other nations, of course: Messner and Habeler, Doug Scott and Greg Child. But no single country could boast such a strength and depth of climbing talent. Within that Polish team, with its dozens of amazing performers, the stars rose to the surface: Jurek Kukuczka, Voytek Kurtyka, Wanda Rutkiewicz, Krzysztof Wielicki, Andrzej Zawada and Artur Hajzer.

But the team was breaking up. Voytek had long ago given up on the big national-style expeditions, preferring to climb in small groups, often with foreign partners. Wanda too had forsaken any sense of Polish loyalty, climbing with whomever she could, depending on the circumstances. Not just in Poland, but everywhere, individual aspirations had taken over where nationalistic goals once ruled. Jurek wanted the Himalayan Crown. Krzysztof was after speed.

They struggled to balance their aspirations with the continuing challenge of financing their dreams. Shortly after climbing K2, Wanda met the person who would help her do just that – Dr. Marion Feik. A lawyer from Vienna, Marion was tiring of her profession in the human rights field and offered to become Wanda's agent and manager. Wanda accepted. Now she could concentrate on what she did best: climbing. Marion would take care of the rest. It was a match that promised long-term stability, a luxury that Wanda had been unable to find in her two attempts at marriage. Their relationship also yielded an invaluable source of correspondence for historians, tracking not only Wanda's career but also her feelings, her doubts, her dreams and her fears.

She wasted little time in Poland and was back in the Himalaya by September of 1986, this time to attempt Makalu, in the eastern part of Nepal. Wanda was in good spirits and wrote from the trek:

Dear Marion   6 September 1986
Your help in organizing this expedition was invaluable. I'm taking your
perfume up to base camp, but I'll eat the ham on the approach march.
I've left European civilization far behind and I'm enchanted by the
landscape below Makalu ....

Ever since Reinhold Messner's achievement, a great deal of media attention was being paid to 8000-metre peaks. But Messner and Jurek weren't
the only ones chasing 8000ers. Swiss butcher Marcel Rüedi was ticking
them off, too. Although none of them had admitted to a "race," everyone
else, including the media, had treated it as such. Wanda too had become
an 8000-metre specialist, and it was likely on Makalu that she began to imagine herself climbing all 14, for both Rüedi and Messner were at base
camp. Impressed with Wanda's performance on the mountain, Messner
pronounced, "Wanda is the living proof that women can put up perform-
ances at high altitude that most men can only dream of. I'm certain that a
woman will have conquered the magic fourteen 8,000-metre peaks within
the next ten years."[47]

Dear Marion   30 September 1986
The normal route up Makalu is not particularly difficult, but it is savagely
strenuous .... One of the worst trials is having to keep retreading the
track in deep snow, often up to your waist and burrowing like a
mole .... I think about you often, and I'm looking forward to your
warm welcome in Vienna.

Although Wanda reached 8000 metres on the mountain, the summit
eluded her. Not so for Marcel Rüedi, who was climbing with Krzysztof.
Krzysztof was faster and reached the summit before Rüedi, who eventually
had to bivouac on the way down without a sleeping bag at 8200 metres.
When Messner and his partners climbed to the summit the next morning,
they were watching out for Rüedi, yet it wasn't until they were descending
that they saw him sitting in the snow with his hands on his ski poles. He
appeared to be taking a short rest. But he was dead. After climbing nine of
the 14 8000ers, he had died in his tracks, apparently not acclimatized to
climb at the pace he was attempting. For Wanda, the 14-8000-metre dream
was just beginning.

❄ ❄ ❄

Although the race was over for him, Jurek was motivated to finish off his last climbs. Artur, now his preferred climbing partner, was just as enthusiastic. Together with Krzysztof, Wanda and Rysiek Warecki, they arranged for a winter permit for Annapurna and were back in Nepal by the New Year of 1987.

Wanda didn't confine her activities to Annapurna.

Dear Marion   11 January 1987
... I was busy in Kathmandu working the system to get more permits
for the future. I just can't slow down, even in Nepal....

It had been Jurek's idea to invite Wanda on the trip, although none of the other climbers were particularly excited about climbing with her. If Jurek invited her, then he could climb with her, they reasoned. She didn't climb as fast as the others; she bivouacked too often; and she always brought too many gadgets. Jurek wasn't all that keen to climb with her, either, but he had a practical reason for inviting her. Wanda had a film commission from an Austrian network, and she would bring some badly needed cash. In fact Jurek had often commented to Celina that climbing in the Himalaya was not for women. Celina disagreed with him and, in her quiet way, was a strong supporter of Wanda, who she thought was brave and strong for choosing this tough climbing lifestyle.

They established base camp by January 20, but their time was desperately short: the permit expired on February 15. Annapurna in any season is one of the most dangerous of the 8000-metre peaks. A winter attempt nudged it into another dimension altogether. They were on the north side of the mountain where they saw not one ray of sunlight, not even an hour or two of forgiving warmth to look forward to. Except at base camp, it was just constant cold and shade.

Since Jurek had done the organizing, there was a lot of food, at least. Rysiek had recently returned from the Tyrol, bringing a supply of delicious Austrian *Speck* (bacon). Everyone on the team was looking forward to sampling it. When they reached base camp they rummaged through barrel after barrel: no *Speck* to be found. Their disappointment was mitigated by the amusing sounds emerging from Jurek and Wanda's tent. The other climbers giggled each night as they listened to the strange smacking sounds. Their imaginations ran wild. "We thought, oh boy, Celina will be jealous," Artur said. In fact, Celina was a bit worried. She knew that Wanda and Jurek would be sharing a tent on this trip, and, although she admired

Wanda, even saw her as a kind of idol, she was not blind to her feminine charm. As it turned out, her worries were unfounded; when the expedition ended and they were packing up base camp, Artur discovered a pile of *Speck* containers tucked under Jurek and Wanda's tent. The suspicious noises had been more gastronomical than anatomical.

Initially the climbers made good progress on their cold, dark mountain. They were resting in base camp before taking another load of gear and food higher up the mountain when Wanda fell ill with a fever and sore throat, as she often did early in an expedition. She opted out of the next load-carrying trip. Jurek, Krzysztof and Artur began packing up. As usual, Artur wanted to take more gear, and Jurek, as always, wanted to take more food. He belonged to the group of alpinists who, regardless of the altitude, liked to eat well.

Wanda wasn't part of this packing up, so she was in the mess tent, chatting with Rysiek. Artur approached the tent and overheard them speaking.

"I know these sons of bitches. They're going to try to get to the top now," Rysiek said.

"Do you really think so?" Wanda asked, obviously surprised.

"Well what would they be waiting for?"

When Artur entered, Wanda asked him directly, "Is it true that you are going to try and get to the top?"

Artur was caught. This was a much more difficult question than appeared at first glance. He knew that it might be possible to try for an early summit bid and that if any of them could do it, it would be Jurek and him. They climbed quickly and were still acclimatized from Manaslu. But they hadn't been on the mountain long and the highest camps were not yet in, so the chances of getting to the top right now were very unlikely. The answer was therefore both yes and no. He didn't know what to tell her, so he deferred to Jurek. "I just follow the leader," he said. "If the leader stops, I stop. If the leader goes, I go. If the leader backs down, I back down. I'm not the one to make the decision."

Wanda saw through the deflection and became angry, accusing Artur of scheming behind her back. She stomped out of the tent in search of Jurek. Upon being questioned, he said that, yes, if there was a chance to go to the summit now, why would they wait? It seemed obvious. She became enraged. She wasn't ready yet. It was all happening too quickly. "If, as you say, there is a chance that you'll go all the way to the summit, what will happen to me?" she demanded of Jurek. "You know that I can't try for the summit right now. I think that you should designate someone to stay behind and be my partner for a later summit attempt."

Artur had sidled up to the pair and overheard her request. He was dumb-founded. "This 'to designate' sounded so curious to me," he exclaimed. "She was forcing Jurek to become a true general manager, as if we were on a big expedition. I knew this kind of management from books and all of a sudden it looked as if I would still be able to see all these mistakes and blunders first-hand."

There were three eligible partners for Wanda: Jurek, Krzysztof or Artur. Jurek designated himself. And so the unofficial climbing team of Jurek and Artur was, for the time being, broken up. Jurek assigned Artur to Krzysztof. The wily Artur tried to process what had just happened. He knew that Krzysztof, even though he wasn't as successful or as psychologically tough as Jurek, was in even better physical condition. But Jurek was more driven. Either of them would make a formidable partner. "To put it bluntly, switching partners can be compared to getting out of a Toyota diesel into a gasoline Mazda," he finally concluded.

By the time they reached 6800 metres, all four were climbing together. They were just 300 metres above Camp III when nightfall forced them to bivouac. Everyone was tired and Wanda still felt ill, possibly suffering from anemia, a condition that had plagued her on and off since Everest. They planned to descend the next day, rehydrate, continue to acclimatize and then come back up the mountain for a serious summit bid. Krzysztof and Artur were in their tent, preparing for bed. All of a sudden, from the neighbouring tent, came Jurek's question: "Who is going to come with me and try to get Camp V set up tomorrow?"

Wanda knew she wasn't well enough acclimatized. It would be a waste of effort for her to try and climb higher now, and the summit was still more than 1200 metres above them. It was an easy decision for her; the answer was no.

Krzysztof was not completely acclimatized either. But he was a faster climber. He could probably go higher and get safely down. Yet he was also smarting from the repercussions of the recent death of his good friend Marcel Rüedi. When Rüedi, climbing slower than Krzysztof, had opted to stay behind and rest on the way down, Krzysztof had agreed. After Rüedi died in his tracks, Krzysztof had been criticized for "leaving his partner" on the mountain, and he was worried about getting into a similar situation with Wanda. But before he could begin to respond to Jurek's challenge, Artur shouted as loud as he possibly could, "Meeeeeeeeeeee!"

❋ ❋ ❋

The circumstances leading to the summit team of Jurek and Artur were curious. On the one hand, the two were clearly the most able, since they were still acclimatized from their previous climb. On the other, Krzysztof was much more experienced than Artur and was perhaps a more obvious choice for Jurek. About Jurek there never seemed any doubt: he was always the most ambitious and most willing to suffer for a summit. Annapurna in winter was no exception. Wanda was probably never a serious candidate for a fast ascent, even though she had brought most of the financing. In the end, the summit team was decided in that moment when Artur seized the day, yelling out his eagerness to go.

Artur worried about Krzysztof, who by now had developed a big reputation. He not only climbed fast but also expected others to perform at his level. Some called him a "harsh leader" who bossed people around and wanted things done quickly – his way. He was a small person with a big attitude. Certainly bigger than Artur's. And his ambitions were enormous. Maybe Krzysztof would hold a grudge against him. Artur was experienced enough to know that relations between big egos on big mountains can sometimes produce big problems. He remembered Kangchenjunga in January, when Krzysztof had positioned himself so carefully and craftily in order to assure himself a summit bid. And the South Face of Lhotse in 1985, when Krzysztof had left the expedition abruptly after Rafał Chołda's death, declaring that any further effort would be a lost cause. Krzysztof knew when to cut his losses. That was clear. But for the moment, Artur was willing to risk hard feelings for the chance to climb higher with Jurek.

Jurek and Artur didn't stop at Camp V. On February 3, just 16 days after arriving in base camp, they reached the top of Annapurna.

Their achievement was remarkable, not only because of the speed with which they climbed it but also because of the winter storm that hit them near the top. They were forced to climb the last bit blind, following radio instructions from below. Krzysztof remembered the moment the pair trudged into base camp, Jurek's joy as he waved his arms, singing a popular Polish song at the top of his voice: "I love you, Life."

Krzysztof and Wanda tried one more time, but she was extremely weak from a lingering bronchial infection; it was only her dogged determination that initiated their second attempt. Krzysztof knew it was doomed even before they began. He saw the enormous effort it cost Wanda to try again, knowing that just a few months earlier she had been standing on the summit of K2. He understood the physical and emotional ordeal she had endured on that mountain, and he tried to convince her to ease up. "I told her a thousand times: 'Messner went up with the Sherpas. Is he great?'"

"He is," Wanda acknowledged.

"Then take the Sherpas, they will help you," he implored. But Wanda wanted to do it her way, to be the first, to do it without help.

"A difficult woman," Krzysztof said, "an extraordinary woman."

Krzysztof had initially been impressed, even awed by Wanda. But as he grew to know her better his admiration faded. "Not an easy woman. Very hard – hard-headed," he said.

He told a story about when he, Jurek and Wanda had been invited to Switzerland to participate in some medical tests on high-altitude climbers. One of the procedures, which was supposed to determine the condition of their altitude-impaired brains, was a memory test. The scientists would make statements such as, "On January 13, at 6:10 a.m., a ship with a draught of 260,000 tons sank in Hamburg harbour. Sixteen children and 31 adults drowned, among them 7 women and 15 men, 3 seamen.... At 1:10 p.m., a rescue team consisting of 47 people set out. Three rescuers died during the operation." The climbers would then be asked to repeat it.

"Is a seaman the same as a man?" joked Krzysztof.

"Your brain has more holes than mine," Jurek taunted.

"Yes, but yours are bigger," retorted Krzysztof.

They played around with the questions and answers, not taking the exercise terribly seriously. That evening, Wanda appeared at their door with a slight frown furrowing her brow. "Jurek, how many of those rescuers drowned?" The two were flabbergasted and laughed at her earnestness.

"That's ambition!" exclaimed Krzysztof.

He complained that she refused to follow traditional expedition rules and protocol. More important, he felt, along with quite a few others, that when Wanda was on an expedition there was always more work to be done, often for her benefit. Alek Lwow agreed that she tended to use people for her own goals on expeditions and that, particularly as she began to age, she gravitated to climbers who were better and stronger than her. She certainly wouldn't be the first – or the last – aging climber to adopt this strategy. Even Messner admitted that if it hadn't been for the strength of Hans Kammerlander, his partner on Lhotse, his last 8000er, he never would have summited. Krzysztof worried that, although Wanda was a star – the biggest in Poland's climbing history – physically, she was slowing down to a dangerous level.

The Annapurna winter defeat was bitter for Krzysztof who, in later years, developed an obsession for winter climbs. He had come very close on

Annapurna but had given up his attempt for his partner, who wasn't even his partner but Jurek's partner. "Annapurna was the first peak that I didn't climb," he said. "I was with Wanda. No, *Kukuczka* was with Wanda."

At the end, despite the obvious fact that she had been invited to Annapurna primarily for her money – not because they wanted to climb with her – Wanda just seemed happy to have survived.

> Dear Marion   18 February 1987
> The events of the last three weeks seem quite straightforward when I
> sit and write them down, but in fact I have survived some of the worst
> perils of my life. The route on Annapurna was a very dangerous one....
> I was in poor condition, with a bad cough.... Thank you for remem-
> bering my birthday.

Like her contemporaries, Wanda devoted her entire life to Himalayan climbing. Although her 10th-floor apartment on Sobieskiego Street in Warsaw was neither beautiful nor elaborate, it housed her equipment and provided her with a home base. The view out her window of the sea of rooftops and endless blocks of concrete was monotonous and grey. But it really didn't matter, since she was hardly ever there.

Marion managed her as best she could, but there was never enough time to do all the things Wanda wanted to do. Wanda's ambitions far exceeded climbing. She recorded interviews, wrote reports, filmed and edited, lectured and solicited sponsors – all activities essential to the life of a professional alpinist. She confided to Marion, "I live for the mountains, but I don't live only *by* the mountains. I'm not just a climber, and I don't ever want to be just a climber."[48] Still, she was realistic about her creative talents, saying, "I'm one of those who is competent, but not talented.... But I'm grateful for even the modicum of talent that I have."[49] She soon developed a pattern of overcommitment that gradually wore her down.

Krzysztof's career was heating up; winter climbing was becoming one of his specialties. Following the carnage of the 1986 summer season on K2, he joined Andrzej Zawada's winter expedition in 1987. Affectionately known as the "K2-million-dollar-helicopter-expedition," it was a lavish affair. They had arranged for their equipment to be carried in by 250 porters in October. But heavy snowfall stopped the caravan partway up the Baltoro Glacier, and they abandoned the bags halfway to the base. When the team arrived in late December, the bags were strewn everywhere. They had reached slightly higher than 7300 metres when the fierce cold winds of the Karakoram winter chased them off. Broad Peak too was a failure.

These disappointments, plus a failed winter attempt of Nanga Parbat, didn't deter Andrzej. He remained excited about the future of winter climbing, making two attempts on Makalu and five attempts on Nanga Parbat over the next few years. Even as he grew older and his physical prowess waned, his vision never wavered.

❄ ❄ ❄

It had been a busy 14 months for Jurek. In January of 1986 he had stood on the top of Kangchenjunga. In the summer he had climbed a new route on the South Face of K2. Autumn saw him complete a new route on Manaslu and, by the beginning of February 1987, the winter ascent of Annapurna. He was at number 13. Only one to go – Shishapangma.

Located in China, Shishapangma presented some organizational and financial challenges. Four years earlier, Jurek had toyed with the idea of sneaking across the border with Voytek for an illegal ascent. But times had changed, and for this final 8000er, he wanted it all above board. Jurek and Janusz Majer first tried to organize a permit with some Chinese Mountaineering Association officials who were visiting Poland. The Chinese offered the period between November 10 and December 15, 1986. "What a date!" stormed Jurek. "Neither summer nor winter!" He and Janusz interpreted this as a diplomatic refusal, and they requested a different time. The answer was no. The next step was to accept the Chinese invitation to Beijing to continue the discussions. But there was a problem: the Chinese trip would cost money – in a currency they didn't have.

They packed for the big city: jacket, tie and their very best shoes. Once in Beijing, the two indulged in sightseeing tours in a comfortable Mercedes bus. They slept soundly in a good hotel and ate some excellent meals. But on the main issue – how to get and pay for the permit – they made no progress at all. They finally managed to schedule a meeting with the top official on the last day of their visit. The night before the meeting, Jurek and Janusz hatched their plan: they would invite some Chinese climbers to Poland and offer to cover all the costs in Polish złotys. In return, they would ask for the Shishapangma permit.

The Chinese official was guarded with his response. "Ah yes, this could be of some interest to China," he said. "It is very important for Chinese climbers to gain experience in other mountain ranges. You would cover all the costs in Poland?"

"Yes, absolutely. All the costs. It would be a great honour for us," Janusz enthused.

Jurek chimed in at this opportune moment. "Perhaps you could include the costs of this 'organizational' week in Beijing as part the Chinese contribution to our partnership?"

The Chinese official looked up from his papers with a serious expression. In the spirit of international cooperation, he nodded. "Yes, gentlemen, that would work." They shook hands.

Relieved, Janusz and Jurek topped up their budget by inviting a number of foreign climbers to Shishapangma. And so it transpired that Jurek's Shishapangma expedition of summer 1987 included French, American, Mexican and British climbers, along with Janusz, Artur and Wanda.

A succession of storms confined them to base camp, where Janusz was struck down by a particularly virulent case of altitude sickness. The rest tucked in to a wide range of international cuisine, and Jurek endeared himself to all the other climbers with his cooking skills. They were a merry lot, getting along with a minimum of posturing. They rested, slept, visited, read and ate as much as possible, waiting for their chance to climb.

When the weather improved they all headed up the mountain. With such a diverse group of people, all with different goals and ability levels, they drifted off to their individual routes and camps, a situation that suited Jurek. He seemed quite relaxed on his last 8000er, confident in his abilities and no longer burdened by the race with Messner.

Jurek wanted to climb Shishapangma by a new route up the West Ridge and then ski down the peak, just to add interest. Wanda wanted to become the first Pole to climb it (she was second, just after Ryszard Warecki), and was on the standard route with Carlos Carsolio and several others. Artur was ambivalent about being on a mountain with Wanda again. He was young and strong and judged her as already past her prime, despite her achievements and her standing in the community. But he needn't have worried about being bogged down by Wanda; he was teamed up with Jurek.

Artur and Jurek made the first ascent of the West Ridge, crossing the previously unclimbed West Summit, then continuing over the Central Summit and along the connecting ridge to the Main Summit. This was the first time the sharp ridge connecting the Central and Main summits had been crossed. When they arrived on top on September 18, they were alone. It was already quite late in the day, but they were used to high-altitude bivouacs. As the two friends stood on top, peaceful and quiet, the sun sank below the horizon, releasing a kaleidoscope of hues: salmon, terracotta, vermilion, ochre and mauve.

The normally taciturn Jurek was finally moved by the experience. After eight years of wandering around in the highest mountains on Earth, he had done it. Never in his most daring dreams had he imagined such a feeling of joy as he stood on the summit of his final 8000er, the last bead on his "Himalayan rosary," as he called it. If Goethe was right when he wrote in his *Theory of Colours* that the "highest goal that man can achieve is amazement," Jurek had succeeded.

A couple of days later, after Jurek had skied down the mountain, everyone celebrated at base camp with a flag-festooned cake to mark his success. Fourteen flags for 14 summits. Messner sent a telegram to Jurek, saying, "You're not number two. You're magnificent." And so he was. His record on the big peaks was second to none – not even to Messner's – for he had chosen to do them in very sporting style. The "hard way," as some put it. And in half the time.

Surrounded by his friends from home and from other parts of the world, Jurek was perfectly content. He had achieved his dream. Even more important, he was in the mountains he loved.

❄ ❄ ❄

In sharp contrast, Wanda's reaction to her own fine performance on Shishapangma revealed scant satisfaction: "It's a wonderful moment, when I feel utterly exhausted and utterly happy at the same time. I'm delighted to have another damned peak over and done with, but that moment at the summit is also the end of something – the signal to turn about and begin to return to ordinary life. Whenever you achieve something, you're standing at the end of another road....".[50] Perhaps she was thinking of a future road for herself, one that involved more creativity and less brute strength.

Ewa Matuszewska suggested that she might consider buying a shop to sell outdoor clothing and equipment. With her fame, it would almost certainly be a success, and it could provide a career after her climbing days were over. Wanda scoffed at the idea and accused Ewa of trying to force her into a life as a shopkeeper.

But Wanda's brother Michael knew she was considering other possibilities. She had floated the idea of buying an old, abandoned castle, fixing it up and operating it as a high-priced hotel. Not a bad idea, thought Michael, but not for Wanda. He knew she could never settle down long enough to make it work. He had watched for years as she had drifted about, dropping in to the family home just long enough to reconnect between expeditions. He was amused by these events, for his mother, who was thrilled by her fame, would explode in a flurry of action, assembling the rest of the family. "Wanda's coming. Wanda's coming!" They would troop in for the obligatory family dinner and then wouldn't see her again for months on end.

By 1987 Wanda had become increasingly reflective about her dangerous lifestyle. "I take all my emotions to the mountains with me," she wrote to Marion, "so any fighting I do is with myself, not the mountain…. What you can't do is dominate the mountain. Mountains never forgive mistakes, which is why I keep up a dialogue with them…. When I'm up in that thin air, suffering at every step, I'm able to reach deep into my inner self and in those moments I have a certainty that someone is helping me."

She was expressing what so many Himalayan alpinists feel at altitude – a rational acceptance of danger, combined with a psychic bond to a benevolent higher power, that elusive third man. There are countless stories from extreme situations on windblown ridges and avalanche-scoured walls in which alpinists draw on a supernatural power that appears to come from without. Voytek, Jurek and Krzysztof had all experienced the sensation numerous times. As Greg Child explained, "Going to blow-your-mind high altitude creates a world inside of ourselves."

Despite her awareness of her own mortality, however, Wanda ultimately knew that she was addicted to adventure and danger. "I can't live without them," she wrote in a letter to Marion.

CHAPTER THIRTEEN

FALLEN GIANT

*The summit of the mountain, the thunder of the sky, the rhythm
of the sea, speaks to me ... And my heart soars.*
— CHIEF DAN GEORGE, *MY HEART SOARS*

Krzysztof had already tried the magnificent South Face of Lhotse twice
before he finally climbed the mountain on the last day of 1988 by its regular route. In fact, the South Face had become a kind of "Polish problem,"
just as Everest had been for the British and Nanga Parbat for the Germans.
Back in 1985, Krzysztof, together with Mirosław "Falco" Dąsal, Walenty
Fiut and Artur Hajzer, had climbed the Lhotse face up to 8250 metres before they were turned back. Two years later he and Artur inched a little
higher, to about 8300 metres. They spent one night in a snow cave but then
fled from the winds that battered them, rappelling three long, tedious kilometres down the face.

When Krzysztof returned to Lhotse in 1988, he was suffering from a
climbing accident on Bhagirathi in India's Garhwal region. The doctor's
report was clear: lung trauma of the chest with compression of the eighth
thoracic vertebra, a condition in which the patient has to be immobilized
to prevent further spinal cord trauma. No more mountaineering.

The doctor didn't know his patient. When Krzysztof received an invitation to climb Lhotse in winter, he responded with a yes, and then wedged
himself into a special corset to stiffen his spine. The invitation came from
a Belgian team that included his close friend Ingrid Bayens. Knowing the
Polish talent for winter climbs, the Belgians invited Krzysztof, Andrzej
Zawada and Leszek Cichy to help them with the task. Four climbers headed up at the end of December and reached 6400 metres in the Western
Cwm, between Lhotse and Everest.

Illness defeated all but one – Krzysztof. The only chance to claim the
summit was to go alone, so the day before New Year's Eve he laced up his
corset and got underway. Camp III had been unoccupied for a couple of
weeks, and the howling winter winds had destroyed the tents. He huddled
in the ruins of one and waited out the night. The next morning he continued on up the regular route and reached the summit.

It was the first winter ascent of Lhotse, and it was solo.

Going down was much harder than going up. Downclimbing exacerbated his back injury, which was now excruciatingly painful. Twenty steps at a time were all he could manage. He would then lie down on the slope to relieve the pain, a precarious manoeuvre on the steep, icy slope. Even worse, he kept falling asleep. Looking back, Krzysztof shook his head in disbelief at his actions on Lhotse. "Four months after my accident. Alone, in winter, and in a corset! But I did it." When his doctor read about the climb in the newspaper, he declared Krzysztof "stupid." Krzysztof was inclined to agree.

Krzysztof and Artur went back to the South Face of Lhotse one more time, in 1989. Reinhold Messner had pulled together an international dream team for the attempt, but the expedition lacked a cohesive approach. Each climber wanted the prize for himself, and they never jelled as a team. The expedition failed.

At the same time, a major tragedy was rolling out on the West Ridge of Everest. An 18-member international expedition led by Genek Chrobak from Poland put two Polish climbers on the summit; of the 10 Poles on the trip, however, only five returned. The mountains had been killing Polish climbers steadily each year, but usually only one or two at a time. Not this time.

Elizabeth Hawley's fall report summed it up: "Too many Poles had died."

❄ ❄ ❄

When Jurek completed his 14 8000ers, Celina was relieved. She doubted he would leave expedition life forever, but maybe now he would take a break, at least for a while. The Olympic association had awarded him an honorary medal to sit alongside all the other gold medals from the Polish government. He had been named "Man of the Year" in Poland, and most people thought Jurek would *retire* from Himalayan climbing. But for Jurek, the race had been just that – a race. It hadn't destroyed his love for the high mountains or his lofty ambitions for interesting and challenging routes. One route in particular held his interest.

Jurek was consumed by his nemesis – the South Face of Lhotse. Some climbers were calling it the most important face in the Himalaya. After his defeat on the face, Messner would declare that it would be impossible to climb in the 20th century – possibly in the 21st. Jurek thought otherwise.

He had been thinking about this face ever since he first saw a photograph in a calendar, 12 years before. Back then it was completely beyond his comprehension as a climbing objective. But in 1981, Voytek had suggested it, and Jurek had agreed that it might be possible; he trusted Voytek's judgement. Instead, they went to Makalu. Jurek had already made a couple of serious attempts, but when he heard that Messner had given up, he became excited. His competitive juices were still very much alive. He immediately applied for a permit, confident that he would have no problem finding good climbers for his team.

Jurek was in Italy, packing up his clothes at a friend's apartment near Rome when the landlady summoned him for a phone call. The news was devastating. Five of Poland's best climbers dead on Everest. "Everything changed at that moment," he said. "The faces of my partners flashed in front of me. The weirdest feeling came over me as if I wanted to take a step back, erase everything. Irrationally I felt responsible. I just wanted to hide. To be alone."[51]

He caught the next train to northern Italy, shut the door to his compartment, slumped down in his seat and held his head in his hands. His team was gone. His friends were dead.

As he pondered the situation, the rational side of his brain urged him to slow down. Take it easy. Take a break. For the next two weeks he waged a private debate about Lhotse. He even constructed graphs, with for and against columns. Finally he decided to do things the way he always did – by instinct. His inner voice was clear about Lhotse's South Face: it was now or never. Messner had tagged him correctly when he described him as the most intuitive of Poland's great climbers.

In June Jurek told the Katowice club that he was going back to the South Face of Lhotse that autumn and was looking for good partners. Artur and Krzysztof were back from their third attempt on the face, but, although they were confident they could finish the route, they were frustrated with Lhotse and had promised to give it a rest for a year or two. Artur had also been involved in the heroic Everest rescue effort and was burned out. Both declined Jurek's invitation and tried to convince him to postpone his plan. They wanted to climb it with him. Such an ascent would be the best revenge on this mountain that kept sending them home empty-handed. But not now. After the Everest tragedy, Janusz was fed up, too. Everyone yearned for the comforts of home and flat ground for awhile. Even Jurek's sponsors pressed for a delay until 1990.

But Jurek was in no mood to wait. His protégé, Artur, had announced that spring that he was going to try to climb all the 8000ers in a year. Jurek was slightly irritated, for this audacious plan would upstage his own accomplishments. Artur and his team were in the process of raising the million dollars they thought it would cost, when they received a blunt refusal from the Pakistani authorities for the permits they needed for the five Karakoram peaks. End of plan.

The removal of that particular irritant, plus Messner's insistence that the South Face of Lhotse was unclimbable, only fuelled Jurek more. Now was his chance. He knew the face; he knew a good part of the route; and he thought he knew how to finish it. But he couldn't do it alone.

Jurek was frustrated that he couldn't convince his favourite partners to join him. He was impatient, calling climbers from all over Poland. "I would either have to take young angry ones or really old veterans," he said. "I chose the latter."[52] Shortly before leaving, Ryszard Pawlowski agreed to be Jurek's partner on Lhotse.

Ryszard was from the Katowice club, but he and Jurek had only roped up together once before, coincidentally on the South Face of Lhotse. Tall and lean, with a deeply lined face radiating determination, Ryszard didn't have Jurek's vast experience, but he had a respectable climbing résumé, with ascents in North and South America, the Alps, the Caucasus, the Pamirs and the Tien Shan, and a climb of Broad Peak.

Ryszard had moved to Katowice from Northern Silesia at the age of 14 when his parents decided that his best chance for a decent life was to attend mining school. There, he received free food, accommodation and an education that included theoretical and practical training in coal mining. He worked 10 long years in the coal mines as a result of that training and considered himself lucky to have had any job at all. Even during Poland's worst years, the Soviet Union's appetite for Polish coal was insatiable.

Ryszard showed a natural aptitude for sports. At first it was judo. Next he turned to climbing. He joined the Katowice club and soon knew all the other regulars, including Jurek. For most climbers, the club was the next most important thing to family. Since Ryszard had no family nearby, the club meant everything to him. He soon began working on the rope-access jobs, painting and cleaning smokestacks along with the other Katowice climbers. Finally he quit the coal mines altogether, combining his rope-access work with stints as a climbing instructor at the local crags.

Celina recalled that Jurek's normal pre-expedition routine was a little different this time. The last days before he and Ryszard left for Lhotse were even more chaotic than usual. Jurek usually took a lot of equipment and food from Poland on his expeditions. Barrels and barrels of food! But this time he took almost nothing. Just one pack.

Celina came to the railroad station to say goodbye. She remembers it clearly: Jurek standing there, with just his small rucksack. There were so many people jostling about, attending to last bits of business with Jurek, that she never had a chance to say a proper goodbye. At one moment there was a crowd of people; the next moment the train had left. "I had no choice, so I just walked to the car and went home," she said.

❄ ❄ ❄

Jurek kept a journal on the climb.

His September 6 entry was all about practical matters: who was fixing lines, who was putting in the camps, the weather. He didn't write about personal issues, just the desire to keep moving, perhaps a little more quickly.

By October 17 he appeared stressed. "All night there was a huge wind … coming down the valley. Air pressure is jumping all over the place…. What's going on? We are frustrated. I feel like we have lost the first round. We are racing towards the time when the fall winds will come. Now we have to make quick decisions and we are going back down. At 10 we are at base camp."

Ryszard recalled that Jurek didn't seem all that happy. He was jumpy. They were both frustrated with the weather, although they agreed that the route was superb. They wanted it badly. Maybe too badly. Would they somehow be different when they got to the top? Would they be closer to the people they envisioned themselves to be?

Before they left for their summit attempt, Jurek wrote his plan for the next few days in his journal:

> 23rd and 24th – descent
> 26th – caravan back to Kathmandu
> 3rd November – Kathmandu
> 20th November – meeting in Italy
> 2nd December – back to Katowice

By October 24, Jurek and Ryszard were in the high camp. They left at 8 a.m. The weather was perfect.

Their last bivouac was between 8200 and 8300 metres. The good weather held. For days they had been battling with the cold and their private demons of weakness and fear. Now they felt a small ray of hope. Ryszard was calm, absorbing the wonderful silence. He began to think that they might just climb this face. Their long multi-month battle was nearing its end. The South Face was finally giving them a chance. He felt like one of the chosen ones who, if they succeeded, would enter into the history books of Himalayan mountaineering.

They neared the summit ridge, just a few metres from the col where Krzysztof and Artur had spent a night in a snow hole in 1987, so close to the top. There remained just one difficult stretch – a rock slab on which a light skiff of snow rested. They had a single 80-metre, seven-millimetre rope.[53] It was abnormally thin, but they had chosen this diameter, as well as dispensing with the usual second rope, in order to save weight and increase their speed.

Ryszard looped two slings over a rocky outcrop for a belay. As Jurek led out on the single line, he pounded in a piton after about 20 metres. Ryszard watched his every move. "I was belaying him and giving him all of my good thoughts," he said. "Jurek climbed on with confidence, not slowing perceptibly when he reached the snowy slab."

❄ ❄ ❄

Celina was in Katowice with their eldest son, Maciek, while their youngest, Wojtek, was staying at the Istebna cottage with his grandmother. In the early-morning hours of October 24, Wojtek had a nightmare. He was with his dad going up and down in an elevator. Up and down. Up and down. The motion was sickening. He wanted out. It wouldn't stop. Even Jurek was helpless to make it stop. Wojtek became frightened and awoke, screaming for his grandmother. It was 4 a.m.

❄ ❄ ❄

Still at his belay, Ryszard watched as Jurek inched his way up the snow-covered slab. There were only a few metres left on the face. He could see Jurek's profile etched clearly against the dark blue sky. Where the wall ended, a snowy ridge went up toward the summit. Jurek plastered himself against the wall. Ryszard caught his breath. With his hands, Jurek groped for better holds. His crampons scratched about on the smooth surface.

Time slowed for Ryszard during those moments. "'Jurek, watch out,' I whispered in my mind. All of a sudden my partner started to slide slowly along with a layer of snow." Jurek's crampon had slipped. He clawed with his axes and flailed with his feet but he had lost his balance. Ryszard watched from the belay as Jurek fell. "I was helpless," he said. "He got greater and greater speed. He started to bounce off the rock. My fears grew. I went inside myself and prayed. I could do nothing except hold the rope. Ping. The piton pulled out. He continued falling. Is this the end? My God!"

Ryszard clenched the rope in his hands, ready for a sharp tug. Jurek's weight on the end of the rope threw him against the rocks. For a moment Ryszard panicked when he feared his belay might pull out, but it held. Everything seemed as if in slow motion, but it was done in a flash. "Just for a moment I heard the sound of the ice axe hitting the rocks. I saw Jurek's red mitten fall slowly."

Then Ryszard's world stood still. There was complete silence. He craned his neck, looking down for Jurek. He should be just below. But no, the piton that came out would mean the fall was significantly farther. Maybe he was injured. It was then that Ryszard noticed the thin, worthless rope in his hand. "There was no weight on it. I lifted it easily. Up and down. Up and down."

He pulled the rope toward him. There was only a two-metre length of line left. The end was frayed. It had broken against some sharp rocks from the force of Jurek's fall.

The time was 9 a.m. – about 4 a.m. in Poland.

Ryszard had no idea how far Jurek had fallen. Jurek had been carrying the radio, so Ryszard was unable to call base camp, and their location on the mountain was out of sight from camp. Nobody but Ryszard had seen the accident.

"My partner – the greatest climber in Poland, my friend – had just fallen in front of my eyes. I had to do something."

Continuing up never entered his mind. He thought of only two things: find Jurek and get off this mountain alive. He downclimbed as carefully as he could for a few metres until he came to a section of old, sun-bleached fixed ropes. He pulled at the tangled nest until he found a decent length of not too badly decomposed rope. He concentrated intensely as he cut the old ropes to construct a makeshift rappel. He started down the South Face, rappelling the steepest sections and downclimbing the easier bits, headed for the tent, which he recalled was at 7900 metres.

Hour after hour he continued. His mind raced. The fall flashed in front of him over and over although he struggled to wipe the image from his mind. Concentrate. No mistakes. As daylight receded his world became murky. Finally it was completely dark. He knew he had to stop for fear of making a fatal error, but where was the tent? He was sure he must be near it, so he rummaged around in his pack for his headlamp. His hands were clumsy, and his brain was jumbled. He couldn't make the headlamp work. Then he dropped it. There was no way to avoid it: a second bivouac at 8000 metres.

※ ※ ※

The next morning Ryszard passed his tent in disgust. It was about 100 metres from where he had bivouacked. He continued down, and at midday he saw his friends from base camp coming up toward him. They were worried about Ryszard and Jurek since they had heard nothing for two days. Ryszard explained what had happened, and they could see he was shattered from the experience. They helped him down to Camp III at 7000 metres, and the following day they reached base camp and began a full-scale search effort. They looked for Jurek everywhere in the massive, complex maze of rock and ice, gullies and gendarmes. Their efforts were futile.

※ ※ ※

As Celina went about her morning chores, Wojtek's grandmother called her about his nightmare. Celina listened to the story and comforted Wojtek as best she could, assuring him that it was just a dream. She continued with her day.

Later that morning, there was a knock on Celina's door. She walked over and looked out the glass door that opened into the hallway. There stood Janusz Majer and his wife, Zosia. "My stomach dropped," she said.

※ ※ ※

Ewa Matuszewska remembered the day the doorbell rang and there was Wanda, standing on the step, a devastated look on her face and a bottle of vodka in her hand. She stormed into the kitchen and demanded a couple of glasses.

"What is wrong?" asked Ewa. "You look terrible."

"I am," Wanda replied. "Jurek is dead."

Wanda ranted and railed about how strong Jurek had been, about what an exceptional climber he had been, all the while knocking back glasses of the clear, potent liquid. "If Jurek can die in the mountains, any of us can," she concluded. Jurek the strong one. Jurek the dependable one. She slammed down the empty glass, wiped her tears, left the apartment and roared off.

Voytek was angry when he heard about Jurek's death. He blamed the tragedy on Jurek's blind trust in God, which prevented him from heeding obvious dangers. "And that attitude was definitely, I'm 100 per cent sure, responsible for this tragedy," Voytek said. "Jurek hardly ever failed, and when he did, it shook him to his core. Deeply religious, he would demand of his God, 'Why did you do this to me? I never did anything wrong in my life. I followed your way. I didn't deserve it. Why? Why?'"

On the other side of the world, in Mexico City, Carlos mourned the loss of Jurek, for he had become his close friend. "He talked so much with me," Carlos said. "He was so tough and direct – a bit like Šrauf. Nobody was as tough as Jurek." Then softly, with a slight tremor in his voice, he added, "Later … he was not so tall, he was losing some hair, he had a little stomach. When you saw him in the street, you would not guess that he was the best climber in the world. He was the best in the history of Himalayan climbing."

Climbers around the world were stunned that the indestructible Jurek was dead. For a while, Polish climbers lost heart and their confidence wavered. Artur stopped climbing. The entire country mourned.

❄ ❄ ❄

All Souls' Day, November 2, 1989. It was a cold, grey day with a thin, steady drizzle. The Katowice Cathedral was packed with mourners. Hundreds of people – family members, climbing partners, friends and strangers – gathered to pay their respects to Jurek Kukuczka, symbol of bravery and courage for countless Poles. The pure harmonies and clear voices of the Requiem Mass reverberated off the soaring stone walls, warming their hearts, moving them to tears. When the service ended, the echoes faded and silence settled over the church. Just then, a mournful brass salute filled the vaulted space as a small group of trumpeters from Jurek's family village, Istebna, played their last farewell. Quietly and reverently, everyone filed out of the cathedral.

Celina needed to be practical. She had to cope with a life after Jurek. They had never really planned for the future. "We didn't do that in Communist times," she explained. "There was no point. We just lived." But now the future was here, and she was alone with her two boys, aged nine and four. Because a body was required for Jurek's life insurance to be paid, the official report stated that the team had found him and buried him in a crevasse. She had the insurance money plus a bit of rental income, but she was thankful they had never developed an extravagant lifestyle. The children were her main focus; they were her responsibility, and they gave her strength. The climbing community quietly supported her, but their respect for her privacy sometimes left her feeling cruelly alone. Celina was strong. She had learned how to build a life for her family during all those years Jurek had gone to the mountains. But this was new: now she had to learn how to mourn. There was no one to teach her that.

She smiled at her memories of their 14 years of marriage. Fourteen years isn't a long time, and she knew that their physical time together was much less – maybe half that. "When we were actually together, the time was very good. It was good times for both of us," she said.

Schools began calling her from all corners of the country to come and help them celebrate when they renamed themselves after Jurek. She chuckled when Polish citizens were asked to vote on the name for a particularly important school. There were two choices: Pope John Paul II or Jerzy Kukuczka. They chose Kukuczka. These occasions brought her a quiet pride: hundreds of freshly scrubbed faces gazing up at her, asking her questions, thanking her for their hero Jurek. Even Katowice named an entire city district after him. His memory would never fade in Poland – she was sure of that.

Although she had often pleaded with Jurek to take her to a base camp of one of his mountains, it wasn't until 2009 that Celina finally made that trek. She journeyed to the South Face of Lhotse to pay homage to her husband and others who had died on the great face. Their son, Wojtek, now 30, was overwhelmed at the size of the face. After spending a night at base camp, gazing at the wall in various lights and watching the tiny figures of climbers through his binoculars, he better understood Krzysztof's assessment of Jurek's death: "He died a mountaineer's death in classic circumstances: a very steep wall, a fall, a severed rope and the final drop down the precipice."[54]

❄ ❄ ❄

As for the South Face of Lhotse, Krzysztof had completely lost interest. "There is no more unknown on the South Face of Lhotse," he said. "I know every inch of it." Ryszard agreed, and besides, enough Polish people had already died on the face. But the final word came from the expedition's deputy leader, Ryszard Warecki, with his sad but accurate statement: "Also, from the stock of best climbers, only a few are left in Poland."

CHAPTER FOURTEEN

CARAVAN OF DREAMS

If I am a legend, then why am I so lonely?
—JUDY GARLAND, ATTRIBUTED

Wanda's success in the high mountains didn't come easily. For every Himalayan giant she climbed, she was forced down twice as often, sometimes because of bad weather and dangerous conditions, but most often because of illness and persistent injuries. It happened again on Makalu in 1990. When illness once more eroded her overall conditioning, she began to doubt her abilities. And doubt soon spiralled into depression and fear.

> Dear Marion   30 April 1990
> ... I've been feeling very depressed, with my usual uncertainties about the mountain, exacerbated by doubts about my health. Writing to you helps because I know that you understand these things....

She didn't make the summit and wondered if her luck had turned. She decided to change her strategy. Instead of going to the Himalaya once a year for one or two expeditions, she decided that, with her particular physiological makeup, it would be better to do them all as fast as possible. But this would take money – and superb fitness. Her equipment was tattered; her tents were too small; and her boots didn't fit properly. She needed to find an exceptionally generous sponsor. And she needed time to train.

But at the moment she was in Asia, so, instead of going home to recover from Makalu, she headed east to Pakistan to join an expedition to Gasherbrum I. At 8068 metres, it was the highest of the Gasherbrum group, and she wanted it badly.

When Wanda first arrived at the mountain, she appeared uninterested in the other climbers. She was completely focused on her own goal and seemed to lack basic understanding of her teammates' aspirations and abilities. Communication with them was minimal, which limited her judgement of the situation, since she refused to consider any opinions other than her own. On Gasherbrum I, her uncompromising style seemed to contrast even more than usual with her personality off the mountain, which was much less obstinate and even somewhat shy. To climb with Wanda one had to be exceptionally thick-skinned, as well as clear-minded about one's own goals. Otherwise, it was easy to be manipulated into serving her ambitions. She was so focused and driven.

But this expedition was special for Wanda because she had fallen in love with a German neurologist and long-distance runner, Kurt Lyncke. He had joined a team nearby on Gasherbrum II, mainly to be near her. Their relationship was fresh and passionate, providing endless entertainment for the other climbers as the two lovers exchanged endearments on the radio. Wanda radiated joy and energy. She even confided to her friend Ewa that she and Kurt were "preparing for old age together," a highly unusual concept for Wanda.

When Wanda summited Gasherbrum I, it was her sixth 8000-metre peak. Hoping to capitalize on her fitness and acclimatization, she marched over to nearby Broad Peak, taking Kurt and two others, with the intention of racing up the mountain in three days. This would give Wanda her seventh 8000er – and all of the Pakistani peaks that she would need for her collection.

Things didn't work out as planned. On their very first day on the mountain, Kurt slipped and tumbled 400 metres. Wanda saw it happen. By the time she reached him he was already dead. She was completely shattered. She had finally found a man with whom she felt she could share her passion for the mountains, and the rest of her life. It had been difficult for her to find someone in total harmony with her – someone free and independent. She claimed to have been ready for a third marriage, believing that this time it could be for life. "He stimulated me, released me from my natural introversion and helped me to blossom," she said of Kurt. It's difficult to say whether, over time, their mutual infatuation would have faded, or if her need to climb would have exceeded her love for Kurt. But it had looked promising.

Back in Poland, she visited her friend Ewa, who broached the subject of Kurt. "Are you going to be able to cope?" she asked. Wanda looked away and thought a minute before she answered.

"You know, I feel like I don't have anything holding me back anymore and now I'm going to fulfill my plan to the full." Ewa shrugged slightly, then looked down in resignation, for she knew what was coming.

Wanda threw herself into her work: lecturing, travelling, marketing herself and her dreams and, crucially, finding those all-important sponsors. Marion worked full time to raise money for the growing expenses. Unlike many other Polish climbers, Wanda didn't paint factory towers. Her strategy was different. She knew the value of her charisma and the uniqueness of her ambitions, and with Marion's help she learned how to make it pay.

Wanda's judgement again appeared suspect as she presented her public rendition of the Gasherbrum I expedition. According to her press release she had climbed it with one woman in light expedition style. She *mentioned* a Polish Gasherbrum expedition whose base camp she had used, and she gave some credit to a "group of men" with whom she had shared the route up to 6000 metres and who had set up her Camp II. But that was it. From that point on it was as if Wanda and her partner, Ewa Panejko-Pankiewicz, had been on the mountain alone. This was not the case. Although her unsuspecting sponsors were impressed, many climbers were puzzled by her revisionism.

Throughout the confusion, Marion remained her perfect friend and manager. She was fascinated by Wanda's powerful personality, and she wasn't threatened by her climbing achievements, in part because she wasn't a climber herself and didn't completely fathom what was involved. She simply saw an attractive, intelligent woman who lived on the edge, a woman well acquainted with death, highly motivated and ambitious – a woman with enormous needs. Some were financial, but not all.

Marion's goal was to help Wanda realize her potential, but her most important contribution was in providing Wanda with a sense of stability. She organized her lecture tours, negotiated her contracts, found her sponsors and arranged her travel. A large, matronly woman, she assumed a kind of motherly role even though she was actually younger than Wanda. Their relationship was clearly unbalanced, but Marion wasn't the only one giving. Marion's life was enriched by the excitement and variety that Wanda's adventures brought. Some observed that Marion was enchanted, even in love, with Wanda. Many wondered about the nature of their relationship; although it was never completely clear, Wanda took great comfort in Marion's loyalty. Ultimately, her friendship with Marion was probably the only long-term relationship Wanda could have tolerated. As Wanda herself once stated in a lecture in Vienna, "I cannot resist the mountains, and that is why I have chosen the single life."

After Kurt's death in 1990, Wanda distanced herself from deep personal commitments. A former climbing partner observed, "Nobody loved Wanda ... a woman like her, beautiful and brilliant, reaches the age of 50 and ... she still has no one in her life." Although not yet 50, it was true that Wanda had never been so emotionally bereft. But her situation was certainly not unique. Devoting their early years to climbing leaves many middle-aged alpinists somewhat solitary, alone with their photographs, their memories and the occasional climbers' reunion.

Still, there were people who cared for Wanda. Alek Lwow was one. "Personally, I loved Wanda…. She was like an older sister to me," he said. "When I started climbing I was very young – 16. And she was already famous…. Of course I understood that we were not equal. She was aggressive. She was complicated. But I loved her."

However, Wanda's loss of friends to the mountains was staggering. In a televised interview after returning from Broad Peak, she reminisced in a flat, emotionless tone about the many partners she had lost through climbing, people with whom she had gone on expeditions or who were members of her close circle of friends: over 30 of them were now dead. "That's a tragic amount," she intoned. "Many times I contemplated … why … why I endure all of this. I know what life is. I'm fearful when climbing." She looked straight at the camera and added, "I know the value of life, and not only of my own." Then she seemed to lose confidence, dropping her eyes as she continued. "Every one of us has his own other life. We have our loved ones, but … climbing has become a part of my life. A passion that engulfs everything so that I can't quit it, just like I can't quit my own life."

❆ ❆ ❆

From 1987 to 1992 Voytek continued to search out futuristic lines, including three more attempts on K2, two of them on its West Face – his second obsession, after Gasherbrum IV. But his efforts weren't limited to K2. With a Swiss climber, Erhard Loretan, Voytek succeeded on an extremely difficult, 29-pitch route up the 1000-metre East Face of Trango Tower, and then headed to Cho Oyu and Shishapangma with Erhard and another Swiss partner, Jean Troillet.

Erhard was a favourite climbing partner for Voytek, the best since Alex and Jurek. But in 1990 on Cho Oyu their friendship was strained to the breaking point. From the beginning, Voytek was pushing to summit Cho Oyu and Shishapangma in quick succession. Erhard and Jean agreed. Their plan was to first acclimatize and then climb each mountain in one push: no tent, no stove and almost no food. Just their clothing and a limited amount of equipment. They came to call their approach "night naked" climbing.

For three weeks they waited for the bad weather to clear at the base of the Southwest Face of Cho Oyu. Voytek was a bit distracted by thoughts of his newborn son, Aleksander. The smallest things irritated him. Even the gurgling sounds of Erhard's water bottle drove him crazy. Erhard, in turn, seemed oddly aggressive and angry on the trip, sometimes yelling uncontrollably at Voytek for perceived transgressions.

One such explosion erupted over a discussion about pitons. Erhard wanted to take just two up the mountain. Voytek pushed for six.

"Okay, you take everything," Erhard yelled and threw the equipment down.

Voytek retorted, "Erhard, you lost a partner on a face for just that reason." They settled on six.

While they waited for the weather to improve, they fumed at the irritating pattern that had emerged: clearing skies at night, clear in the early morning, snow beginning by 10 a.m., then a bit of sun followed by more snow, clearing again at night. They became impatient. Finally they hatched the idea of climbing at night. The weather seemed most stable during the night and they had no intention of being on the face very long, anyway – just one continuous push to the summit. Climbing quickly throughout the night would put them in the summit area in the morning hours, when the weather traditionally broke down. Since the terrain was much easier high on the mountain, it seemed like a reasonable plan. They discussed the pros and cons all afternoon and decided to leave at dark.

They stopped at the base of the wall to cook their last meal before going up, trying to ignore the avalanches rumbling down the face. Then it started to snow. "Beautiful big flakes, coming down like Christmas," Voytek recalled.

Jean and Erhard were intent on going, despite the change in weather pattern. But Voytek had reservations. Jean looked at Voytek and said, "You don't look good, do you have a problem?"

"I think it's dangerous," Voytek replied.

"Do you have some bad feeling about going up?" Jean insisted.

"I think so."

"Do you think something might happen?" Jean pushed harder.

"I can't say that for sure, but I think it's dangerous."

Erhard said nothing.

Voytek gave in to his instincts that night and decided to go back to camp. Jean and Erhard would go up without him. Voytek started down, sad and unbelievably tired, as if he had just returned from five days of climbing. He was psychologically and physically destroyed.

As he trudged back to camp he tried to analyze his condition. He knew he had lost the power of his imagination, but where had it gone? How could he have even imagined climbing this mountain, feeling as weak as he did? Still, in this unhappy state he knew it was better to retreat and live rather than stubbornly push on into unacceptable danger. He plodded down for two hours, slipping and sliding on the loose scree, morose yet relieved. The retreat ended abruptly when he stumbled into a yak. In his exhaustion he had confused its glistening eyes with the distant lights of the tents. A short time later he arrived at the camp and headed to the kitchen tent to make some tea. Over the hiss of the gas stove he heard rustling movements outside. Someone was coming into the camp. "Who is there?" No answer. He poked his head outside. Through the murk he saw them: Jean and Erhard. "What happened?" Neither said a word.

The next day Erhard continued the silent treatment, but Jean explained what had transpired: an avalanche had roared down when they were about 100 metres up, almost wiping them off the wall. Wisely, they had turned around.

A few days later the weather changed and they climbed their new route to the summit non-stop.

They rested just one day in base camp. The next, they walked down to the valley below. Two days by jeep, and they were at the base of Shishapangma. Their plan was to climb a new route on the South Face, just left of the Yugoslav route. The style was the same – "night naked" – one single push with just four candy bars, four bottles of liquid, 30 metres of seven-millimetre rope and four pitons. They even left their harnesses behind.

Near the top they came up against a steep section of mixed rock and ice. Jean and Erhard chose the most obvious weakness through the difficulty, but Voytek spied a more interesting possibility. Although it was a steeper line, he thought it would provide a shortcut to the col between the West and Central summits. He was buoyed by the Cho Oyu climb and felt strong and confident. Besides, this shortcut looked "interesting."

It was more than interesting and, after a few moves, Voytek was stuck. When he looked up for a way out he saw that it became even more difficult. He felt that he might fall. He tried again, a little to the left. Just the same. He moved up a bit more and then realized that it led nowhere. He would have to downclimb this technical ground, which would be a much greater challenge than going up. After 100 metres he made it down, albeit somewhat shaken. Chastised by his bad decision, he headed over to the original line, which Erhard and Jean had already climbed. They were now more than an hour ahead of him, and he later described his mood at this moment as "alone and sad."

The three reached the Central Summit of Shishapangma just six days after Cho Oyu. The team had climbed new routes on both peaks. Both ascents had been non-stop and were done in alpine style. A new standard of climbing in the Himalaya had been set. It was Voytek's farewell to the 8000ers, and it was an achievement of the highest class. "After finishing a climb like this you feel a sort of catharsis," Voytek explained. "You are just a happy creature."

Despite his euphoria, Voytek was destroyed by Erhard's attitude toward him. During their end-of-expedition Swiss fondue feast, Voytek tried to express his happiness and gratitude for what they had done together. Jean was close to tears. Erhard was very quiet. It's not uncommon to experience tension during an expedition, but Erhard's expression of it seemed excessive and, perhaps, final. Voytek couldn't understand why, for he harboured no hard feelings toward Erhard. Years later Erhard expressed a change in attitude when he publicly stated, "I would go to hell with Voytek: if Voytek calls me, I will go with him anywhere."

Voytek remained puzzled. "It is funny. Before – and later. But not during." Voytek later wondered if he had been too pushy on that trip. He had specific ideas and ambitions and he had tried to convince the Swiss of them. Maybe he had pushed too hard.

❅ ❅ ❅

Cho Oyu and Shishapangma were Voytek's last great climbs in the Himalaya. His departure from that arena was elegant in several ways: he managed to save a friendship; he pushed the concept of lightweight climbing to an unusually high standard; and he survived.

Voytek's safety record in the mountains was impeccable. Despite his penchant for extremely difficult and dangerous climbs, he avoided accidents and tragedy. It wasn't because he had a particular aversion to death. "I think we should accept death more. Touch it even," he said. He had certainly touched it, but he had also been able to step back from it. He wasn't afraid to turn away from a climb. His 30-year career was studded not only with outstanding triumphs but also with hasty and strategic retreats.

Many climbers commented on Voytek's almost mystical decision-making process, and they sometimes laughed at his seemingly illogical decisions to leave a mountain. But they might have been succumbing to that potentially deadly mountaineer's illness: a gradual dulling of sensitivity to risk, combined with a sense of immortality. This desensitization can take a climber beyond the barrier that separates life and death. Voytek guarded that sensitivity fiercely, relying on it to alert him to important emotions, particularly fear.

Voytek's son, Aleksander, said that his father attributed his avoidance of accidents to being "the biggest coward in the world." Voytek readily admitted fear, defeat and retreat. Although he sometimes termed it basic cowardice, in moments of reflection he wondered if it could have been wisdom.

His safety record held for his partners, too. Dozens of the best alpinists from Voytek's generation ended up dying in the mountains, even some of his closest partners. But never while climbing with him. With so many climbers attempting such ambitious targets, a certain amount of indifference to risk permeated the community. Yet altitude paid no attention to attitude, and the tragedies mounted, sometimes because the climber's objective and his ability were not equal and sometimes because of simple mistakes with equipment or technique. Nonetheless, fatalities almost always occurred when climbers stayed too long at altitude. Most who died were solid, experienced mountaineers, often around the age of 50, and with decades of experience.

Jurek's fate was one such example. Angry and saddened by his death, Voytek was quite outspoken: "He was taking too many chances, definitely. I did not think it was proper. And the basic proof is that he lost something like five partners." He declined to say that Jurek's death in the mountains was inevitable, but it seemed predictable. At some point Voytek became afraid of Jurek: so many of his partners had died. In fact it was only during the four-year period in which the two teamed up that Jurek kept tragedy at bay. Voytek viewed Jurek's as a dead-end situation in which Jurek kept pushing higher and higher on unprotected ground. "There was no retreat for him," Voytek said. "He would never back down. He was that kind of person."

But Voytek remains puzzled by his own flawless record. "I simply don't know why even the smallest hair of my body did not fall off throughout a few decades of climbing..." he reflects. "When I think about it, I get cold feet." He looks up, a concerned furrow creasing his brow: "Will I have to pay for this at some point?"

❄ ❄ ❄

Wanda had hinted at her 8000er plan to Ewa, and in 1990 she went public. She called it her "Caravan of Dreams." Later that year she and Marion issued a press release to prospective sponsors and the media. "My project is to climb eight peaks higher than 8000 metres – Cho Oyu (8201), Annapurna (8091), Dhaulagiri (8167), Manaslu (8163), Makalu (8485),

Lhotse (8516), Broad Peak (8051), and Kangchenjunga (8586) – in a little more than one year. No woman has ever braved such an enterprise," she said, adding, "I shall be the first."

If she succeeded, she would also be the first woman to climb *all* 14 of the 8000ers, a plan that Carlos was convinced was nothing more than a marketing strategy – like his and Jurek's and others' – to find funding for more Himalayan expeditions. "This was not a goal," he said. "It was a tool." Wanda's brother Michael worried about the plan. The Caravan of Dreams was like a machine, and once Wanda started, he knew it would be difficult for her to stop.

Her first target was Kangchenjunga, a mountain she'd tried before. She chose Ewa Panejko-Pankiewicz as her climbing partner, and they joined a Yugoslavian expedition in March of 1991. They nearly succeeded, but the expedition was called off when two Yugoslav climbers died near the summit. The first mountain in the Caravan of Dreams had not cooperated.

In August Wanda raced over to Cho Oyu, sometimes considered the easiest of the 8000ers. She joined a Polish/International team led by Krzysztof Wielicki, and by September 26 she stood alone on its summit.

One down, seven to go.

She was back in Kathmandu by September 29 and immediately moved on to Annapurna's South Face. First climbed in 1970 by Chris Bonington's British team, it remained an impressive prize. On the first day of Wanda's summit attempt a falling rock slammed into her thigh so violently that at first she thought it had been refractured. But it was just severely bruised, and, by lifting her leg with her hands at each step and taking a healthy dose of painkillers, she felt able to continue. Her climbing partner, Bogdan Stefko, thought otherwise. Both he and Krzysztof Wielicki, leader of the expedition, encouraged her to go down. She said no. So the men joined up as partners, leaving Wanda on her own. She understood their decision but was still disappointed when they left her to climb the peak alone.

Dear Marion   28 October 1991
… I never seem to be lucky with male partners. I would never want to
hold anyone up or be a burden, but I was very upset. . . . I had no
choice but to say, 'Don't bother about me, I'll sort myself out.' . . .
It was a pity that I had no real friends among the other expedition
members and had not had time to strike up any new friendships,
but that was because of my own decision to attach myself to an
expedition of relative strangers and climb with instant partners. . . .

Early in the morning on October 22 she met Ryszard Pawlowski on his way down from the summit. His hesitation in answering her route-finding questions appeared to betray a concern that if he gave her too much information it would allow her to claim the summit even if she didn't make it. She interpreted his reticence as an insult. Ryszard later insisted he was just trying to remember all the details, and added, "It's a shame she didn't mention that I gave her the rest of my tea and my food."

Wanda continued up alone and, at sunset, became the first woman to reach the summit of Annapurna by its South Face. As the light faded, the valleys slipped into darkness. She rotated slowly, in a daze, staring at an increasingly featureless black chasm. Her thoughts drifted to God and the Church and the gap that, for her, had widened between them. She instinctively knew she was in the most beautiful church in the world. She could feel God's presence keenly. She didn't need incense or bells or liturgy, just the sharp, thin air.

She reached into her pack and fumbled with her camera. Although she managed a couple of pictures before the shutter froze, she was unable to get the "money" shot of herself on the summit. In frustration she threw the camera down, then she thought better of it. She stuffed it back in her pack and just stood quietly, absorbing the enormity of what she had done and what still lay before her – the descent. She did not radio base camp.

Wanda started down in the moonlight but soon lost her way, wandering off route onto some steepening ice slopes. With an injured leg and a headlamp that no longer worked, she wisely reversed her steps up to more level ground at 7800 metres where she could reassess her options. There, she dug a bivouac platform where she spent what she later described as, "quite a pleasant night in my bivouac bag." The next morning she continued down to Camp II, where she radioed to base camp to announce her summit victory.

Krzysztof didn't believe her. He had watched her through his binoculars and was sure she had turned around short of the summit. He suspected that it was an honest mistake because she was probably hallucinating. "If you say you reached the summit, I won't contradict you, but personally I don't believe it." Although he later retreated from his hardline stance, he maintained his doubts.

Wanda was devastated. This was the worst experience she had endured in all her years of climbing. They had come to the mountains as friends but were parting more like angry wolves from rival packs. Rumours of doubt about her summit preceded her back to Poland, and the media fed on them.

Ewa was in the middle of the furor, her phone ringing off the hook, journalists demanding answers. She assured them that when Wanda returned she would explain everything. She defended her friend, saying, "I know Wanda well enough. This is too large, too serious of a matter for Wanda to say she reached the summit without having done so." Polish Himalayan climber Piotr Pustelnik agreed on the seriousness of the charge, saying that it was the worst accusation a climber could face.

In addition to this new crisis, it was obvious to everyone that Wanda was still very depressed about Kurt's death. She confided that she felt more and more isolated. She had the feeling that everyone was waiting for her to slip up. Ewa observed that Wanda grew extremely paranoid during this time, categorizing anyone who dared to say anything negative about her as her enemy. A telling video clip of her shows a still beautiful, mature woman glancing over at the video camera, forcing a smile, then reverting immediately to a haunted, tortured expression.

It wasn't long after the Annapurna debacle that Ewa began working with a respected publisher called *Solidarity Weekly*. As Ewa's attention shifted to her new work, Wanda sensed the loss of yet another friend and accused Ewa of abandoning her. Ewa was probably her closest friend throughout these years, but even she admitted it was a difficult friendship. "To be close friends with someone, you need to share time and opinions and ideas together," she said. "Wanda never had time. She was always on the run." She was isolating herself, one person at a time.

Then Wanda developed her roll of film from Annapurna. When compared with other accepted summit shots, her single hazy image taken almost at dark seemed to prove her claim. The sports committee of the Polish Alpine Association declared that Wanda *did* reach the summit. Artur and Janusz were part of that committee, and both were adamant that the photo proved her claim. "That photograph means something to me," Artur said. "I had previously been on that summit and could comment on the photo. It definitely shows that she was there."

Alek Lwow disagreed. "The photograph showed nothing," he scoffed. "I saw this photograph.... It shows a dark ridge and a higher point. She was close, but not on the top." Alek was convinced that since the alpine association couldn't prove that she *hadn't* climbed it, they had to accept her word that she *had*.

Wanda was relieved at the association's conclusion, but her shock at the mistrust brought her unwelcome, ever-present companions: anxiety, loss of confidence, and loneliness. Anna Czerwińska, who had also been asked for proof of her Lhotse and Shishapangma summits, was convinced that Wanda never fully recovered from her shock and depression following Annapurna. "There was no one around to help her," she said. "Wanda's loneliness really must have been beyond human strength."

Krystyna Palmowska pointed to Wanda's leg injury from Mt. Elbrus, years before, as the main cause of her depression. "It turned out to have long-term consequences because she never let it heal properly," she said, referring to the 1982 K2 expedition, during which Wanda had marched to base camp on crutches. Krystyna was sure Wanda's leg had deteriorated steadily during the years of climbing. "At the same time, her determination rose, so the gap between physical ability and ambition was opening in a dangerous way," she added. For Krystyna this raised a red flag, and she even considered advising Wanda to leave climbing. But Krystyna was absolutely sure that any warnings would have been in vain.

Over time, several stories emerged about what might have happened on Annapurna. Nobody could say for certain exactly which day Wanda summited. The final determination was that Wanda must have lost consciousness and didn't know herself. When Krzysztof and the others saw her climbing up, that's likely what she was doing. But why? Either she was headed back up to get a better photo or she had forgotten she had already climbed it. She lost a day and almost her summit victory. There was no way to know which version of the story was the truth.

There was another factor, too. Wanda had now climbed eight of the 14 8000-metre peaks. So had Krzysztof. There was no woman even close to that. Her only competitors were men.

As her isolation intensified, Voytek was one of her few remaining friends. He and Wanda had first met at the climbing cliffs near Wrocław. She was a beautiful young woman then, and he had even been a little infatuated. They had become good friends, and although they had never climbed together, they were frequently on the same expeditions. He had watched her career, seen her develop as a climber and then as a leader. He understood her ambitions and demons, and he watched her butt heads with others in the community. He understood why people were offended by her: in part because of her strong character and her unbridled ambition. He thought her behaviour sometimes bordered on lunacy, such as the time she hobbled into K2 base camp on crutches and he and Jurek had to carry her for the last two hours. But Voytek was a loner, too, and perhaps as a result of that the two never clashed.

❄ ❄ ❄

Meanwhile, Wanda's less tolerant but equally ambitious Annapurna team-mate Krzysztof was on fire. He had never been fitter, stronger or more clearly focused. He loved everything about his life: the mountains, the physical challenge and the enthusiastic support from his teammates. The little Boy Scout had found his uniform, and it fit him well.

In 1990 he had gone to Dhaulagiri and climbed the 8167-metre peak's normal route on April 24. He came down to base camp with energy to spare. He had nothing particular to do and no place to be, so he decided to go back up onto the East Face to try for a rapid one-day solo ascent of a new line. The 2400-metre face had already been climbed by Voytek and company in their 1980 alpine-style ascent, but Krzysztof was looking at another possibility a little farther left.

Fully acclimatized from his jaunt up the normal route, Krzysztof set off alone at 11 p.m. He took very little with him, for he didn't intend to be up there for long. Just a couple of litres of liquid, some candies, his radio, a camera, four pitons, four ice screws, two ice axes and a 30-metre length of rope (which he promptly dropped). The moon illuminated the night, and he made quick progress up moderate terrain. It steepened at an ice chute, but he moved up confidently and, at the top, stopped for a brief rest and a sip of his hot drink. But the higher he climbed the more difficult it be-came. He had no way of knowing what to expect, since he'd never been on the route before. When a particularly difficult section appeared, with ice covered by loose, unconsolidated snow, he struggled for two long and dangerous hours.

"I had a kind of hallucination – not because of lack of oxygen but be-cause of the situation, because of fear," he recalled. "I felt that somebody was with me. When I tried to go right, I was looking for somebody to ad-vise me . . . it shows that in a difficult situation you need a friend, a mother or a lover. So I created one for myself."

Past the dangerous bit, he lost his way in the rocky section above, but he finally found a way out of the confusing terrain and topped out on the summit ridge at 3 p.m. He was at 7800 metres and the wall was climbed. But he was still some distance from the summit. It had now been snowing for an hour. His survival instinct clicked in, and he decided to go down, wary of a bivouac with absolutely no equipment. He found a tent that had been left by his friends and he started making tea – for *two* people. Even though he was in a relatively secure position now, the hallucination remained vivid.

Many other Himalayan climbers have had similar experiences with hallucinations, including Carlos Carsolio, who cherished them. Carlos learned that, after the first time, they became easier to induce. He was convinced that such illusions were proof of a channel opening within him. "I looked for such moments," he said. "It was a kind of spiritual addiction."

Krzysztof later admitted that, on this climb, he went beyond the "thin red line." Despite the "failure" to reach the summit a second time, his climb was widely considered an outstanding achievement and an indication of the future.

Above all, Krzysztof was fast. That was Wanda's problem: lack of speed and time. After her failed attempt on Dhaulagiri, the timeline for her Caravan of Dreams plan was now at risk. It would be impossible to finish off the six remaining peaks in the next year. Some people close to her thought – and hoped – that she might abandon the plan altogether. But that was not to be. Instead, she extended it by just one season.

CHAPTER FIFTEEN

LAST CLIMB

I never seek death, but I don't mind the idea of dying on the mountains.
It would be an easy death for me. After all that I've experienced,
I'm familiar with it. And most of my friends are there in
the mountains, waiting for me . . .
—WANDA RUTKIEWICZ, *A CARAVAN OF DREAMS*

Before each expedition, Wanda had a ritual. She would return home to re-ceive her mother's blessing. After talking about the coming trip, Maria would make the sign of the cross on Wanda's forehead. They would em-brace and Wanda would leave, emotionally prepared to climb.

Wanda was almost 50 years old when she returned to Kangchenjunga, the third-highest mountain in the world. This would be her third attempt to climb it. When Wanda visited her mother for the pre-expedition tradi-tion, Maria sensed a shift. Wanda looked like she was made of stone, as if she wasn't really there. After a brief conversation she backed away from her mother; it was time to go. Maria ran after her daughter, calling, "Wanda, wait. You haven't said goodbye! And the cross . . ." Wanda stopped, staring straight ahead as her mother blessed her. But it was clear to Maria that her mind was already on the mountain.

Carlos Carsolio was leading the six-person expedition, hoping to tick his fifth 8000er. Wanda knew the handsome dark-haired climber from previous climbs. Although she had a chest infection, her leg hurt and she was tired from her last two expeditions, she nevertheless felt good about this trip; she was among friends. Carlos knew she had plenty of problems back home, but here in the mountains she was relaxed and motivated. Her eyes were shining with happiness. The 30-year-old Carlos adored and admired Wanda's willpower and her particularly sensuous style of toughness. They would make a good team on the North Face: her experience and his youth-ful strength.

> Dear Marion, 26 March 1992
> I got to base camp a couple of weeks ago. Tomorrow Carlos and I are
> going up to Camp I and on to the end of the fixed ropes at 6900

metres, below the north col, where we are going to set up Camp II. It's a hard climb . . . there are dangerous potential avalanches and very strong winds. . . . I didn't get off to a very good start on this expedition. . . . Time is rushing by . . . I'm sitting at the ends of the earth, cut off from all the things that are important elsewhere, but enjoying the isolation. As I lie in my tent at base camp I have a vivid picture of you and I feel that you're not really far away. . . . I send you all my best thoughts and my fondest words. So far removed from you, I wish I could make them more expressive. I need you and I bless the good fortune that brought our ways together. All my love, Wanda.

The climb didn't go well. The sacred massif of Kangchenjunga, with its five separate peaks, seemed to be repelling them. The weather was wild. Two climbers on the expedition became ill from eating too many canned mangoes and had to descend to base camp. Two more suffered from serious frostbite and fled the expedition. In the end, only Carlos and Wanda remained high on the mountain.

Dear Marion,   2 May 1992
Nothing is going according to plan. We've been foiled by the weather. Snowstorms and thunderstorms all at the same time. . . . I'm a little stressed because the route isn't all that easy. . . . And I'm worried because I feel alone. I don't know what you're doing right now and where you are. I'm sending my best thoughts and lots of love . . . from this faraway place. And I am really thankful that we have met. I need you.
Love, Wanda.

Wanda and Carlos began their summit attempt on May 7. Two days later they left Camp I and made good progress upward. By Camp III, however, the snow became deeper, and their progress slowed. Carlos pushed on to Camp IV, but Wanda became bogged down along the way, so she decided to bivouac at 11 p.m. Carlos climbed through the night and arrived at the ice cave at Camp IV at 6:30 a.m. Since the next day was extremely stormy, Carlos rested alone in camp. Wanda finally appeared at 7 p.m., weary from her efforts in the blowing snow. Her stove no longer worked, and they used Carlos's stove and their last supplies of fuel to melt snow and rehydrate.

The morning of May 12 dawned clear, so at 3:30 a.m. they crawled out of their tent and headed up toward the summit. Planning to climb quickly, they left almost all of their bivouac gear behind. The younger and more powerful Carlos pulled ahead, plowing through the deep snow while Wanda lagged behind. She was climbing extremely slowly. Carlos reached the summit at 5 p.m., alone.

Three hours into his descent, at about 8300 metres, he came upon Wanda. She had dug a little snow cave under an overhanging rock and was crouched there, trying to stay warm. The night was cold and clear, with a light wind.

"Wanda, are you okay?" Carlos asked as he shone his headlamp on her half-hidden face.

"Yes, yes, I am just resting. I'm going slowly, so I will rest here a bit and go up tomorrow. All I need is some water. Do you have some?"

As Carlos crouched down beside her he could see the determination in her eyes. Still, he urged her to reconsider.

"You should come down. It's still a long way – hours – to the top. Listen, the snow is deep and the ridge is not easy and I drank all my water hours ago. I'm sorry. Please come down with me."

"No," she insisted. "I'm staying. I'll just wait for the sun and then I'll go. I can do this." Carlos could see that she was shivering inside her bivouac sack. "I don't want to come back to this mountain again. But I'm cold. Can I have your down pants? Just for tonight?"

Moved by her plea, he could do little but try to convince her to descend the mountain. "I'm sorry, I have nothing else. I need them. I'm near the end. Come down with me. We can go together to Camp IV and then tomorrow to Camp III. There we can drink something."

She refused him. "I just need you to tell me about the ridge."

Defeated and almost delirious, Carlos explained every detail he could remember. He urged her one more time to come down, but he didn't push. After all, this was the great Wanda Rutkiewicz; she must know her own limits. He could see that her mind was very clear, but she looked pathetically small and cold in her cave.

"Don't worry," she said, reading his concern. "We'll see each other below. I'm just going to have a little rest, and then I'll get going for the summit . . ."

After 10 minutes Carlos continued down, stumbling in the night, his limbs almost frozen and his thoughts running wild. He was worn out from the day's effort, and the exchange with Wanda had further depleted him emotionally. His headlamp threw just a small orb of light that twisted and writhed with each movement of his head. He knew he was on the edge, and it frightened him. Focus. Down. Live. He couldn't think of Wanda.

Up in her snow cave, Wanda struggled to get comfortable. She had no tent, no sleeping bag, no stove and no water. Just her bivouac sack, a head-lamp, 20 metres of rope, extra gloves, extra goggles and a few candies. A slight breeze had picked up and now snuck around the edge of her cave and into her thin bivy bag, draining her body core of warmth.

She had been alone on mountains before, even abandoned at altitude. But this was different. The decision to stay and climb was hers alone. There was only Carlos on the mountain now, and with each passing moment the distance between them grew.

Although nobody can know exactly what she was thinking, she surely rehearsed the route in her mind. Ahead of her lay endless snowy slopes, then the pinnacles where she would need to traverse over the ridge to the south side of the mountain, then finally the climb up the summit ridge. Hours of struggle remained. She looked at her watch. Only 17 minutes had passed since Carlos had left.

Fear nibbled at her resolve. Daylight promised bravery and hope, but night on a mountain brings only darkness and death.

❄ ❄ ❄

Carlos waited three days at Camp II, but Wanda never appeared. He left a fully equipped tent for her, knowing it was useless. On the way to Camp II he had a powerful sensation that she was dying. "She said goodbye to me," he said. "I was very focused, but suddenly my mind was filled with her presence, her femininity. I felt it very strongly."

Emotionally and physically destroyed, he left Camp II to continue down. On a short section between fixed ropes he lost his concentration and fell, catching hold of the rope at just the last moment. "Don't worry. I will take care of you," he heard Wanda's voice in his head. Sobbing, and wracked with guilt, he continued on to base camp. There were no climbers left on Kangchenjunga to mount a rescue attempt. On May 21 another storm moved in and Carlos left the mountain.

The tent at Camp II was soon buried by snow. All that was left on Kangchenjunga's five peaks were the wind and the snow and the cold.

Dear Marion,   27 May 1992

I want to share my grief at Wanda's death with you . . . as Arek told you, there was nothing we could have done. I waited for her at 8000 meters, and again at Camp II, until I was certain she couldn't still be alive. . . . I couldn't dissuade her, even though she was very tired and had no sleeping bag, no cooker, no water and no food. We don't know whether she died in her bivouac cave or on her way up to the summit or on her way down; all we know is that she is gone for ever. We loved Wanda. Carlos.

Reuters ran a story about her disappearance as soon as word reached Poland. The next Saturday evening, Ewa was home alone. She went to bed early and fell asleep almost immediately. Around 3 a.m. the phone rang. She answered it and heard Wanda's voice.

"Ewa . . ."

"My God, Wanda, where are you? We are all tearing out our hair."

"I am really cold. But please don't cry."

"Why aren't you coming back?"

"I can't right now . . ."

Ewa woke up and realized she had been in the middle of a terrifying nightmare. She glanced at her night table and was horrified to see that the handset was off the phone.

The next morning, she called Wanda's mother to tell her the strange story. In a calm voice, Wanda's mother expressed little surprise, adding that one of her friends had run into Wanda, walking down the streets of Wrocław. She had been dressed in white and was very, very cold.

❄ ❄ ❄

When Wanda first announced her Caravan of Dreams project, she stated that "living means risking, means daring; not to dare is not to live." She insisted she did not go to the mountains for life-threatening thrills but to experience "exceptional achievement." "Stuff your rucksack with no more than your needs for the next few days and head for the summit," she said. "Do in a few weeks . . . what would take an expedition several months."[55] What she hadn't taken into account was the recovery time needed between these exhausting climbs. Acclimatization was one thing, but physical stamina was altogether different. Because of this, most people assumed that Wanda simply ran out of strength on the mountain.

Or did she?

Three Italians climbing Kangchenjunga in 1995 spotted what they first thought was a tent lying on the snow on the mountain's southwest face. They looked more closely and saw that the pink and yellow tent had legs. Upon closer examination, they saw that the body was missing a leg and was nearly decapitated. Who could it be? Then they realized it was a woman. Only a handful of women had been on the mountain up to this time, including Wanda and a Bulgarian woman, Iordanka Dimitrova, who had disappeared on the mountain in 1994. They concluded it must be Wanda.

The location of the body was intriguing. When Carlos left her she was hunkered down on the Northwest Ridge. Everyone assumed that she had succumbed to the elements in her bivouac. The broken body found on the Southwest Face suggested she might have died not resting but climbing. Despite the cold and her lack of food and water, it was possible – though unlikely – that Wanda had pushed herself once again, this time beyond her limits, to somewhere around 8450 metres on the summit ridge. And then she had fallen.

When the Italians revealed their gruesome find back in Europe, they were met with skepticism. Wanda's former climbing partner Anna Czerwińska scoffed at the idea, saying that the colour of the suit was wrong. "Wanda was too vain," she said. "Wanda would never be caught dead in pink!" Carlos couldn't remember what colour her suit was on the climb, yet everyone agreed that Wanda had indeed owned a pink and yellow Valendré suit. But a small packet of medicine with a Bulgarian label that was found in one of the pockets pointed more toward the Bulgarian woman, and it was this conclusion that was drawn by many, including Elizabeth Hawley.

Because no body was recovered, and because her mother refused to believe she was dead, the official report of Wanda's death in Poland was confused and muted. Her brother Michael tried unsuccessfully to launch an expedition to locate her body. There were problems with the insurance, and the entire affair was handled in an inconclusive manner.

❄ ❄ ❄

Wanda's tragic death hit the climbing community hard. There had already been so many Polish fatalities, starting long ago in the Hindu Kush, then continuing year after year in the Himalaya: the horrendous loss of Poles on Everest, Jurek on the South Face of Lhotse, and now Wanda. It was beginning to look like a war with the mountains, and the Poles appeared to be losing.

Climbers were conflicted about the cause of Wanda's death. Her decision to stay on the mountain rather than descend with Carlos was considered rash by many. Surely she must have known she was ill-equipped to spend yet another night at altitude. There were real technical difficulties ahead of her, and she was already worn out. She still faced an entire day's climb – and then the descent. Many felt that Wanda had broken all the rules on Kangchenjunga, perhaps because she knew she was running out of time.

By the time Wanda went to Kangchenjunga she knew she was not invincible. Jurek's death had shattered the illusion that she could keep returning to the mountains forever. "Every road has its beginning and its end," she had said. But it's unlikely she had lost her will to live. She had wanted to be on Kangchenjunga, and she had been happy and content while she was on the mountain, climbing with the young Carlos. When she needed to show real strength, however, not just in getting up the peak but in admitting defeat, she couldn't do it. Her stubbornness and pride and ambition defeated her in the end.

Most Polish climbers gave her full marks for her brilliant climbing career. A few thought she had been "lucky," but they also admitted that not all of her luck had been of the good variety. Despite her sometimes difficult personality, climbers felt an enormous emotional loss at her death. They had cared more about Wanda than they realized. It was clear to most that her mountaineering accomplishments were years ahead of her time. When Elizabeth Hawley weighed in with her opinion, she was unequivocal: "Wanda Rutkiewicz will go down in history as one of the greats of mountaineering."

Still, not everyone agreed, particularly those who had come too close to Wanda's burning flame and been singed. Wanda's former husband, Dr. Helmut Scharfetter, was bitter and blunt in his assessment. "Wanda was both a child of her time and a climber of her time. Mountaineering has moved on, but Wanda was a product of the Eastern bloc system of those days. . . . Her 'Caravan of Dreams' project was like jumping off a high wall: a sure recipe for the kind of death that Wanda had always wanted. The kind of expedition climbing that she knew was as dead as she is. And she could never have bourne [sic] to live with herself as an ageing, unattractive ex-climber."[56]

If he was right, she certainly wouldn't have been the only Himalayan climber to fear old age more than pain or hardship. Perhaps she had prepared herself – and others – for this day by limiting her ties. She left few personal effects and no emotional baggage. Wanda had travelled lightly on the earth.

Krzysztof felt that this was the real flaw in her life. "Wanda did one mistake," he said. "She left husband; she left family; she left friends. She had no one to come back to. She had no job, no profession, no garden, no other interests. She had no fallback position. She had nothing. She was completely alone and there was nobody to help guide her." It's true that Wanda could walk the streets of Warsaw and be recognized by everyone; but there was nobody waiting for her at home.

Her words of advice to those mourning Jurek a few years before now seemed appropriate for her: "We should not presume to judge those who seek out danger on the world's highest places or demand to be told the meaning of what they do," she said at the time. "Simply, when they pay the ultimate price for their passion, we should remember them . . ."

CHAPTER SIXTEEN

THE LONELIEST CROWN

*The unhappiest people I know these days are often the ones in motion,
encouraged to search for a utopia outside themselves.*
— PICO IYER, *THE GLOBAL SOUL*

I've looked at clouds from both sides now.
— JONI MITCHELL, "BOTH SIDES NOW"

Poland's first real election took place in October 1990. By December 22, Lech Wałęsa – electrician, protester, prisoner and Nobel Peace Prize recipient – was now President Lech Wałęsa.

By 1995 Poland's massive foreign debt was paid off. But political reorganization hadn't lived up to expectations, and Wałęsa, who had galvanized his country and performed brilliantly as a leader of Solidarity, functioned less well in government. There were too many meetings, too much consultation, too much compromise. He was defeated in the 1995 election and replaced by a Communist candidate.

The outside world was stunned. But it didn't surprise the Poles, and it didn't particularly worry them, because an *elected* Communist government was a far cry from the previous regime that had been forced upon them. They expected results from their elected officials; the Solidarity party hadn't delivered. They searched diligently for the right leadership, electing seven different governments in as many years. It was almost as if they were revelling in a glut of free electoral votes. Progression to a fully functioning democracy was not easy. It had been decades since the Poles had been given any responsibility for choosing their own government, and their roster of experienced governors was limited; most had fled abroad. It isn't surprising that there was a shakedown period while Poland felt its way as a fledgling democracy.

But the Poles persevered, for that was their tradition. Much of their history had been a struggle for survival. The preceding 50 years had been most brutal, fighting two wars and providing the battleground for a third. Their battered nation had been handed over to the Soviets as a gift, but they outlasted both their invaders and their masters. Somehow, without violence, Poland had become the first Communist state to emerge as a free nation. Poles would then watch the Berlin Wall fall and Czechoslovakia emerge from domination with their 1989 "Velvet Revolution." It would take two more years for the Ukraine.

❄ ❄ ❄

It was during this hopeful time that Krzysztof Wielicki reached his full potential as an alpinist, spending more time in Asia than in Poland. In 1992 he attempted Gasherbrum I and led a successful expedition to Manaslu. In September of 1993 he climbed a partial new route on Cho Oyu, following the West Ridge all the way to the summit with Italian Marco Bianchi. Krzysztof felt so fit that he considered going up the mountain again, this time alone, in a day and by a new route. He was just about to start when his climbing partner came over to his tent, put a hand on his shoulder and asked, "What are you looking for? What do you want to prove? For us, you are already the best." Krzysztof was unnerved by the discomforting questions. He reconsidered, and stayed in camp that night.

Immediately after, he headed to Tibet, for another 8000er: Shishapangma. Fresh from Cho Oyu, and feeling somewhat confused and frustrated by the difficult questions raised by his teammates, he needed to challenge himself. The South Face seemed a likely candidate. Krzysztof started up alone on October 7, 1993, and 20 hours after leaving base camp he reached the summit.

Shishapangma was Krzysztof's 10th 8000-metre summit. It was now clear to him what he had done and what he could probably achieve: all 14. Four peaks remained, all in Pakistan.

He'd already been to K2 twice before, but in 1994 he returned with Voytek, New Zealander Rob Hall and American Carlos Buhler. Their objective was the West Face. They reached 6800 metres but had to turn back because the conditions were too dangerous and their fixed lines had become coated with ice. They tried again on the easier Basque Route on the South-southeast Spur. Voytek, who was fixated on the West Face, decided that the Basque Route was not to his liking so he went down. The other three continued. Hall, who was using oxygen, reached the summit, but Carlos and Krzysztof, who were not using supplemental oxygen, finally turned back, unknowingly just a maddening few dozen metres from the summit.

Frustrated by K2, Krzysztof secured permits a year later for both Gasherbrums I and II. Now a full-time professional alpinist, he was with other international high-performance athletes: Ed Viesturs from the US,

Rob Hall, Carlos Carsolio and a fellow Pole, Jacek Berbeka. Krzysztof climbed like a finely tuned instrument, and he expected a perfect performance each time. He wanted to climb Gasherbrum II in a day, as he had done so many times before. But even Krzysztof's body needed to acclimatize, and on GII he needed a bit more time. Still, he summited just four days after his teammates, alone. Next it was on to Gasherbrum I, the highest in the group at 8068 metres. Since the base camp was the same as for Gasherbrum II, the two peaks made an efficient double objective. He and Carlos, both now perfectly acclimatized from their Gasherbrum II ascent, reached the top of GI on July 15. Only 17 days had passed since their arrival in base camp, and they had already climbed two 8000-metre peaks.

Krzysztof obviously needed K2 for his 8000-metre quest, so 1996 found him back, for the fourth time. This time he approached it from the Chinese side, hoping to make a complete ascent of the North Buttress, including the top part, which had yet to be climbed. As the route was covered with loose, unstable snow, the team changed plans and moved over to the Japanese Route. That summer's monsoon had been even worse than usual, resulting in horrendously dangerous snow conditions on the mountain. If they had been prudent, they probably would have gone home. But they didn't.

On August 10, five climbers headed up from their high camp at 7800 metres. Two gave up, but three continued on: the two Italians – Marco Bianchi and Christian Kuntner – and Krzysztof. At 8200 metres the snow became soft and deep. Krzysztof was out front, breaking trail for three long hours. He would lift one leg, push the snow forward, plunge down with his foot, trying to consolidate the powdery snow enough to hold the weight of his body, then thrust his ice axe as deep as possible and repeat with the other leg. Over and over again. After a few steps he would lean over his ice axe to rest his heaving body for a few moments, trying to stabilize his raspy, shallow breathing. He would straighten his back and begin again. There was no point in thinking about this endless suffering. Just keep moving up. It wasn't until 8 p.m. that the three stood on the summit of the second-highest mountain in the world.

A few minutes were all they allowed themselves, for it was already dark. They were not expecting to bivouac and had brought no bivouac equipment with them. But it was clear they would have to, and they were dangerously close to the summit – a sure ticket to disaster. It very nearly was. Krzysztof knew he needed to stay awake at all costs, so he silently sang every song in his musical repertoire: scouting songs, traditional folk songs and war ballads. It didn't take long to get through them, so he repeated the playlist, all night long. Eventually dawn crept over the mountain and they were able to move once again. They made it down, with some help from their teammates and a nearby Russian team.

❈ ❈ ❈

With K2 completed, Krzysztof had only one mountain left to climb: Nanga Parbat. His plan was to climb it immediately after K2, joining up with an expedition led by Jacek Berbeka. But when he called his friends on the mountain, he was horrified to learn that they were already back in Poland! Because his K2 climb had taken longer than expected, they had gone home. He would have to climb Nanga Parbat alone. Climbing friends in Poland knew what he was considering, so they contacted Krzysztof and urged him to come home; it was too late in the year and a solo attempt would be dangerous. Be patient, they advised. Krzysztof grappled with his decision: Poland or Nanga Parbat. He decided he would at least go to the base camp, just to take a look. He arrived on August 26 to find it eerily deserted. Such a lovely setting, with its lush grassy meadows, but nobody there. What should he do?

A cautious climber would have studied the mountain, making mental note of the major features on the peak, the weather patterns and the best possible escape routes. A patient climber would have enjoyed camping in the meadows, revelling in the peace of mind that comes with knowing that this climb is not for now but for another time. A wise climber would have gone home, probably a little disappointed, but thankful to have survived another season in the Karakoram and excited about plans for the following year.

But Krzysztof was fully acclimatized. He had only one peak remaining to finish off his Himalayan Crown. His internal clock was racing. This was not a Polish Himalayan Crown: Jurek had already won that honour. It wasn't even a Polish first ascent of Nanga Parbat; that too had been done. Getting up Nanga Parbat, now and quickly, was a very personal goal for Krzysztof. He decided to head up the Kinshofer Route alone, but he didn't know where to start. He queried some residents of the nearest village, eliciting looks of stunned disbelief: a lone climber, so late in the season, and he doesn't know the way! But he assured them he was legitimate, explained the situation and convinced them to show him the beginning of the route.

With one pack on his back and another on his front, he started up the Diamir Face at midnight. The lower section snaked amongst a labyrinth of steep couloirs, where he found a wide assortment of rope fragments and ladders left by previous expeditions. Not knowing which were solid, he found it difficult to choose between them. By 7 a.m. he had reached the Eagle's Nest, a rocky tower that provides good protection against avalanches from above. He found a tent left over from Berbeka's team and crawled in.

Then his nightmare began. An abscessed tooth flared up, threatening to force him down to safer elevations. The pain was excruciating. He found a bottle of antibiotics in his pack and read the prescription: one pill every six hours. He swallowed four. The pain subsided, but that night's sleep was a torment of hallucinatory dreams. He thrashed around the tent, in and out of his sleeping bag, vacillating from shivering with cold to sweating from a panic-driven fever. He had lost all sense of where he was on the mountain and was catatonic with fear at every noise. Half-awake, he re-lived large segments of his life: the Boy Scout uniform he had loved so dearly; his Lhotse corset; the moment on Dhaulagiri when he had crossed the "red line"; his beautiful daughter. He considered going down but knew that was even more dangerous than staying where he was until he regained control of his fears. And his loneliness. On his first climb on Everest, everybody was cheering. On this one, he was terribly alone.

The next morning he felt slightly better, so he continued up. When he came across a tent from a previous expedition, he crawled in and melted snow and drank tea until 3 a.m. Finally, agitated and nervous, he knew it was time to go. The weather conditions appeared to be stable, with only a slight breeze. He was still a long way from the summit, and although the terrain was not terribly difficult, it was complicated. He had to focus; not only did he need to get up this thing but he also had to remember the way down.

At 10:30 a.m. on September 1, he stood on the top, 20 days after summiting K2. There were no witnesses. For the first time in his career, he felt the need to take photographs to prove it. "But you know what was most important?" he later said. "Nobody asked. Nobody asked for proof." He gazed around at the amazing panorama: the Karakoram to the northeast, the Hindu Kush to the northwest, and farther north, in the distance, the Pamirs.

Very carefully, he picked his way down the tricky terrain. It was more difficult now for he often had to face the ice, front-pointing over the steepest sections. In three hours he reached his last tent spot. Since it was still daylight he continued. Down. Down. Darkness came, and he kept going. When he finally slithered off the last bit of glacier, he was greeted with a rousing burst of fire from a Kalashnikov rifle. "The whole village was watching your climb, we saw everything, you do not have to tell anything," his sirdar exclaimed.

Krzysztof felt neither victorious nor jubilant. He had just become the fifth person to climb the Himalayan Crown, after Messner, Jurek, Erhard Loretan and Carlos Carsolio. He had started his brilliant Himalayan career as a youngster on Everest in winter, awash with the warmth of camaraderie and Polish pride in their collective victory. This latest mountaineering milestone felt somewhat lonely in comparison. Going for the record was a different experience than going for the adventure. Just as Wanda had felt after her Shishapangma ascent, climbing all of the 8000ers was simply something "done."

In a small stone house, far from his loved ones, he lit a candle and made some tea. As he warmed his hands on the metal cup, he asked himself, "Has anything changed in my life?" Strangely, he felt exactly the same: no better, no worse, no happier. No real relief. "I knew only that I would be back in the mountains," he said.

❄ ❄ ❄

There were so many iconic climbers in those 20 years of the Golden Age of Polish Himalayan Climbing. Each had their specialty and all left a legacy.

The greatest export of the era was unquestionably Voytek: the thinking man's climber, visionary and philosophical. He is remembered still for his uncompromising choice of lines. On some he succeeded; on others he failed. But his vision was always inspired. He didn't enter the race for 8000-metre peaks like Jurek and Wanda but instead made his name on the massive frozen faces, big technical walls and high-altitude traverses of the Himalaya. He was motivated by beautiful lines, difficult lines, futuristic lines. He eschewed fixed ropes and big expeditions, preferring the flexibility and independence of two- or three-person teams. And it was on the international stage that he shone brightest.

The charismatic Andrzej Zawada galvanized an entire generation of Polish climbers to expand the boundaries of what was considered possible and excel in the winter climbing arena. He made them proud to be Polish and helped them become the best in the world.

Krzysztof was the tiger, racing up his peaks. Next, he assumed Zawada's mantle, withstanding the cruelties of winter and leading the next generation of climbers on winter ascents of the highest mountains on Earth.

Jurek was one who did it with grace. The mountains made Jurek, and Jurek became the best man he could be in the mountains. During those two decades, he became a symbol of courage and bravery for countless people, not just climbers. He was undoubtedly the most famous, in part because his 8000-metre quest was easily grasped by the general public, who embraced him as a national hero at a time when Poles needed one badly. What they might not have known, but every alpinist did, was that his standards were impossibly high. For Jurek, if it wasn't a new route or a first winter ascent, it was hardly worth doing. "Jerzy Kukuczka was simply the best," Krzysztof said. Many people asked Jurek why he climbed, but he didn't really have an answer. "I went to mountains and climbed them," he said. "That is all."[57]

Equally driven, and years ahead of her time, Wanda earned a record on the 8000ers that would not be matched by another woman for 15 years. Her Caravan of Dreams plan would take nearly two decades for a female mountaineer to realize. It was in the field of women's climbing that Wanda's efforts were the most significant.

Each of these stars had his or her own *idée fixe*. For Wanda it was to be the first woman to wear the Himalayan Crown; for Jurek it was Lhotse's South Face; for Andrzej and Krzysztof it was all about winter climbs; and for Voytek it was the West Face of K2. They, and the army of climbers who joined them, created a powerful Himalayan legacy. With the exception of individual stars, such as Messner and Habeler, the Poles ruled the climbing world in the 1980s and 1990s. Their determination and pride and ability to suffer allowed them to excel, just as the British had in the 1970s and the Slovenians and Russians would in the decades to come.

❄ ❄ ❄

Russian artist Wassily Kandinsky had a theory about colour and people that he wrote about in his 1911 work *Concerning the Spiritual in Art*. It was as if he knew these Polish climbers. "Orange is like a man, convinced of his own powers. . . . The power of profound meaning is blue . . . it is concentric motion. . . . Red rings inwardly with a determined and powerful intensity. It glows in itself, maturely, and does not distribute its vigor aimlessly." Wanda. Voytek. Jurek.

They were geniuses. They knew how to live with uncertainty. They manipulated an impossible system so well that they were able to realize their dreams. They travelled, saw the world and lived lives of adventure and intensity. They had the perseverance of pioneers and the values of patriots. Their dynasty has crumbled, but for 20 golden years they were the best in the world.

EPILOGUE

Do not forget those who stay in the mountains, keeping vigil by campfires, guarding high passes. The passes you wanted to cross. Their haughty persistence, you may call it madness. But think back to those days when you had dreams, too ... Be not hasty to forget those who stayed in the mountains, those determined to last. Maybe they still tread the nebulous path that you abandoned.
— TRADITIONAL POLISH SAYING

It is December of 2009, and I am at yet another mountain film festival, this one in Warsaw. The theatre is full, but the energy differs from the Katowice gathering more than 15 years before. The audience jostles and chats as they enter the cinema. I watch the hustle and bustle and ask my Polish friend what they are talking about. Their animated conversations are about their jobs, she explains, their careers, their weekends at the crags and the mountain-bike trail they discovered last week.

I catch sight of two older women with weather-beaten faces and a special look in their eyes. "Who are they?" I ask.

"Ah yes, it's Anna and Krystyna, two Himalayan veterans from Wanda's generation," my friend replies. "And over there is Leszek, talking with Krzysztof, both here to introduce a film." They stand out in sharp contrast to this young, urban crowd.

❋ ❋ ❋

I spent the next weeks traversing the sub-zero, wind-scoured country, meeting with climbers and historians as well as with surviving family members of those who had died in the mountains. Hours and hours in kitchens and living rooms, peering at historic photographs and devouring the stories from another era. I learned that, now, in the first decade of the 21st century, Poland still claims a host of climbers, but few are active in the tallest peaks. Most are interested in rock climbing or climbing in the Alps and the Tatras.

The shift is due, in part, to the loss of experienced climbers from the golden years. An astonishing 80 per cent of the best high-altitude climbers died in the great ranges during that era, raising the question of whether there wasn't an underlying appetite for annihilation amongst that generation. Despite a few still-active Himalayan climbers from the previous generation, such as Krzysztof, Artur, Anna Czerwińska and Piotr Pustelnik,

212

there are only a handful of young tigers now. Perhaps the Golden Age climbers left an imprint of suffering and martyrdom that the younger generation didn't want to accept. Or perhaps not enough of the veterans remained to coach and nurture the next generation. Where are the great partnerships, such as that of Jurek and Artur, or Zawada and his "boys"? There remains a dearth of deep experience in that magic combination of organization, fitness and high-altitude miles.

The climbers of the past became as strong as they did by climbing in the highest peaks, year after year, for months at a time. This they accomplished despite – and even because of – the political and economic upheaval that existed at the time. Polish climbers manipulated the Communist-style system and made it work for them. They created a black-market economy that financed their climbing lifestyle. They didn't enjoy the same standard of travel as other expeditions. There was no money for Sherpas. They used trucks instead of planes and did not rely on foreign supplies. But after each expedition the climbers would split the balance of the remaining cash and return to Poland better off than when they left. "We were rich guys in Poland after the expeditions," Artur explained. That business model no longer works, because with democracy came inflation; prices in Poland are now much higher than in Asia.

Government support for the climbers has also dropped dramatically. And to make expedition climbing even less appealing, it's now entirely possible to earn a good salary and pursue a challenging career in Poland. There is little motivation to leave those high-paying jobs for months on end in the Himalaya. There is so much more to lose. As each of the Himalayan powerhouses – Britain, Poland, Slovenia and Russia – improved their standards of living and economic situations, fewer of their climbers were willing to commit themselves to the mountains. It would entail a vow of poverty, no longer much in fashion. In 1993 Voytek wrote in his *Polish Syndrome*, "Almost physically I sense in Poland the subsiding of the great mountain inspiration. I believe it is being replaced by the onerous aware-ness of a new era and the necessity of meeting its demands." Adversity shapes the best climbers; prosperity is not as inspiring.

The state of Poland itself has fundamentally changed. Now part of the European Union, Poland is much less isolated. Everyday life more closely resembles what most of us endure in the Western world – the hectic sched-ules, the multi-tasking and the impossible deadlines – making it almost impossible for even the most well-meaning to find time to connect with wild places. As 19th- and 21st-century capitalism shoves 20th-century socialist ideals aside, an increasing amount of Western junk fills Poland's streets and homes, cluttering the landscape and the mind.

With growing consumerism, the influence of the Catholic Church has also waned. As has Poles' interest in their past. When General Wojciech Jaruzelski, the man who declared martial law on December 13, 1981, went back on trial for his sins committed almost 30 years ago, most Poles weren't all that interested. They have lives to live, jobs to keep, deadlines to meet.

❄ ❄ ❄

Anna Milewska, wife of Andrzej Zawada, the undisputed leader of the Golden Age climbers, welcomed me into her home and recounted stories for hours on end in broken French, our only common language. Andrzej had died in 2000 after a short, intense battle with cancer, and she proudly showed me the journals and photographs documenting his remarkable life. Anna protested that, after 50 years of climbing and almost 37 years of marriage, it wasn't fair for Andrzej to have died so soon; he had enough mountain dreams for another 200 years' worth of life.

Most of the surviving heroes of the Golden Age have created impressive and productive lives. All have published books about their climbing careers. All except Voytek, who maintains that he will write his story when he's good and ready, when he can adequately express his thoughts, which, he feels, are equally if not more important than his accomplishments in the mountains. Krzysztof, Artur and Janusz have built successful outdoor equipment businesses, and Ryszard is a high-altitude guide. Janusz Onyszkiewicz has served his country with honour in the European Parliament, while Voytek's early smuggling activities have morphed into a successful import business specializing in Asian products. He still climbs regularly, and at extremely high levels, on his local rock crags. His Himalayan musings are sometimes nostalgic, such as when he cranks up Dire Straits on his car stereo and speeds along, remembering those precious days with Erhard, Jurek and Alex. More often the musings are cerebral, about having transformed high mountain ridges into a home for extended periods of time, about having become intimate with the mountains – a blessed place for him. But for Voytek, what's done is done. "Why brood over the past when the present offers much more mystery and charm?"

Just as they are for Voytek, the old stories are a map for Janusz, a map for new and unpredictable experiences. The people, the landscapes, the diverse cultures and the adventure – all played an important role for Janusz. So when his big climbs ended, he kept exploring on his own terms. He remembers those golden years, with their icy winds and exposed bivouacs; he looks at the photographs and feels the laughter and the tears. He recreates those days in his mind and savours the memories. But he doesn't retreat into the past.

So many Golden Age alpinists are dead, and only a few younger climbers are interested. But Artur hasn't given up on his dreams for the highest peaks.

Artur was the youngest but also one of the most motivated from the old guard. He had seven incredibly prolific climbing years from 1983 to 1989. But in 1990, he quit. He had lost Jurek, his partner, after all. He had given up on the South Face of Lhotse, and the new economic system in Poland made it more difficult to work the black market. With his wife expecting a baby and his knees giving out, there were ample reasons for stopping. But the most fundamental was that, after the deaths of five Polish climbers on Everest, and Jurek's on Lhotse's South Face, the young, brash and talented climber realized that he was not immortal.

Now, however, more than 20 years later, he again seems willing to accept risks in order to blaze new ground in the cruel Karakoram winter. In recent years the somewhat wary and still powerfully built Artur has returned to high-altitude expeditions: Broad Peak in summer; Nanga Parbat in winter together with Krzysztof; Dhaulagiri in summer; and Broad Peak again, in winter. He summited Nanga Parbat in 2010 and returned soon after for a winter attempt of Broad Peak. The allure of winter climbs remains for those who still remember the glorious taste of Golden Age climbing.

As Anna Milewska and I exchanged stories, I told her about the time I had met Andrzej in Katowice and had asked him why he insisted on leading expeditions to the highest mountains in winter. The tall, elegant Pole had looked down the full length of his meandering nose and declared, with a twinkle in his eye, "Because Himalaya in summer are for women!" His pronunciation of women, which sounded like "vimmen," added to the finality of his answer. Anna laughed, "That's Andrzej – of course you know he was joking." Maybe so, but it seems it's still only men who are inspired by his winter vision.

The two Himalayan veterans, Krzysztof and Artur, have not given up on Andrzej's dream to complete the Himalayan Crown in winter. Perhaps for both of them it is as Krzysztof says, "You can change your hobbies, not your passion. With time, it fills all spheres of your life. Winter in the Himalaya is still a great challenge. At this time of year, the mountains are a mystery, and the unknown attracts."

This is part of Poland's legacy – seven Himalayan 8000ers climbed in winter: Everest, Manaslu, Dhaulagiri, Cho Oyu, Kangchenjunga, Annapurna and Lhotse. It took 17 years to do it.

Krzysztof and Artur have a plan, to climb the rest of the 8000ers in winter with a Polish team. But their plan is expensive. Climbing in winter costs more because it's not uncommon to use helicopters to set up base camp. They have other tactics in mind, like acclimatizing in entirely different valleys to fend off the debilitating boredom of months on end in the same wintry base camp. Still, even with experience, adequate funding and helicopters, the success rate is only 10 per cent; those odds are not attractive to many.

But for Krzysztof, who already has three first winter ascents under his belt – Lhotse, Everest and Kangchenjunga – the daunting odds provide greater interest. He maintains that the most important factor for success on a mountain, particularly in winter, is teamwork. He knows there are still a few very good Polish Himalayan climbers, but he worries about their strong commitment to teamwork: they seem more focused on individual ambitions. Some Polish climbers worry that Krzysztof, also, is too preoccupied with his own personal challenges and speed to make a great leader. Like Wanda, he wants the summits too badly. Even his friends say that he's not quite ready; that he has too many personal goals. "Either you have to get older, or do some more climbing to get it out of your system," they say. Ignoring their skepticism, Krzysztof sees himself as the successor to Andrzej, a man he loved and admired and whose footsteps he's proud to follow. "Winter is for tough people," claims Krzysztof. "For those who will walk in the footsteps of Andrzej Zawada. His standards were very high."

Despite Krzysztof's enthusiasm, he has recently become a father again, and his focus has shifted. He is joined by others in a serious loss of confidence in Polish winter aspirations. Some say that there isn't enough experience in Poland, and that those who have it are either "too old" or "too fat." Krzysztof and Artur may have to look farther afield, or mentor some of the younger Polish climbers to round out their dream team. After decades of tragedies, the death of Piotr Morawski on Dhaulagiri in 2009 was another critical blow to the nation that too that too's cache of experienced Himalayan climbers. Only Krzysztof, Artur, Anna, Piotr Pustelnik and Kinga Baranowska, Poland's current favourite, remain.

Blond and beautiful, Kinga is following in Wanda's footsteps, with seven 8000ers under her belt already, including Wanda's last mountain, Kangchenjunga, in 2009. She considers Wanda her idol and mentor and admits to wistful feelings about the early female expeditions of the 1970s. "I've never experienced anything like that. There aren't enough female climbers now in Poland to make it happen."[58] But Kinga isn't interested in winter climbs. She seems content to repeat the historic achievements of previous generations rather than create new milestones for herself.

When Artur returned to high-altitude climbing, he expressed disappointment with progress in the Himalaya in the intervening 15 years. "People climb faster, and lighter," he said, "but nothing really new." That may not be completely fair, particularly in the arena of winter climbs. Although the Poles scooped seven winter firsts and revolutionized the concept of winter Himalayan climbing during the 1980s, three more 8000ers only recently toppled. Polish climber Piotr Morawski and Italian Simone Moro climbed Shishapangma in mid-January 2005, making Simone the first non-Polish climber to top a Himalayan giant in winter. His critics called it luck, but he proved them wrong when he teamed up with Russian Denis Urubko four years later to climb Makalu in February. And then came their astonishing winter ascent of Gasherbrum II in 2011 – the first of the Karakoram giants to fall in winter.

In Poland the momentum has stalled. Leszek Cichy, now in his late 50s and still slender and fit, shrugs his shoulders in disbelief at the changes. "In our days there was a queue," he says with an easy smile. "There were climbers everywhere." With over 2,000 active Polish climbers at the time, it's not surprising that the queues were long for many of the Himalayan giants. Leszek maintains that very few climbers – only 10 or 20 in the entire world – are now interested in winter ascents or difficult climbs. "The rest are on Everest," he says. Ryszard thinks that winter climbing for the Poles is doomed – in part, he thinks, due to gender politics. "The Polish Alpine Association is only interested in supporting one climber now: Kinga. The rest don't have a chance." In Poland, if it's not a new route, a winter climb or a female ascent, there is very little support.

Still, there seems to be a minor resurrection. Piotr Pustelnik finished off his 14th 8000er on Annapurna in 2010, together with Kinga, for whom it was her seventh. In the same year, another group of Poles were on K2, and there is Artur's success on Nanga Parbat. And winter plans continue for the Karakoram giants.

Yet there is a palpable difference. The magic of the Golden Age is over. It seems to have passed away, along with so many magnificent climbers. But their legacy, and the magic they created to build that legacy, remains up in the cold thin air of the world's highest peaks, inaccessible to those who do not want to climb that high, to take those risks, to reach for the same sort of greatness.

It's waiting there for those who do.

ACKNOWLEDGEMENTS

As I've indicated in the Prologue, the seeds of this book were planted 20 years ago in Antibes, France, when I first met Wanda Rutkiewicz at a mountain film festival. They were nurtured a few years later when I met several of the most accomplished Polish climbers in Katowice, Poland. Over the next couple of decades, I grew to know a number of these climbers well, both through my work with the Banff Mountain Film Festival and at various meetings in all corners of the globe. Their history and traditions, their accomplishments and motivations, and their quirky personalities all resonated for me.

I waited for someone to write their story. No one did. With the encouragement of my publisher and a few close writing friends, I decided to tackle it. I can't adequately thank the Polish climbers and surviving family members who so kindly supported me throughout this long and interesting process. Their enthusiasm and generosity caught me entirely off guard. It is because of their written accounts, their letters and photos, their libraries, and the untold hours they spent with me in person at their kitchen tables, on the phone and on email, that this book exists.

But I should be very clear that this is not the definitive history of Polish Himalayan climbing. I concentrated on certain personalities and specific climbs rather than cramming the details of this vast, complex and impressive history into one book. Many significant ascents and important Polish alpinists are not included. I apologize to any who might feel slighted or ignored.

An early supporter of the book was the Adam Mickiewicz Institute in Warsaw, an organization that recognizes mountaineering as an important part of Polish national culture. I would like to thank the institute for supporting my research and choosing this book to help represent Polish culture within the European Union at the 2011 summer celebrations surrounding Poland's elevated role in the European Parliament.

I would also like to thank those who agreed to interviews with me, some of which went on for days: Kinga Baranowska, Michael Blaskiewicz, Carlos Carsolio, Grzegorz Chwoła, Leszek Cichy, Jim Curran, Anna Czerwińska, Wojtek Dzik, Nina Fies, Roman Goledowski, Artur Hajzer, Bogdan Jankowski, Celina Kukuczka, Wojtek Kukuczka, Janusz Kurczab, Voytek Kurtyka, Erhard Loretan, Alek Lwow, Janusz Majer, Ewa Matuszewska, Anna Milewska, Simone Moro, Krystyna Palmowska, Ryszard Pawlowski, Jerzy Porębski, John Porter, Jerzy Surdel and Krzysztof Wielicki.

Many others provided brief quotes and opinions on this history, for which I am grateful: Barry Blanchard, Carlos Carsolio, Kurt Diemberger, Steve House, Reinhold Messner, Doug Scott, Freddie Wilkinson and others.

Thanks go to Karolina Born for early research; to Keese Lane and Katie Ives at *Alpinist*; and to Stephen Goodwin and John Town at the *Alpine Journal* for their enormous assistance. I owe a debt to Anke Smit of Pro-Physio for her help when I really needed it. And thanks to Lindsay Griffin, whose Himalayan-database of a mind scoured the manuscript for climbing history errors.

I was blessed with an overabundance of wonderful photos, thanks to the help of so many: Nicholas Blaskiewicz and the Rutkiewicz Archive, Arlene Blum, Carlos Carsolio, Wojtek Dzik, Artur Hajzer, Bogdan Jankowski, Wojtek Kukuczka and the Kukuczka Archive, Janusz Kurczab, Voytek Kurtyka, Alek Lwow, Janusz Majer, Anna Milewska and the Andrzej Zawada archive, Jerzy Porębski and Krzysztof Wielicki. Thanks, as well, to Roman Goledowski for helping with the Zawada archive, Marek Kłosowicz for providing photos from his film series, and Jerzy Porębski and Janusz Kurczab for providing photos from their film/book series. Thank you to Ludwik Wilczyński for allowing me to quote from an unpublished essay, and a huge thank you to Janusz Kurczab for providing the brief history of Polish Himalayan climbing that provided the backbone of the Appendix.

And there are those who provided good critical reads, such as John Murrell, Leslie Taylor, Anne Ryall, Kate Harris, Bob A. Schelfhout Aubertijn, Roman Goledowski, and the faculty of The Banff Centre's mountain writing program – Marni Jackson and Tony Whittome – as well as the rest of my writing colleagues in the program. I owe a huge debt of gratitude to Leslie Miller, Marni Jackson and Meaghan Craven for their editing skills, and to Don Gorman and his team at Rocky Mountain Books for believing in and supporting this project.

But of all the people who helped me out, Julia Pulwicki deserves my greatest thanks. My research for this book included a couple of dozen hefty tomes on Polish climbing history – in Polish, of course. Imagine my relief when a mutual friend introduced me to Julia, a Polish-Canadian physicist living in Calgary, who climbs! We spent most of one winter together as she translated countless pages of fascinating stuff. If Julia ever tires of her physics experiments, I know she will have an excellent future as a translator.

And finally, I thank my husband, Alan, whose patience with me when I disappeared into the world of Polish climbing bordered on saintly.

APPENDIX

CHRONOLOGY OF MAJOR POLISH HIMALAYAN CLIMBS
(1971–1996)

Year	Goal	Leader & Members	Achievement
1971	Karakoram, Kunyang Chhish (7852 m)	Andrzej Zawada 13 members	**Kunyang Chhish** 1st ascent: Zygmunt A. Heinrich, Jan Stryczynski, Ryszard Szafirski, Andrzej Zawada, 26.08.1971
1972	Hindu Kush, Noshaq (7492 m)	Janusz Kurczab 11 members	**Noshaq** Southwest Face 1st ascent: Jan Holnicki-Szulc, Janusz Kurczab, Krzysztof Zdzitowiecki, 20–22.08.1972
1972	Hindu Kush, Akher Čagh (7017 m) Koh-e-Tez (7015 m)	Ryszard Koziol 10 members	**Akher Čagh** Northeast Face 1st ascent: Piotr Jasiński, Marek Kowalczyk, Voytek Kurtyka, 3–5.09.1972; **Koh-e-Tez** North Ridge 1st ascent: Alicja Bednarz, Ryszard Koziol, Voytek Kurtyka, 25.08.1972
1973	Hindu Kush, Noshaq (7492 m)	Andrzej Zawada 10 members	**Noshaq** 1st winter ascent: Andrzej Zawada, Tadeusz Piotrowski, 13.02.1973.
1974	Nepal Himalaya, Kangbachen (7902 m)	Piotr Młotecki 15 members	**Kangbachen** 1st ascent: Wojciech Branski, Wiesław Klaput, Marek Malatyński, Kazimierz Olech, Zbigniew Rubinowski, 26.05.1974
1974	Karakoram, Shispare Sar (7611 m)	Polish–German Expedition Janusz Kurczab 14 members	**Shispare Sar** 1st ascent: Hubert Bleicher (DE), Leszek Cichy, Marek Grochowski, Jan Holnicki-Szulc, Andrzej Młynarczyk, Herbert Oberhofer (DE), Jacek Poreba, 21.07.1974 **Ghenta Sar** (7090 m) 1st ascent: Janusz Kurczab, 21.07.1974
1975	Karakoram, Broad Peak Central (8011 m)	Janusz Fereński 15 members	**Broad Peak Central** 1st ascent: Kazimierz Glazek, Marek Kesicki, Janusz Kulis, Bogdan Nowaczyk, Andrzej Sikorski, 28.07.1975

Year	Goal	Leader & Members	Achievement
1975	Karakoram, Gasherbrum III (7952 m) Gasherbrum II (8034 m)	Wanda Rutkiewicz 15 members	**Gasherbrum III** 1st ascent: Alison Chadwick-Onyszkiewicz, Wanda Rutkiewicz, Janusz Onyszkiewicz, Krzysztof Zdzitowiecki, 11.08.1975 **Gasherbrum II** Northwest Face 1st ascent (upper part): Leszek Cichy, Janusz Onyszkiewicz, Krzysztof Zdzitowiecki, 1.08.1975 **Gasherbrum II** 1st female ascent: Halina Krüger-Syrokomska, Anna Okopińska, 12.08.1975
1976	Karakoram, K2 (8611 m)	Janusz Kurczab 19 members	**K2** Northeast Ridge (new route to 8400 m): Genek Chrobak, Wojciech Wróż.
1977	Hindu Kush, Koh-e-Bandaka (6843 m) Koh-e-Mandaras (6631 m)	Polish–British Expedition Andrzej Zawada 9 members	**Koh-e-Bandaka** Northeast Face 1st ascent: Voytek Kurtyka, John Porter (GB), Alex MacIntyre (GB), 9–14.08.1977 **Koh-e-Mandaras** North Face 1st ascent: Piotr Jasiński, Terry King (GB), Marek Kowalczyk, Andrzej Zawada, 10–14.08.1977
1978	Nepal Himalaya, Kangchenjunga South Peak (8476 m), Kangchenjunga Central Peak (8473 m)	Piotr Młotecki 25 members	**Kangchenjunga** South Peak 1st ascent: Genek Chrobak, Wojciech Wróż, 19.05.1978 **Kangchenjunga** Central Peak 1st ascent: Wojciech Brański, Zygmunt A. Heinrich, Kazimierz Olech, 23.05.1978
1978	Garhwal Himalaya, Changabang (6864 m)	Polish–British Expedition Voytek Kurtyka 5 members	**Changabang** South Face 1st ascent: Voytek Kurtyka, Alex MacIntyre (GB), John Porter (GB), Krzysztof Zurek, 20–27.09.1978

Year	Goal	Leader & Members	Achievement
1978	Hindu Kush, Tirich Mir East (7692 m)	Stanisław Rudziński Polish–Yugoslav Expedition 15 members	**Tirich Mir East** 1st ascent: Jerzy Kukuczka, Tadeusz Piotrowski, 10.08.1978; 2nd ascent: Michał Wroczyński, Miro Stebe (Yug) Matjaź Veselko (Yug), 11.08.1978; 3rd ascent: Vinko Berćić, Janez Śuśerśić, Jerzy Ożóg, 13.08.1978.
1978	Nepal Himalaya, Mt. Everest (8848 m)	Karl Herrligkoffer German–French Expedition 1 Polish member	**Mt. Everest** (13 members summited) 1st ascent by a European woman, 1st ascent by a Pole and 3rd ascent by a woman: Wanda Rutkiewicz, 10.16.1978.
1979	Nepal Himalaya, Ngadi Chuli (7835 m)	Ryszard Szafirski 6 members	**Ngadi Chuli** 1st ascent: Ryszard Gajewski, Maciej Pawlikowski, 08.05.1979
1979	Karakoram, Rakaposhi (7788 m)	Sher Khan Ryszard Kowalewski 7 Polish members 5 Pakistani members	**Rakaposhi** 2nd ascent new route from the north: Ryszard Kowalewski, Tadeusz Piotrowski, Sher Khan, 1.07.1979; 3rd ascent: Andrzej Bieluń, Jacek Gronczewski, Jerzy Tillak, 2.07.1979; 4th ascent: Anna Czerwińska, Krystyna Palmowska, 5.07.1979.
1979–1980	Nepal Himalaya, Mt. Everest (8848 m)	Andrzej Zawada 20 members	**Mt. Everest** 1st winter ascent: Leszek Cichy, Krzysztof Wielicki, 17.02.1980
1980	Nepal Himalaya, Dhaulagiri (8167 m)	International Expedition Voytek Kurtyka 4 members	**Dhaulagiri** East Face 1st ascent: René Ghilini (FR), Voytek Kurtyka, Alex MacIntyre (GB), Ludwik Wilczyński, 18.05.1980
1980	Nepal Himalaya, Mount Everest (8848 m)	Andrzej Zawada 15 members	**Mount Everest** South Pillar 1st ascent: Andrzej Czok, Jerzy Kukuczka, 19.05.1980
1980	Karakoram, Yazghil Dome South (7440 m) Distaghil Sar East (7700 m)	Ryszard Kowalewski 5 members	**Yazghil Dome South** 1st ascent (in alpine style), Andrzej Bieluń, Jacek Gronczewski, Ryszard Kowalewski Tadeusz Piotrowski, Jerzy Tillak, 25.07.1980. **Distaghil Sar East** 1st ascent (in alpine style), the same team, 26.07.1980.

Year	Goal	Leader & Members	Achievement
1981	Nepal Himalaya, Annapurna (8091 m)	Ryszard Szafirski 8 members	**Annapurna** South Face (new route): Maciej Berbeka, Bogusław Probulski, 23.05.1981
1981	Nepal Himalaya, Makalu (8485 m)	Voytek Kurtyka 3 members	**Makalu** Northwest Ridge (new route): Jerzy Kukuczka, 15.10.1981
1981	Karakoram, Masherbrum Southwest (7806 m)	Piotr Młotecki 8 members	**Masherbrum Southwest** 1st ascent, Andrzej Heinrich, Marek Malatyński, Przemysław Nowacki, 17.09.1981.
1982	Nepal Himalaya, Makalu (8485 m)	Adam Bilczewski 20 members	**Makalu** West Face 1st ascent: Andrzej Czok, 10.10.1982
1983	Karakoram, Gasherbrum II East (7758 m) Gasherbrum II (8034 m) Gasherbrum I (8080 m)	Jerzy Kukuczka, Voytek Kurtyka	**Gasherbrum II East** 1st ascent, 23.06.1983; **Gasherbrum II East–Gasherbrum II** traverse, 29.06–1.07.1983; **Gasherbrum I** Southwest Face 1st ascent, 20–23.07.1983
1983	Karakoram, Broad Peak (8051 m)	Anna Czerwińska, Krystyna Palmowska	**Broad Peak** 1st female ascent: Krystyna Palmowska, 30.06.1983
1983	Garhwal Himalaya, Thalay Sagar (6904 m)	Polish-Norwegian Expedition Janusz Skorek	**Thalay Sagar** Northeast Pillar 1st ascent: Andrzej Czok, Hans-Christian Doseth (NO), Frode Guldal (NO), Havard Nesheim (NO), Janusz Skorek, 16–23.08.1983
1983	Garhwal Himalaya, Meru North (6400 m)	Danuta Wach 6 female members	**Meru North** 1st female ascent: Aniela Lukaszewska, Ewa Panejko-Pankiewicz, Danuta Wach, 8.09.1983; Monika Niedbalska, Ewa Szcześniak, 15.09.1983
1983	Kishtwar Himalaya, Arjuna (6230 m)	Bogumil Slama 7 members	**Arjuna** 1st ascent: Tomasz Bender, Przemyslaw Piasecki (West Face of **Arjuna South**), 12–17.08.1983; Jerzy Barszczewski, Mirosław Dąsal, Zbigniew Skierski (West Face of **Arjuna Central**), 14–18.08.1983

Year	Goal	Leader & Members	Achievement
1983	Karakoram, Batura Sar V (7531 m) Batura Sar VI (7462 m)	Władysław Wisz 12 members	**Batura Sar V** 1st ascent: Zygmunt A. Heinrich, Marek Kowalczyk, Volker Stahlbohn (D), 31.08.1983; **Batura Sar VI** 1st ascent: Jan Jaworski, Paweł Mularz, Andrzej Paulo, 2.09.1983
1983	Nepal Himalaya, Mt. Api (7132 m)	Tadeusz Piotrowski 8 members	**Mt. Api** 1st winter ascent: Andrzej Bieluń, Tadeusz Piotrowski, 24.12.1983
1983–1984	Nepal Himalaya, Manaslu (8163 m)	Lech Korniszewski 11 members	**Manaslu** 1st winter ascent: Maciej Berbeka, Ryszard Gajewski, 12.01 1984
1984	Karakoram, Broad Peak North (7490 m) Broad Peak Central (8011 m) Broad Peak Main (8051 m)	Jerzy Kukuczka Voytek Kurtyka	**Broad Peak North** West Rib 1st ascent: Jerzy Kukuczka, Voytek Kurtyka, 13–15.07.1984; **Broad Peak North–Broad Peak Central–Broad Peak Main** traverse 1st ascent: Voytek Kurtyka, Jerzy Kukuczka, 13–17.07.1984
1984	Karakoram, Broad Peak (8051 m)	Janusz Majer 4 members	**Broad Peak** fastest ascent (from ABC to the summit and back in one day): Krzysztof Wielicki, 14.07.1984
1984	Nepal Himalaya, Manaslu (8163 m)	Janusz Kulis 8 members	**Manaslu** South Ridge 1st ascent: Aleksander Lwow, Krzysztof Wielicki, 20.10.1984
1984	Nepal Himalaya, Yalung Kang (8505 m)	Tadeusz Karolczak 10 members	**Yalung Kang** South Pillar 1st ascent: Tadeusz Karolczak, Wojciech Wróż, 7.10.1984; Leszek Cichy, Przemyslaw Piasecki, 10.10.1984
1984–1985	Nepal Himalaya, Dhaulagiri (8167 m)	Adam Bilczewski 10 members	**Dhaulagiri** 1st winter ascent: Andrzej Czok, Jerzy Kukuczka, 21.01.1985
1984–1985	Nepal Himalaya, Cho Oyu (8201 m)	Andrzej Zawada 13 members	**Cho Oyu** 1st winter ascent (by new route – Southeast Pillar): Maciej Berbeka, Maciej Pawlikowski, 12.02.1985; Zygmunt A. Heinrich, Jerzy Kukuczka, 15.02.1985
1985	Western Himalaya, Nanga Parbat (8126 m)	Pawel Mularz 13 members	**Nanga Parbat** Southeast Pillar 1st ascent: Carlos Carsolio (MX), Zygmunt A. Heinrich, Jerzy Kukuczka, Sławomir Łobodziński, 13.07.1985

Year	Goal	Leader & Members	Achievement
1985	Western Himalaya, Nanga Parbat (8126 m)	Dobrosława Wolf 5 female members	**Nanga Parbat** third female ascent: Anna Czerwińska, Krystyna Palmowska, Wanda Rutkiewicz, 15.07.1985
1985	Karakoram, Gasherbrum IV (7925 m)	Voytek Kurtyka Robert Schauer (AT)	**Gasherbrum IV** West Face 1st ascent: Voytek Kurtyka, Robert Schauer, 13–20.07.1985
1985–1986	Nepal Himalaya, Kangchenjunga (8586 m)	Andrzej Machnik 20 members	**Kangchenjunga** 1st winter ascent: Jerzy Kukuczka, Krzysztof Wielicki, 11.01.1986
1986	Karakoram, K2 (8611 m)	International Expedition Maurice Barrard (FR) 4 members	**K2** 1st female ascent: Wanda Rutkiewicz, Liliane Barrard (FR), 23.06.1986
1986	Karakoram, K2 (8611 m)	International Expedition Karl M. Herrligkoffer (DK)	**K2** South Face 1st ascent: Jerzy Kukuczka, Tadeusz Piotrowski, 3–8.07.1986
1986	Karakoram, K2 (8611 m)	Janusz Majer 8 members	**K2** Southwest Pillar *Magic Line* 1st ascent: Petr Bozik (SK), Przemyslaw Piasecki, Wojciech Wróż, 3.08.1986
1986	Nepal Himalaya, Manaslu (8163 m)	Jerzy Kukuczka 5 members	**Manaslu** East Pinnacle (7992 m) 1st ascent: Carlos Carsolio (MX), Artur Hajzer, Jerzy Kukuczka, 9.11.1986 **Manaslu** Northeast Face and East Ridge (new route): Artur Hajzer, Jerzy Kukuczka, 10.11.1986
1986–1987	Nepal Himalaya, Annapurna (8091 m)	Jerzy Kukuczka 6 members	**Annapurna** 1st winter ascent: Artur Hajzer, Jerzy Kukuczka, 3.02.1987
1987	Tibet Himalaya, Shishapangma (8027 m)	Jerzy Kukuczka 13 members	**Shishapangma** West Ridge 1st ascent: Artur Hajzer, Jerzy Kukuczka, 18.09.1987
1987–1988	Nepal Himalaya, Langtang Lirung (7225 m)	Wojciech Maslowski 10 members	**Langtang Lirung** 1st winter ascent: Mikołaj Czyżewski, Kazimierz Kiszka, Adam Potoczek, 3.01.1988

Year	Goal	Leader & Members	Achievement
1988	Karakoram, Haramosh (7397 m)	Janusz Baranek 10 members	**Haramosh** 1st ascent (from the south), Mieczysław Jarosz, Kazimierz Malczyk, Marek Pronobis, 28.07.1988; Janusz Baranek, Andrzej Mostek, Kazimierz Wszołek, 30.07.1988.
1988	Karakoram, Trango Tower (6238 m)	Voytek Kurtyka, Erhard Loretan (CH)	**Trango Tower** East Face 1st ascent: Voytek Kurtyka, Erhard Loretan (CH), 13.07.1988
1988	Nepal Himalaya, Annapurna (8091 m)	Jerzy Kukuczka 13 members	**Annapurna I East** (8010 m) South Face and East Ridge (new route): Artur Hajzer, Jerzy Kukuczka, 13.10.1988
1988–1989	Nepal Himalaya, Lhotse (8516 m)	International Expedition Herman Detienne (BE)	**Lhotse** 1st winter ascent: Krzysztof Wielicki, 31.12.1988
1990	Nepal Himalaya, Dhaulagiri (8167 m)	Krzysztof Wielicki 6 members	**Dhaulagiri** East Face (new route): Krzysztof Wielicki, 9–10.05.1990
1990	Tibet Himalaya, Cho Oyu (8201 m)	Voytek Kurtyka, Erhard Loretan (CH), Jean Troillet (CH)	**Cho Oyu** Southwest Face 1st ascent: Voytek Kurtyka, Erhard Loretan (CH), Jean Troillet (CH), 21.09.1990
1990	Tibet Himalaya, Shishapangma Central (8008 m)	Voytek Kurtyka, Erhard Loretan CH), Jean Troillet (CH)	**Shishapangma** Southwest Face (new route): Voytek Kurtyka, Erhard Loretan (CH), Jean Troillet (CH), 3.10.1990
1993	Tibet Himalaya, Shishapangma (8027 m)	Krzysztof Wielicki	**Shishapangma** Southwest Face (new route): Krzysztof Wielicki, 7.10.1993
1996	Nepal Himalaya, Annapurna (8091 m)	Waldemar Soroka, 13 members	**Annapurna** Northwest Ridge 1st ascent: Andrzej Marciniak, Władysław Terzyul (UA), 20.10.1996

POLES WHO CLIMBED ALL PEAKS ABOVE 8000 M

Name	First	Last	O₂ Used
Jerzy Kukuczka	1979	1987	Everest
Krzysztof Wielicki	1980	1996	Everest (winter)
Piotr Pustelnik	1990	2010	Everest, K2, Kangchenjunga, Lhotse, Makalu, Manaslu, Annapurna

NOTES

1 Barbary Rusowicz, *Wszystko o Wandzie Rutkiewicz*, 1992.

2 Gertrude Reinisch, *Wanda Rutkiewicz: A Caravan of Dreams*, 2000.

3 Ewa Matuszewska, *Uciec jak najwyżej: nie dokończone życie Wandy Rutkiewicz (Escaping to the Highest: The Unfinished Life of Wanda Rutkiewicz)*, 1999.

4 *Bularz 91*, Klub Wysokogórski Gliwice.

5 Ibid.

6 Reinisch, 2000.

7 Wanda Rutkiewicz, *Na jednej linie*, 1986.

8 Anna Milewska, *Zyciez Zawada*, 2009.

9 Reinisch, 2000.

10 Ewa Matuszewska, *Lider: górskim szlakiem Andrzeja Zawady*, 2003.

11 Jerzy Porębski, *Polskie Himalaje:Women in the Mountains*, Artica, 2008.

12 Reinisch, 2000.

13 Thomasz Hreczuch, *Prostowanie zwojów*, 2006.

14 Jerzy Kukuczka, *My Vertical World*, 1992.

15 Reinisch, 2000.

16 Anna Milewska, *Zyciez Zawada*, 2009.

17 Kukuczka, 1992.

18 Ibid.

19 Reinisch, 2000.

20 Kukuczka, 1992.

21 Artur Hajzer, *Atak rozpaczy*, 1994.

22 Alex MacIntyre, "Broken English," *Mountain* no. 77 (1981).

23 Voytek Kurtyka, "The Gasherbrums Are Lonely," *Mountain* no. 97 (May–June 1984).

24 Marek Kłosowicz, *Ścieżka gór (Way of the Mountain): Wojciech Kurtyka*, TVN, S.A. Poland, 2007.

25 Voytek Kurtyka, "The Gasherbrums Are Lonely," 1984.

26 Voytek Kurtyka, "The Path of the Mountain," *Bularz 88–89*.

27 Ibid.

28 Reinisch, 2000.

29 Voytek Kurtyka, "The Shining Wall of Gasherbrum IV," *American Alpine Journal* (1986).

30 Johnny Cash covered "Hurt" on his 2002 album *American IV: The Man Comes Around*. "Hurt" was written by Nine Inch Nails' Trent Reznor and was first recorded by Nine Inch Nails on their 1994 album *The Downward Spiral*.

31 Greg Child, "Seeking the Balance: A Profile of Doug Scott, the Great Survivor," *Mixed Emotions*, 1993.

32 Greg Child, "Between the Hammer and the Anvil," *Mixed Emotions*, 1993.

33 Voytek Kurtyka, "The Shining Wall," *Alpinist* no. 2 (Spring 2004).

34 Kukuczka, 1992.

35 Hajzer, 1994.

36 Jim Curran, *K2: Triumph and Tragedy*, 1987.

37 Ibid.

38 Reinisch, 2000.

39 Ibid.

40 Curran, 1987.

41 Reinisch, 2000.

42 Twenty-three years passed between K2's first and second ascents, and, even today, climbers who reach the summit have a one in 10 chance of not returning alive.

43 Kukuczka, 1992.

44 Jerzy Porębski, *Polskie Himalaje: The Great Tragedies*, 2008.

45 Ibid.

46 Ludwik Wilczyński, *The Polish Himalayan Boom 1971–79*, unpublished.

47 Reinisch, 2000.

48 Ibid.

49 Rusowicz, 1992.

50 Reinisch, 2000.

51 Jerzy Kukuczka, *Mój pionowy świat*, 1995.

52 Ibid.

53 Numerous reports erroneously describe the rope as six millimetre and used, purchased in a Kathmandu second-hand equipment shop. Ryszard confirms that it was seven millimetre and new.

54 Kukuczka, 1992.

55 Reinisch, 2000.

56 Ibid.

57 Kukuczka, 1992.

58 Jerzy Porębski, *Polskie Himalaje: Women in the Mountains*, Artica, 2008.

SELECT BIBLIOGRAPHY & SOURCES

BOOKS

Ardito, Stefano. *History of the Great Mountaineering Adventures*. Vercelli, Italy: White Star, 2000.

Atanasow, Piotr, et al., eds. Ewa Abgarowicz et al., photo eds. *Wprowadzenie*. Vol. 1 of *Wielka encyklopedia gór i alpiniszmu*, Małgorzaty i Jana Kiełkowskich, general eds. Katowice: Stapis, 2003.

———. *Góry Azji*. Vol. 2 of *Wielka encyklopedia gór i alpiniszmu*, Małgorzaty i Jana Kiełkowskich, general eds. Katowice: Stapis, 2005.

———. *Góry Europy*. Vol. 3 of *Wielka encyklopedia gór i alpiniszmu*, Małgorzaty i Jana Kiełkowskich, general eds. Katowice: Stapis, 2007.

Birkett, Bill, and Bill Peascod. *Women Climbing: 200 Years of Achievement*. London: A & C Black, 1989.

Child, Greg. *Mixed Emotions: Mountaineering Writings of Greg Child*. Seattle: The Mountaineers, 1993.

Coffey, Maria. *Explorers of the Infinite: The Secret Spiritual Lives of Extreme Athletes, and What They Reveal About Near-Death Experiences, Psychic Communication, and Touching the Beyond*. New York: Tarcher Penguin, 2008.

Craig, Robert W. *Storm and Sorrow in the High Pamirs*. New York: Simon & Schuster, 1977.

Curran, Jim. *K2: The Story of the Savage Mountain*. London: Hodder & Stoughton, 1995.

———. *K2: Triumph and Tragedy*. Seattle: The Mountaineers, 1987.

Czerwińska, Anna. *GórFanka: Moje ABC w skale i lodzie*. Warszawa: Annapurna, 2008.

———. *GórFanka: Na szczytach Himalajów*. Warszawa: Annapurna, 2008.

Davies, Norman. *God's Playground: A History of Poland*. Rev. ed., vol. 2, *1795 to the Present*. Oxford and New York: Oxford University Press, 2005.

Diemberger, Kurt. *The Endless Knot: K2, Mountain of Dreams and Destiny*. London: Grafton Books, 1991.

Echevarria, Evelio, et al., eds. *Góry Ameryki*. Vol. 4 of *Wielka encyklopedia gór i alpiniszmu*, Małgorzaty i Jana Kiełkowskich, general eds. Katowice: Stapis, 2009.

Fanshawe, Andy, and Stephen Venables. *Himalaya Alpine-Style: The Most Challenging Routes on the Highest Peaks*. London: Hodder & Stoughton, 1995.

Hajzer, Artur. *Atak rozpaczy*. Gliwice: EXPLO, 1994.

Hreczuch, Thomasz. *Prostowanie zwojów*. Warszawa: Annapurna; Katowice: Stapis, 2006.

Isserman, Maurice, and Stewart Weaver, with sketches by Dee Molenaar. *Fallen Giants: A History of Himalayan Mountaineering from the Age of Empire to the Age of Extremes.* New Haven: Yale University Press, 2008.

Kandinsky, Wassily. *Concerning the Spiritual in Art.* New York: Dover, 1977. First published 1911 by R. Piper & Co. Verlag, Munich, as *Über das Geistige in der Kunst.*

Kukuczka, Jerzy. *My Vertical World: Climbing the 8000-Metre Peaks.* Seattle: The Mountaineers, 1992.

———. *Mój pionowy świat, czyli 14 x 8000 metrów.* London: Wydawnictwo ATI, 1995.

Łubieński, Tomasz. *Pocztówka.* Warszawa: Czytelnik, 1962. Reprinted in *Bularz 91.*

Lwow, Aleksander. *Zwyciężyć znaczy przeżyć.* Krakow: Hudowski & Marcisz, 1994.

Matuszewska, Ewa. *Lider: górskim szlakiem Andrzeja Zawady.* Warszawa: Iskry, 2003.

———. *Uciec jak najwyżej: nie dokończone życie Wandy Rutkiewicz (Escaping to the Highest: The Unfinished Life of Wanda Rutkiewicz).* Warszawa: Iskry, 1999.

McDonald, Bernadette, ed. *Extreme Landscape: The Lure of Mountain Spaces.* Washington, DC: National Geographic Society, 2002.

McDonald, Bernadette, and John Amatt, eds. *Voices from the Summit: The World's Greatest Mountaineers on the Future of Climbing.* Washington, DC: Adventure Press, National Geographic, in association with The Banff Centre for Mountain Culture, 2000.

Milewska, Anna. *Życie z Zawadą.* Warszawa: Oficyna Wydawnicza Łośgraf, 2009.

O'Connell, Nicholas. *Beyond Risk: Conversations with Climbers.* Seattle: The Mountaineers, 1993.

Pawłowski, Ryszard. *Smak gór.* Seria Literatura Górska na Świecie. Katowice: Infomax, 2004.

Reinisch, Gertrude. *Wanda Rutkiewicz: A Caravan of Dreams.* Ross-on-Wye, UK: Carreg Ltd., 2000.

Rusowicz, Barbara. *Wszystko o Wandzie Rutkiewicz.* Toruń: Comer & Ekolog; Piła: ZG, 1992.

Rutkiewicz, Wanda. *Na jednej linie.* Warszawa: Krajowa Agencja Wydawnicza, 1986.

Sale, Richard, and John Cleare. *Climbing the World's 14 Highest Mountains: The History of the 8000-metre Peaks.* Seattle: The Mountaineers Books, 2000.

Salkeld, Audrey, ed. *World Mountaineering.* Vancouver: Raincoast Books, 1998.

Viesturs, Ed, with David Roberts. *K2: Life and Death on the World's Most Dangerous Mountain*. New York: Broadway Books, 2009.

———. *No Shortcuts to the Top: Climbing the World's 14 Highest Peaks*. New York: Broadway Books, 2006.

Wielicki, Krzysztof. *Korona Himalajów: 14 x 8000*. Krakow: Wydawnictwo ATI, 1997.

JOURNALS & MAGAZINES

Chandry-Smart, David. "Suffering for Style." *Gripped* 6, no. 08–09 (2004).

Bularz 88/89, Gliwice: Klub Wysokogórski, 1989 [title means "fanatic crag-rat with excessive muscles"].

Bularz 91, Gliwice: Klub Wysokogórski, 1991.

Alpine Journal, 1973, 1975, 1979, 1980, 1985, 1986, 1987, 1988, 1990, 1993, 1995, 1996, 1997, 2001.

American Alpine Journal, 1984, 1986, 2001, 2010.

Kurtyka, Voytek, "The Abseil and the Ascent: The Art of Abseiling into the Hell," *The Himalayan Journal* 42 (1984/85).

———, "The Art of Suffering," *Mountain* no. 121 (May–June 1988).

———, "Broad Peak North Ridge," *Climbing* no. 94 (February 1986).

———, "The East Face of Trango's Tower," *American Alpine Journal* (1989).

———, "The Gasherbrums Are Lonely," *Mountain* no. 97 (May–June 1984).

———, "Losar," *Alpinist* no. 4 (Autumn 2003).

———, "New Routes, Cho Oyu and Shishapangma," *American Alpine Journal* (1991).

———, "The Path of the Mountain," *Bularz 88/89*.

———, "The Polish Syndrome," *Mountain Review* 5 (Nov/Dec 1993): 37–47.

———, "The Shining Wall," *Alpinist* no. 2 (2004).

———, "The Shining Wall of Gasherbrum IV," *American Alpine Journal* 28 (1986).

———, "Trango Extremes," *Mountain* no. 127 (May–June 1989).

———, "The Trango Tower," *Alpinism* 1 (1986).

MacIntyre, Alex, "Broken English," *Mountain* no. 77 (1981).

Porter, John, "Changabang, South Buttress," *Climbing* no. 55 (1979).

———, "South Side Story," *Mountain* no. 65 (1979).

FILMS

Kłosowicz, Marek. *Himalaiści: Głód wspinaczki: Krzysztof Wielicki*. TVN, S.A. Poland.

———. *Himalaiści: Karawana marzeń: Wanda Rutkiewicz*. TVN, S.A. Poland.

———. *Himalaiści: Ścieżka gór: Wojciech Kurtyka*. TVN, S.A. Poland.

———. *Himalaiści w strefie śmierci: Ryszard Pawłowski*. TVN, S.A. Poland.

———. *Himalaiści: Życie jest za krótkie: Andrzej Zawada*. TVN, S.A. Poland.

Porębski, Jerzy. *Polskie Himalaje: The First Conquerors*. Artica, Poland.

———. *Polskie Himalaje: The Great Climbing*. Artica, Poland.

———. *Polskie Himalaje: The Great Tragedies*. Artica, Poland.

———. *Polskie Himalaje: The Ice Warriors*. Artica, Poland.

———. *Polskie Himalaje: Women in the Mountains*. Artica, Poland.

Rutkiewicz, Wanda. *Abenteuer am Shisha Pangma*, n.d.

———. *Die Schneefrauen*, 1989.

———. *K2*, 1987.

———. *Requiem*, 1988.

———. *Tango Aconcagua*, 1988.

———. *Wenn du zu dieser Wand kommen würdest?* 1985

INDEX